AVID
READER
PRESS

ALSO BY SUSAN ORLEAN

On Animals

The Library Book

Rin Tin Tin: The Life and the Legend

*The Orchid Thief:
A True Story of Beauty and Obsession*

*My Kind of Place:
Travel Stories from a Woman Who's Been Everywhere*

*The Bullfighter Checks Her Makeup:
My Encounters with Extraordinary People*

Lazy Little Loafers

Saturday Night

JOYRIDE

A MEMOIR

SUSAN ORLEAN

AVID READER PRESS
New York   Amsterdam/Antwerp   London
Toronto   Sydney/Melbourne   New Delhi

AVID READER PRESS
An Imprint of Simon & Schuster, LLC
1230 Avenue of the Americas
New York, NY 10020

For more than 100 years, Simon & Schuster has championed authors and the stories they create. By respecting the copyright of an author's intellectual property, you enable Simon & Schuster and the author to continue publishing exceptional books for years to come. We thank you for supporting the author's copyright by purchasing an authorized edition of this book.

No amount of this book may be reproduced or stored in any format, nor may it be uploaded to any website, database, language-learning model, or other repository, retrieval, or artificial intelligence system without express permission. All rights reserved. Inquiries may be directed to Simon & Schuster, 1230 Avenue of the Americas, New York, NY 10020 or permissions@simonandschuster.com.

Copyright © 2025 by Susan Orlean

All rights reserved, including the right to reproduce this book or portions thereof in any form whatsoever. For information, address Avid Reader Press Subsidiary Rights Department, 1230 Avenue of the Americas, New York, NY 10020.

First Avid Reader Press hardcover edition October 2025

AVID READER PRESS and colophon are trademarks of Simon & Schuster, LLC

Simon & Schuster strongly believes in freedom of expression and stands against censorship in all its forms. For more information, visit BooksBelong.com.

For information about special discounts for bulk purchases, please contact Simon & Schuster Special Sales at 1-866-506-1949 or business@simonandschuster.com.

The Simon & Schuster Speakers Bureau can bring authors to your live event. For more information or to book an event contact the Simon & Schuster Speakers Bureau at 1-866-248-3049 or visit our website at www.simonspeakers.com.

Interior design by Carly Loman

Manufactured in the United States of America

1   3   5   7   9   10   8   6   4   2

Library of Congress Control Number: 2025942604

ISBN 978-1-9821-3516-4
ISBN 978-1-9821-3518-8 (ebook)

For Richard Pine
and
For Chip McGrath
With gratitude and affection

INTRODUCTION

In his great book *Here Is New York,* E. B. White wrote:

> I've been remembering what it felt like as a young man to live in the same town with giants. When I first arrived in New York my personal giants were a dozen or so columnists and critics and poets whose names appeared regularly in the papers. I burned with a low steady fever just because I was on the same island with Heywood Broun . . . Robert Benchley . . . Dorothy Parker . . . Ring Lardner . . . This excitation (nearness of giants) is a continuing thing. The city is always full of young worshipful beginners—young actors, young aspiring poets, ballerinas, painters, reporters, singers—each depending on his own brand of tonic to stay alive, each with his own stable of giants.

I have journeyed in the land of giants, waving my pencil, dreaming. I dreamed of becoming a writer, and then I became one, and now I want to tell you why I wake up every day amazed by that fact. Writing has been the only job I've ever had, the only work I've done since 1978. It feels like I started yesterday, although I'm also aware of how many stories and books I've written and how many years have whipped by. Writing always feels new because you never build equity. Every sentence is a slippery invention, a bit of quicksilver I release to the world, and then it's time to invent the next one. That's why being a writer is never boring, but that's also why it's always a little terrifying, why every time I've sat down to write since 1978, I wonder if this is the time I simply won't be able to do it and words will fail me. But so far, so good.

I noted recently that it has been twenty-five years since I published *The Orchid Thief*, and that unit of time, the quarter-of-a-century monumentality of it, stirred me to think about where I've been and where I'm going, and what I've seen and learned along the way. I've always dreaded the idea of writing a memoir. I'm used to looking outward, not inward; I like to bring attention to hidden worlds, not to my own. I'm proud of my work, and I want as many readers as I can muster, but I hate vanity. I'm used to convincing my subjects that their quiet lives are shimmering and gorgeous and worth talking about, but it's been harder to convince myself of that about my own. Yet here I am. This is my story; please listen.

The process of a journey, of striving for something that offers a sense of belonging and contentment, of traversing the wild mystery of the unknown to arrive at the known, is what it means to be alive. Writing is a recapitulation of that experience. Writing documents the process of traveling from birth to death, from innocence to wisdom, from ignorance to knowledge, from where we start to where we end. Even writing that doesn't seem to be about a journey is at its heart a narrative of the writer's voyage into a new world and toward a grasp of it and then onward to the process of sharing it publicly. I became a writer because I wanted to describe the people and places around me, particularly the ones that were least likely to be noticed. The nooks and crannies of the world, the odd and original shape of people's lives, the passion that we bring to those things that matter to us—the way we try to make our lives make sense and the way we struggle to fit ourselves into the world, the unlikely alignments of disparate elements bounced together by accident or magic—these are the subjects that fascinate me and seem important to understand and illuminate.

Writing is a job, but for me it has always seemed like a mission. I felt called, I really did, to describe ordinary life in a way that revealed its complexity and poetry—to show how rewarding it is to be open to and curious about the world, and how much joy can be found in letting yourself be surprised. I wanted to draw readers in and convince them to appreciate these stories, especially ones they might not think they'd care about or find interesting. Perhaps they would begin to look at the world in a different way, one that was full of curiosity and welcome. I wanted to be a writer because I wanted to show that any life closely examined is complex and can embody both the heroic and the plain. Writing was my effort to make sense of the human experience, of my experience, and I hoped that it might bring a reader to understand and maybe even empathize with a life or circumstance that initially might have seemed strange or impenetrable. When I started my career, I didn't know what I was doing. I made lots of mistakes. Some of my early writing was gimmicky and self-conscious, but even then I was sure of why it was important to do it. Writing is the most meaningful thing I've ever done; it's given me my place in the world. Even when it's frustrating and hard, I know how lucky I am.

Wait—have I forgotten to mention how much fun it is? Being a writer is *so much fun.* It's Make-A-Wish for the curious, an excuse to do anything that seems interesting because there is always a story if you look for it. I would like to meet a woman who has twenty-seven pet tigers! I would like to hang out with backpackers in Bangkok! I want to learn about gospel music, Cuban Little League players, Thomas Kinkade, umbrella inventors, Maui surf girls, Bill Blass, a high school basketball team. I want to go to Bhutan, to a taxidermy convention, to Mount Fuji, to South Africa, to a dog show, to a cat show. I want to talk to everyone and tag along as they live their lives, and because I am a writer, I can.

After I graduated from the University of Michigan in 1978, I drove cross-country from Ann Arbor to Portland, Oregon, where I was planning to spend a year. I dawdled along the way. I'm glad I didn't fly, which would have catapulted me from one piece of my life to the next, from one region to another, from my childhood to my adulthood, from my dream of being a writer to the fact of it actually happening. Instead, I dawdled, gradually easing from my Midwestern roots to my West Coast transplantation, poking into every corner I could along the way. I tromped across sand dunes in Indiana and around the Corn Palace in South Dakota; ate at diners with squeaky screen doors and tabletop jukeboxes along two-lane roads in North Dakota. In Montana, I had drinks with air force officers and hippie carpenters; I stopped for a stroll in Arco, a dismal little town in southern Idaho that was the first city in America to be powered entirely by nuclear energy, where I was sure I was being irradiated by setting foot within the city limits. I filled my tank at the largest truck stop in the world, in Little America, Wyoming. A long-haul trucker I met there offered to strap my car to his empty flatbed and piggyback me to the West Coast. I turned him down on the piggyback but took him up on his offer to drive me around for a while so I could see the world the way he did, from the sky-high cab of his huge truck, peering down on a shrunken universe that looked like an array of Matchbox cars on skinny ribbon roads—tiny, precious things on an infinite game board. Everything changes in significance depending on how you look at it.

At the time of my move, I had just read Dante's *Inferno*—that handy travel guide to hell—and *The Canterbury Tales*, the account of an excursion one spring in the fourteenth century. I had also recently finished William Faulkner's *As I Lay Dying*, the narrative of a macabre expedition by the Bundren family to carry the body of their matriarch, Addie, to her chosen burial place. Those were my literary touchstones. I was under the spell of the emotional arc of a trek and the serendipity of encounters along the way, and I was beginning to understand the importance of a voyage, literal and figurative, to writing. This was the first time I was living it rather than studying it. Since then, the world has changed, and media has evolved; the ways we communicate have transformed and will keep transforming. Still, people continue to want to write, and people continue to want to read what writers have to say. Storytelling persists and endures, evidence of our primal need to make note of our observations, emotions, and experiences and to transmit them to people around us. I wanted—I want, I will always want—to take part in that.

Being a writer is exhilarating, demanding, fascinating. I have had the most wonderful life, a joyride of a life. But at times it can be terribly lonely. I'm surprised over and over again by how solitary the experience of writing is—how the big conversation the writer conducts with the public, the culmination of a desire to gobble up the world and all its contents, comes down, finally, to quiet moments alone.

When I'm writing, the people I have met and the experiences I've had along the way recede, and what I'm left with is the flickering moment I've captured of them and am trying to explain. But soon the next story presents itself, and I embrace it, and for the moment it is what the world is made of. The journey begins again, the story starts over; I gather myself and go out to see what I can see and try to tell it as well as I can. What I write is not only what I feel and see but what is left behind, the flotsam and jetsam of life, the stuff that drifts out of our heads and into history—plucked and pressed between pages, so it will stay fresh forever and never slip away.

ONE

I wish I could tell you how the idea of writing about marrying a ten-year-old boy first occurred to me, but I can't. That's the thing about writing. Some of it is like carpentry: You have pieces of wood and a bag full of nails, and you have an idea of what you're trying to build, so you line up the pieces, and sooner or later the thing you had in your mind is manifest. But some parts of writing, like the lede for my 1992 *Esquire* magazine cover story, "The American Man, Age Ten," aren't like that at all. In those instances, there is no *thing* in your mind to begin with. You don't yet have a picture of what you're trying to build, so your tools and materials are useless clutter. What you do have is your research and observations clanking around in the back of your brain. Every attempt to impose order and meaning on this jumble feels a little like trying to remember a dream. The blankness of the page is epic, glaring, and absolute.

Then, suddenly, you type something. And then you type a bit more. In the case of "The American Man," you type, "If Colin Duffy and I were to get married, we would have matching superhero notebooks." You don't have any idea where the words have come from, but they appear and somehow seem right.

This part of the process baffles and fascinates me, even after doing it for so many years. Writing can seem magical, mysterious. How did I come up with *that*? What synapse fired *that* idea? What pocket did I pull that image out of? The sentences seem to have a life of their own as soon as they appear, as if I had nothing to do with their creation. They exist as a fully realized thing. It's a little miraculous when it happens. What makes writing so challenging is not knowing how to summon that miracle. It comes when it's good and ready. Unannounced, a sentence appears, dewy with invention. The blank page becomes animated, primed to receive more sentences. At some point, you rely less on pure inspiration and lean instead on your carpentry skills and you nail together the story that forms in your mind, but the beginning of the story always demands this wild, unbiddable moment.

I've been asked about the lede of "The American Man, Age Ten" many times. Of all the pieces I've written, it's the one that has been the most anthologized and studied, for many reasons, including the startling fact that *Esquire* let me profile a regular kid when the everyday meat of most magazines is celebrities. I think it's also been a source of interest because, as a lede, it's unusual. I've always fibbed when I'm asked about why I began the piece that way, offering an answer that I've mostly made up. As it happens, writing that story was one of the most panic-inducing moments of my writing career, but it's also probably the easiest way to illustrate what I care about and why I do it.

Here's the truth: In the late summer of 1992, I got a call from an editor at *Esquire* magazine offering me an assignment. I'd dreamed of writing for *Esquire,* and years earlier, I had sent them a query. As I wrote in a letter to my mother, "[The editor] wrote me a very nice note and passed my stuff along to the appropriate people so I'm hoping something will come of it. If they gave prizes away for sheer hustle and letter-writing effort I'd deserve a Pulitzer by now." But nothing came of it. I had no contact with the magazine for the next several years. By the time I got this call, I was much more seasoned: I had been published in four or five national magazines, and I was writing regularly for *The New Yorker*. I didn't have a job or a contract at *The New Yorker* yet, but I had a handshake agreement to contribute regularly. I wanted a more formal arrangement. After much nagging on my part, Robert Gottlieb, then the editor of *The New Yorker*, said he would give me a contract. I was ecstatic. For some reason related to paperwork, the contract wouldn't take effect for a few months. I got the call from *Esquire* right before the contract was to begin. I felt like I was being offered a chance to flirt before my wedding.

I met with *Esquire*'s editor, Terry McDonell, who told me that *Esquire* was planning a special issue about the milestones of men's lives. The project had begun with a piece by Robert Sherrill, who was in his late sixties, called "The Truth About Growing Old." McDonell said that for the next installment in the series, he wanted me to profile actor Macaulay Culkin, to represent the early stages of the male experience. Culkin, who was then ten years old, had already been photographed: The story would be the cover of the magazine that month. "Those were the crazy movie-star-driven days for magazines," McDonell said to me recently. "A number of editors at *Esquire* thought I was nuts to put Culkin on the cover instead of, say, Tom Cruise, but I didn't care."

I was awed by the prospect of writing for *Esquire* and by McDonell himself, an esteemed figure in the magazine world, but he was easygoing and funny and friendly, and he made me feel like I could risk speaking my mind. And that was that I had no actual interest in Macaulay Culkin. I had done enough celebrity profiles to know that the story would be stage-managed and controlled by Culkin's "team." But more than that, I didn't think a story about the life of a tween actor would illuminate the male experience for anyone except, perhaps, a few other tween actors. I was more curious about the inner workings of a regular ten-year-old boy than about Macaulay Culkin. I badly wanted to write a story for *Esquire*, but I wanted it to be a story I was excited to do. I asked McDonell if I could profile an ordinary ten-year-old boy instead.

To my astonishment, he said he thought it was a good idea, and asked if I could turn it in by the end of the month.

I dashed out of *Esquire*'s offices, incandescent with excitement about the assignment and a little stunned that McDonell had agreed to my very altered version of it. Then the challenge of the task hit me. Subverting the assignment wasn't something I'd planned. The idea had simply tumbled out of me. I was surprised to hear myself suggest it. Aaargh, why not profile Macaulay Culkin? It would be so much easier. You don't need to explain a celebrity profile to a reader; you serve it up and that's it, and people are pleased even if the story is featherweight and predictable, because we all have a weakness for reading about celebrities. A story about some unknown kid would require so much more authorial effort. I would have to justify in the piece why I was writing it and why a reader should bother with reading about such a commonplace individual, and I would have to explain why I'd chosen this particular boy rather than some other boy, and I'd have to grapple with the conundrum of "ordinariness"—namely, that something ordinary had to convey something specific and something universal simultaneously. Also, I didn't know any ten-year-old boys. I lived in Manhattan. I rarely saw children in my neighborhood. Even if I did stumble on a neighborhood kid, I didn't want to write about a boy living in Manhattan, because a New York City childhood didn't seem ordinary. I wanted to profile a suburban kid living a life that was more typical, a life with a backyard and a bicycle and a dog. By the time I got home, I was in a sweat. I had gotten what I had wished for and now didn't know what to do with it.

Through the friend of a friend, I secured an introduction to a ten-year-old New Jersey boy named Colin Duffy, and to my pleasant surprise, he and his parents agreed to take part in the story. They actually seemed a little indifferent about it, which was ideal. I told Colin I wanted to spend two weeks with him, which would leave me with a week to write the piece.

I planned to join him at breakfast each morning and then go to school with him and, I hoped, hang around with him in the evening. I still had no idea how I would make this into a story, but it was too late to change course.

The first morning of my reporting, when I showed up at the Duffys' house in Glen Ridge, Colin's indifference seemed to have hardened into something more obdurate. More plainly: He shunned me. Perhaps the oddness of the situation—that an adult woman would be tailing him for two weeks—had sunk in. After a sullen breakfast, we walked to school, and I trailed him by several feet, as if I were a geisha meekly following my master.

I was more of a hit in the fifth-grade classroom, where the kids jostled to get a look at me as if I were an exotic pet Colin had brought in for show-and-tell, but he still wouldn't meet my eye. I squeezed into my tiny classroom chair, my hips squashed, and then I brooded. My despair might have worked in my favor: Seeing how crestfallen I was, Colin began to feel sorry for me, and he cast an occasional gentle glance in my direction. At the end of the day, while we did our classroom chore—cleaning the chalkboard erasers by slapping them together and sending up puffs of dust—he asked me if I'd like to come see his room at home. Would I *ever*! The walls to the citadel had been breached.

My hours of gloom hadn't been an act. I was sure the story was falling apart and that I had blown my chance to write for *Esquire*. But I learned from the experience that being quiet and letting your subject approach you rather than making them feel cornered is the best thing to do. From that point on, Colin and I were shoulder to shoulder, playing video games, shooting baskets, gossiping about the girls in his school and about life and his parents and his dogs and his dreams. Sometimes I think he viewed me as a mythical creature, a chimera—a marvelous hybrid being who could goof around with him as if I were one of his ten-year-old buddies, but with the adult assets of a car and a bottomless stash of quarters for pinball.

SUSAN ORLEAN

* * *

After spending two weeks with Colin and fielding anxious calls from my *Esquire* editor, Bill Tonelli, about my progress, I sat down to write. I immediately realized that I didn't know how to begin or where to go with the story once I started writing. I had two weeks' worth of notes. I had great quotes from Colin and his friends; details about his perspective on the universe; some hard science about the male adolescent brain; my own observations about what being ten looked like and what it provoked in me—namely, a keen appreciation of the poignancy of that particular age, when the gauze of childhood begins to give way to the less enchanted teen years, creating a bewildering phase when those stages of life muddle together. I knew the story would test my conviction that writing about a regular kid, a regular *anything,* was valuable on its own merits. The story had to prove my point. It had to convey why I had taken a perfectly acceptable assignment to do a celebrity profile and substituted a story about a New Jersey boy you might pass in a mall without noticing.

I had to win readers right off the bat. I had to. That's the case with any story, but it is especially so when you're writing about something that's not exotic or well-known. Quite understandably, a reader approaches such stories skeptically, asking why they should read about this unremarkable subject. I picture a battle unfolding in those first sentences between me and the reader: Me, waving my hands and insisting the piece is worth reading, and the reader, grumpily resisting. That battle is pitched, but it's my secret pleasure. I revel in a contrarian urge, a stubborn desire to seduce people into reading something they don't think they care about. I'm not trying to trick anyone. I love these subjects, so I write as if I'm shouting, "You're not going to believe how interesting this is!" I keep shouting until the last sentence is on the page.

When I write, I can't relax until I have a lede that thrills me. I can't write the second sentence until I've written the first. I can't start until I've started, almost as if I'm telling the story out loud, and it would be impossible to do that out of order. Every story feels like a daisy chain to me, the first sentence leading to the second and then the third and so on. Everything depends on the lede. It needs to be a great striptease act, making the most of bated anticipation: You've got to choose carefully which item of clothing to take off first. It has to be enough to intrigue but not give everything away; it has to be arresting enough that it captures readers' attention and makes them eager to know what comes next.

Often I write a lede that's not exactly on the topic, so that it serves as a sort of preamble to the story, an overture before the main event. Other times, if a word or phrase has become important to the piece, I'll riff on it for the lede. A lede doesn't need to preview the story or summarize what the rest of the piece will be about. What's important is that it captivates readers and holds them fast to the page so they keep reading. I have a knack for that, an instinct. I can feel in my gut when a lede works, even if it's oblique.

For two weeks I had been inside Colin's head and I'd seen the world the way a ten-year-old sees it. I was fascinated by the unusual nature of our relationship: We were adult and child, reporter and subject, female and male, and companions all at once, a tangle of roles and rapports. I was enchanted by him; he was a delightful kid. Obviously, I didn't fantasize about marrying him, but I did fantasize about what such a cockeyed notion might have looked like from his perspective. I dove into the imaginary adult world as he envisioned it and tried to convey what it might be to live in it with him, a universe in which childhood folded into adulthood, in which being married mostly meant you had matching superhero notebooks:

> If Colin Duffy and I were to get married, we would have matching superhero notebooks. We would wear shorts, big sneakers, and long, baggy T-shirts depicting famous athletes every single day, even in the winter. We would sleep in our clothes. We would both be good at Nintendo *Street Fighter II*, but Colin

would be better than me. We would have some homework, but it would never be too hard, and we would always have just finished it. We would eat pizza and candy for all of our meals. We wouldn't have sex, but we would have crushes on each other and, magically, babies would appear in our home. We would win the lottery and then buy land in Wyoming, where we would have one of every kind of cute animal. All the while, Colin would be working in law enforcement—probably the FBI. Our favorite movie star, Morgan Freeman, would visit us occasionally. We would listen to the same Eurythmics song ("Here Comes the Rain Again") over and over again and watch two hours of television every Friday night. We would both be good at football, have best friends, and know how to drive; we would cure AIDS and the garbage problem and everything that hurts animals. We would hang out a lot with Colin's dad. For fun, we would load a slingshot with dog food and shoot it at my butt. We would have a very good life.

Quite honestly, I was shocked when I read my lede. I hadn't considered for one minute that this, or anything that sounded like this, was what I would write. I did know it would be useful to start a story about a seemingly mundane subject (a suburban boy) with a sentence that was quite the opposite, ideally one that was a little startling—such as an adult female speculating on marriage to that boy. It had punch. It was transgressive. It was funny, off-kilter, disorienting; it gave little clue about what the rest of the story would encompass, but somehow it propelled the reader forward to find out. It was a good way to mount the argument that I've been compelled by since the first time I ever wrote a story: that anything at all is worth writing about if you care about it and it makes you curious and makes you want to holler about it to other people. In this case, I was genuinely, deeply curious about the life of an ordinary elementary school kid. At first, when I sat down to write the story, nothing came out of my head, and then abruptly it did, fully formed. If writing always made sense, even to the writer, it wouldn't be nearly as interesting.

I held my breath and turned in the piece. I knew it was not what the editors were expecting, but fortunately they embraced it and ran it beside a stunning spread of photos—not of Macaulay Culkin but of Colin Duffy. (One photo of Culkin was used on the cover.) This story was a defining moment for me. I had relied on my instincts, and it worked. I've always marveled that McDonell trusted me so much. His allowing me to do the story my way rather than insisting on the original assignment was a threshold experience in my professional life. In his memoir, *The Accidental Life*, McDonell wrote, "That's the way editing could go sometimes—from marginal idea (Mr. Lonelyhearts) to good idea (Bob [Sherrill] on getting old) to good execution (his piece) to bigger idea (the series about men aging) to great work (Susan's piece)." A breakthrough for sure.

TWO

When did I decide I wanted to be a writer? More to the point, when didn't I want to be one? Writing always felt elemental to me. It was something I wanted to do as soon as I realized it could be done. I wrote my first book, *Herbert the Nearsighted Pigeon,* when I was about five years old. Herbert is estranged from his friends because he needs glasses and can't see them well enough to recognize them. His life is in crisis until he meets a myopic owl who wears glasses. This prompts Herbert to realize what his problem is; he has an eye exam, gets a prescription, and the tide turns. Exit Herbert, wearing glasses, with his reconnected friends.

After *Herbert,* I kept writing. As a teenager, I kept a journal full of weepy, raging, hormonal entries:

> Back to school. I'm mad at everyone. Didn't even call while I was sick. By the way, in ten years I'll be twenty-three.
>
> Back to school again! I really think I'm getting a bit more popular.
>
> Daddy really is unfair. Sometimes I hate him! Hyla told me she hates her father too (another resemblance she and I have).

I kept lists of words I loved and phrases that struck me as beautiful or original—a nerdy habit that I shared with my father and continue to this day. I wrote letters to the editor of *The Plain Dealer* and *The Cleveland Press*. (*Dear Diary, Wrote letter to the editor of the* Press *about the killing of baby seals. Hope it gets in.*) Writing things always felt natural to me, as if it completed the electrical circuit of a thought. A thought didn't quite exist unless I put it on the page. Writing held things fast, clutched them. It pinned experience down, preserving it like a butterfly on a tackboard. Most kids want to hurry time along, but I never did. (As I whimpered in my diary: *I can't believe how fast time goes! It makes me feel sick! Really! Everything changing so much. I hate it!!!*) I wanted to slow time, save it, stop it somehow. I worried that life whooshed by, and that no matter how intense or profound or exciting or sad a moment was, it was gone in an instant, dissolving as if it had never happened and never mattered. The swinging eraser of time moving across experience terrified me. Time moving forward made me sad. Writing protected me. It made things last forever.

The awkward tween years

I started writing poetry when I was young, and time preoccupied me as a poetic subject, too. I published this in my junior high newspaper:

Time moves on
Never slowing
Why must it?
Yet—
It erases the
Pain of some memories
But—
It continues to
Dim others.
Time—
Slow down

Back then I signed my poems "Susi Orlean." I dotted the "i" with a smiley face.

I don't think my parents planned on raising a writer, but I know my inclination started with them. My mother loved to read and dreamed of being a librarian, and she channeled that desire into making her children library-goers from the minute we could walk. Every week she trundled us off to the local branch and allowed us to take out as many books as we wanted. She was a painstaking, careful reader and a deliberate writer. She kept a diary with great diligence and wrote multiple drafts of any correspondence until she was satisfied with the tone. She never would have dreamed of writing for public consumption, but she paid meticulous attention to what she put on the page.

My mother was ladylike and old-fashioned and painfully sensitive. I was the baby of the family, her favorite, and she doted on me, treating every one of my achievements as a huge victory. When I began getting published, she clipped my stories, no matter how small, and kept them in a series of huge scrapbooks. She made copies to share with her friends, her hairdresser, her butcher. Even when I was writing for obscure magazines and barely earning a living from it, she treated me like a star.

My father had a buoyant confidence my mother lacked. He thrived on curiosity. He was a taker of the long way home, a knocker on unknown doors, a talker to strangers. He was small and sturdy and as feisty as a terrier, with red hair that rose from his forehead in scalloping waves. His friends called him Red when he was young. He loved accidental discoveries and the surprise of everyday experience. His interest in other people was expansive and all-inclusive. He chatted with bums and waitresses and farmers and cops as easily as he did to senators and powerful businessmen. He could be somber and ornery at home sometimes, but out in the world he was twinkly.

Even when he was well into his eighties, he liked to while away the day when he visited me in New York by catching whatever bus was passing by and riding it wherever it was going, the more circuitous the route, the better. Then he would catch another bus back. He considered

My mother, Edith, on a trip we took together to Switzerland

this the best way to see the city; that traveling at the inching-along pace of a bus across town was much more interesting than taking a cab to a specific site. Not knowing what he might encounter was the fun of it. A bus ride to who-knows-where was his kind of journey, ambling and rambling and full of serendipity. He didn't need to witness something spectacular to be pleased by the experience. He was happy seeing how life unfolded, what was happening on the street, what people looked like in different neighborhoods, what was being built, what was being demolished.

When I was writing a lot of Talk of the Town pieces for *The New Yorker*, I often got my ideas by wandering around different neighborhoods until something caught my eye. A handwritten sign on a wall, a name on a doorplate, a flyer on a telephone pole, or an unusual magazine at a newsstand would spin me toward a story. I realize now that I picked up this habit from my father. He and I traveled in the same loose-limbed fashion, counting on happenstance and accident to light us up.

My father, Arthur, who was fond of tennis and cars

I am my father's daughter in many ways. I have his wavy red hair and blue eyes and freckles. Being a redhead is more than a mere descriptor: It is a way of being in the world. You stand out. You're noticed. You're a minority of a minority, listed for extinction, identified as different, associated with fieriness, temper; obvious in a crowd. My earliest memory is of being approached by strangers asking my mother if they could touch my hair. I was so young that I was still in a stroller, but even then I understood there was something about me that drew these strangers near.

My parents grew up in Cleveland, Ohio, and remained in Cleveland their entire lives. When they were teenagers, the Great Depression began, and they were shaped by it. My grandfather Samuel Orlinski—my father's father—was born in a village in Poland, then deserted the Russian army and made his way to America. He became a carpenter and builder in Cleveland and somewhere along the way changed his last name to Orlean. Eventually, he did well enough that he owned several apartment buildings. During the Depression, he lost them all. My father, Arthur, was the oldest of four siblings, and he felt responsible for taking care of his family. He put himself through college and then law school. Every time he was faced with a choice about school or work, he opted for whatever offered the most security. He did the necessary thing. Even after his business as a real estate developer flourished and provided my parents with plenty of resources, they always bent toward tangible assets and safe bets, the hard stamp of the Depression still imprinted on them.

My mother, Edith, was born in Hungary in a small, scenic town called Sátoraljaújhely, in the soft hills a few hours northeast of Budapest. Her family lived in a handsome brick house and had fine porcelain, oil paintings, and maids. Her father—my grandfather Lewis—was an accountant. His father had been a doctor. He and my grandmother were assimilated, educated Hungarian Jews who thought of themselves as Hungarians first and Jews second. In the early 1920s, my grandfather put his finger to the wind and became convinced that conditions for Hungarian Jews were souring. He applied for an American visa. In the 1920s, the U.S. had a quota on Jewish immigrants, and consequently, their application was denied. Determined to leave Hungary, my grandfather found a job in the accounting department of American Smelting and Refining Company, in San Luis Potosí, a copper-mining town in eastern Mexico. In San Luis Potosí, my mother and her sister, Eleanor, attended a Catholic school that they loved; it left my mother with an abiding affection for nuns. They walked to school chewing on long sticks of sugarcane, which they loved as well. In my favorite family portrait, my grandfather and grandmother and my mother and her sister are dressed in stiff woolen clothes with high collars and long sleeves—clothes that would have been suited for Sunday lunch in Budapest—but they are standing in front of a row of saguaro cactus, their pale skin blanched by the midday Mexican sun.

After eight years, the family's application for American visas was finally approved and they moved to Cleveland, where my grandmother had cousins. When I was growing up, I didn't know that the rest of their family didn't come to America because they had been killed at Auschwitz. When I was around eleven years old, I saw a photograph of my grandmother's brother. He was dressed in a Hungarian army uniform and had a neatly clipped mustache, a barrel chest, and a faraway gaze. I hadn't known that my grandmother had a brother. I was greedily excited by the picture, imagining that I had stumbled upon a source of many new cousins I didn't know I had. I asked my grandmother where her brother lived. She took a sharp breath and said, "He perished." Had I ever heard the word "perish" before? I don't think so, but I sensed it was a word that discouraged further discussion. My grandmother put the photograph in a drawer and never spoke of it again.

When I was young, I was embarrassed that my mother hadn't been born in the United States. No one ever would have known it, since she was thoroughly American in her manner and affect, and she didn't have an accent. No one would have cared, anyway. But I wanted my mother to seem modern, and coming from a place like Hungary didn't seem modern at all. By the time I was an adult, though, I reveled in the idea that she was a little exotic, with Europe and Mexico in her background.

When I think of my parents, the word that comes to mind is "sturdy." My parents met playing tennis, which they continued to play until they were in their eighties. But their sturdiness was not just about their athleticism. They were capable, competent people, admirably unspoiled and unsnobbish. They didn't deny themselves comfort, but they had no patience for indulgence or laziness or fragility. They had no airs. My father worked until he died, at ninety-two. My mother had a part-time job from the time I was five. They both were happiest when they were getting things done. They inspired me with their resourcefulness, their intrepidness: their sturdiness.

I assume there was a spell when my parents enjoyed each other's company, but that was before my time. They shared so many qualities, but they managed to rub each other wrong. By the point when I was paying attention, they had settled into a tense, weaponized coexistence that was held together tenuously at best. Our house had a center hallway that was open to the ceiling of the second floor. An internal balcony on the second floor overlooked the front door and foyer. Voices moved as easily as air throughout the house, and if you sat on the second-floor balcony, you could hear everything being said on the first floor. I spent a lot of time sitting on that balcony with my sister, eavesdropping on our parents bickering downstairs, and scurrying into our bedrooms the minute we heard the rubbery creak of a shoe on the stairs. If I could say something valuable came out of this miserable pastime, it would be that I became adept at listening while staying out of sight, which seems like good training for a future writer. But it was a costly education. I was frequently crippled with worry about my parents' relationship. I became attuned to any ripple of discord around me—a hypervigilance that is useful for a writer but hell on one's nerves. My parents had remarkable stamina for battling each other.

Even into their nineties, they squabbled about anything and everything. They hurt each other's feelings until the day they died.

We lived in Shaker Heights, a woodsy, sumptuous suburb of Cleveland built in the 1920s as a white Protestant enclave. Beginning in the late 1950s, Shaker Heights deliberately integrated by actively soliciting Black families to buy homes there, making it a rare example of a wealthy town with racial diversity. My junior high was almost all white, but my high school was thirty percent Black. In 1964, the rabbi of my synagogue, Arthur Lelyveld, volunteered to register Black voters during Freedom Summer and was attacked and beaten with a tire iron by segregationists in Hattiesburg, Mississippi. He often talked about the experience at our Saturday-morning services. In 1967, when I was twelve years old, a state representative named Carl Stokes was elected mayor of Cleveland, making it the first major American city to elect a Black mayor. Not long after, my father partnered with a Black developer, George Thompson, and they worked together for years. I tell you this not to rack up points for virtuousness but to clarify what it means to be from Shaker Heights, a place usually known only for its gracious houses and affluent residents. That is true, but it is not the only thing that is true about the town. While its experiment in voluntary integration has had its failings, growing up in Shaker gave me a view of the world that was broader than it otherwise might have been.

My parents were defined by being Jewish. It wasn't a matter of observance or specifics; being Jewish was simply integral to who they were. They enrolled us in Hebrew school when we were toddlers, and we attended two days a week after school as well as Saturday mornings. My father was determined that we get a Jewish education. When I was in high school, I declared that I didn't want to continue Hebrew school, and he made it clear that this was not an option. There were very few things my father was adamant about, but this was one of them. I continued in

Hebrew school. The irony was that my father was an atheist, and he hated attending services, particularly on High Holy Days, because he thought it hypocritical to attend once or twice a year. "People are just going to show off their new clothes," he liked to grumble. Eventually, I saw the logic in what seemed contradictory to me then. He wanted to make sure we knew who we were, to steep us in the cultures and traditions and beliefs of Judaism, so that we could make an informed decision about how we wanted to observe it when we grew up. He couldn't tolerate the phoniness of performative religiosity, the preening display of Rosh Hashanah outfits, and the spectacle of public piety, but he was one of the most deeply Jewish people I've ever known.

My brother was brilliant academically and a superb athlete; he competed in national tennis tournaments. My sister was pretty, shy, artistic, and graceful. I was the clown child, the peacemaker, a tomboy, good at distracting from whatever storm was brewing between my parents. In many early pictures, I'm dressed in a costume. My favorite was a cowboy outfit, complete with a hat and a holster and bright red jeans. I paid for my clowning with stomachaches and headaches and my hyperalertness

My favorite outfit—ready for the Wild West

to strife; I was always primed to perform in hopes of breaking up a fight. I told myself stories to divert myself from worrying about my parents. I played out different scenarios of my life, imagining what would have become of me if my mother's family had stayed in Hungary. Or if they'd stayed in Mexico. Or if my mother had married her first sweetheart, who was an artist. In each of these scenarios, I, or at least the "I" that I turned out to be, wouldn't exist. It was like writing my own horror stories, imagining a jagged hole in the world that my nonexistence would leave.

I was the kind of kid who read until my mother told me to turn out the lights, and then I grabbed a flashlight and made a tent of my bedsheet and kept reading in the humid little refuge I had created. I often fell asleep with a book in my bed and woke up with my cheek glued to it, the texture of the front cover lightly imprinted on my skin. I read books about horses and books about dogs and books about magical kingdoms. Then I graduated to books about governesses hired by handsome, tragic widowers in lonely castles on the darkening moors. In high school, my English teachers introduced me to great literature. I was immediately pulled in. My eleventh-grade English teacher, Mr. Heaps, gave me my first exposure to Faulkner when he assigned *The Sound and the Fury*; reading it, I felt like the top of my head had lifted off, making room for an entirely new way of shaping language and telling stories. To savor it fully, I started reading it a second time before I had finished it the first time, so I had bookmarks in two different places. How the sentences pitched and rolled, the heavy melancholy, the way the story was so finely detailed, the way it built and populated an entire world—I couldn't believe words could do that. I started the book right before winter break. That year my family went to the Caribbean for vacation. All I wanted was to be alone with *The Sound and the Fury*. Every day, when the rest of my family trotted off to the beach, I begged to stay in the hotel room and read. I never dared to think I would write like Faulkner, but the idea that a human could produce such a thing inspired me and made me dream.

When I was in junior high, my yearning to be a writer latched on to some specificity. My parents subscribed to *Life* magazine, which was then in its heyday. The magazine often ran slice-of-life, documentary-style stories. I already knew that I didn't want to be a newspaper reporter, but I couldn't put my finger on what kind of writer I hoped to be except that I knew I wanted to write about what was in front of me rather than what was in my imagination. I loved reading fiction, but I liked the prospect of telling true stories, about whatever topic my inquisitiveness led me to. I wanted to see the world and talk to people and then return to tell the tale.

One week, our issue of *Life* arrived as usual. My brother and sister and I always fought over who got it first, so I snatched it out of the mailbox. I was looking for good pictures of animals—a *Life* specialty and my favorite pastime. As I was flipping through, I noticed a full-page photograph of a middle-aged man leaning against the counter in what appeared to be an exam room. He was wearing wrinkled medical scrubs. His face was blurred by fatigue. I recall he was holding a cup of coffee or doing something that made it clear he was taking a brief pause in an exhausting day. I started to read the story. It was a profile of a doctor, the sole practitioner in a small Midwestern town. The story followed him for one typical workday, dawn until dark, as he delivered babies, stitched up split knees, told someone they had cancer, vaccinated children, comforted dying patients, sent bills, and paid bills.

Reading that story was like hearing a thunderclap: It was the blast that shook me awake and rang in my ears for a lifetime. The content was fascinating, especially for a suburban girl who had no idea what country doctoring entailed. But what mattered most was realizing that a writer could produce a story about something routine—or at least something that wasn't "news"—about someone who wasn't famous, and that the power and purpose of the story was to reveal the truth about another life and nothing more, and that was sufficient to be interesting, to be worth publishing. If the storytelling was good enough, that justified telling it. I'm sure I didn't understand it on those terms at that moment, but something made sense to me for the first time. I knew then that using writing to satisfy my curiosity, and to illuminate the truth in the lives of others, was what I wanted to do.

There is a tenet in Judaism that each person is an entire world. More pessimistically, the Talmud says that anyone who kills a single soul is considered to have killed a complete world. You can interpret this in many ways: for example, that ending a life cuts off an entire universe springing from that person's existence, or that all of reality is intertwined, and the destruction of any part of it is catastrophic to that entirety. I always pictured it as something more individual: that each of us contains an unimaginably rich world, a full universe of thoughts and knowledge and aspirations and reveries, of stories and memories and perceptions and emotions; that the sum of each person is an entire galaxy, unique and whole. If I had to point to one principle that has guided me, inspired me, and taught me how to be in the world as a writer, this would be it.

For a long time, I didn't know that my father dreamed of being a writer. He had never breathed a word of it to me. One afternoon, I was visiting my parents, and my dad and I were hanging out chatting. I was telling him about the Hollywood folks I had interviewed for my book *Rin Tin Tin*. Since my dad was a lawyer and real estate developer, I assumed he had never thought much about how I did my job or what it entailed, so I thought he would find these details interesting.

I knew he had been a champion debater in college. I knew he read the dictionary for fun and rolled new words around in his mouth as if they were candy. He always had a word-of-the-day desk calendar. He wrote fanciful, funny letters to me and my sister and brother at camp and college. ("Dear kids, The ocean waves are high, the wind is strong, and the sun is weak. See you soon, Dad." "Dear kids, As of this moment I have no sunburn and a dry bathing suit. Home soon.") It never occurred to me that he yearned to write for a living, or that he had ever wanted to be something other than what he was. This was probably for the same reason I couldn't picture him as a child, or a young man, or a soldier, or any other version of him that had existed. I couldn't imagine him as anything other than my father. In this way, I was a typical kid: Children, with their vast imaginations, can conjure a monster in the closet, but their imaginations fail when they think about their parents. They are unable to picture their parents having any complexity or history or identities other than the single fact of being parents. That day, during a pause in my monologue about work, my father, who was probably around ninety years old at the time, said offhandedly, "I always wanted to be a writer." I was dumbfounded. And yet it made perfect, poetic sense. His adventurousness, his enjoyment of poking around in new places, his deftness at chatting with strangers—these were the qualities of someone who wanted to tell stories for a living or, at the very least, understood the potency of storytelling. I came to appreciate what a luxury it had been for me to want to be a writer and be able to pursue it rather than being in my father's position of thinking wistfully that it was something he wished he could have done.

My father trained me to be an observer and to be inquisitive, to be comfortable in settings that were unfamiliar or even strange; without saying it explicitly, he trained me to think like a writer. Here's an example: In 1966, when I was eleven years old, there was a week of violent civil disorder in central Cleveland that began after a white bar owner refused to serve water to a Black customer. White suburbanites, already curtailing their trips to downtown Cleveland in favor of new malls outside of town, became terrified of the inner city. I remember classmates telling me that their parents would never venture downtown again. My father had a different attitude. As soon as the unrest settled, he plunked me and my sister and brother in the back seat of his car and drove us to see the neighborhoods that had been in conflict. "I want you to understand that everyone doesn't get to live the way you live," I remember him saying to us. "You are not members of the idle rich." It was not only the prospect of idle children that troubled him; it was the prospect that we might retreat into the bubble of privilege he had created for us and never know a world beyond it and never feel responsible for making that world better. A large part of my father's business was the development of Section 8 subsidized housing. On several occasions, he commanded us each to choose a toy from our many toys, without telling us why we were choosing. Once we had chosen, he put us in the car and drove us to one of his Section 8 projects and had us visit with the children there. Then, at his instruction, we gave our chosen toys to the kids.

I won't pretend that we enjoyed touring the ruined neighborhoods downtown, and we were definitely uncomfortable meeting children we didn't know, and I assure you we did not like giving away our toys. But the experience sank in—the way it forced us to appreciate the existence of the whole city and not only our primped little part of it, and the frankness of seeing things that were harsh and sad but real, and my father's willingness to engage with his tenants in a housing project rather than just building it and cashing the rent checks. The lesson for me was to see the wholeness of life, and not to shrink from the hard parts, and to find the marvel in it, because seeing anything, everything, all of it, is an illumination.

My father recognized the appeal of being a writer. But while he inadvertently prepared me to think like a writer, to see the world like a writer would, he discouraged me from pursuing writing as a profession. We sparred about my career choice for years, and I knew it made him uneasy that I was entering such a wobbly profession, especially one that didn't have a well-defined route to it. It's true that I had no idea how one went about becoming a writer. The path to becoming a newspaper reporter was clear—you took journalism classes and then got internships and stints on a copy desk and went onward from there—but my desire to write long narratives didn't seem to follow any job path I knew.

During my junior year of college, my friend Lisa Klausner gave me a subscription to *The New Yorker* for my birthday. I was aware of the magazine, but I hadn't read it regularly. At the time, *New Yorker* stories loped along page after page, broken up only by occasional illustrations, so at first I thought it was a brick of text that wasn't very engaging. Then I started reading it regularly, and I felt a flash of recognition: *This* was what I wanted to write, and *this* was where I wanted to be published. The story that embodied *The New Yorker* for me, which I read after college, was Mark Singer's 1983 piece "Supers," a profile of five brothers who were superintendents of upscale Manhattan apartment buildings. The story had no urgency, no news peg. It simply described the brothers and their relationship to one another and to the tenants in their building and to New York City—but in doing that, it illustrated a world. The story felt specific and intimate, but at the same time, it showed what a working life feels like, what family means, how humans coexist. I tore the story out of the issue and kept it on my nightstand, like a ticket to a place I wanted to go.

In college, I majored in English and minored in history. I dabbled in other things, taking a few classes in linguistics and psychology and sociology, but I always gravitated back to what I liked the most: reading and writing. I was also very interested in boys and parties. As soon as I arrived in Ann Arbor, I fumbled my way through a bunch of crushes. When I started college I was blindly innocent. Starting in junior high, I always had boyfriends, but I never considered the possibility of actually having sex with them. Coincidentally, I lived in the most liberal dorm on the Michigan campus. It was coed, a room of boys next to a room of girls throughout the entire building, and each hall of students, boys and girls, shared one large, messy bathroom. This was the 1970s, and such gender blending was not the norm at all except in Pilot Program, the niche division I was part of, which was a sort of residential college. I have no idea how the mixed-gender arrangement came about. Because I'd grown up with a brother, I didn't mind the shared arrangement, except that the boys were such slobs. My parents were not pleased, but I explained to them that the students related to one another like siblings and that there was nothing sexual about it. That was true for me, at least. It took a year before I realized that everyone was sleeping with everyone.

I indulged my passion for reading with classes on great American novelists and a seminar on James Joyce. Faulkner's biographer, Joseph Blotner, taught at Michigan, and I took every one of his classes. A reserved, courtly man with a quiet voice and smooth silver hair, he spent decades writing his two-volume Faulkner biography, which was published while I was taking one of his seminars. One day in class, he said he would answer questions about the book. He mentioned somewhat melancholically that when he began the project, his daughter had just been born, and now, as he finally published it, she was finishing college. He was probably the first person I'd ever met who had written a book, and it was the first time I understood how a writing project could consume your life.

During college, my writing consisted of essays for classes and poetry. Writing poetry might seem at odds with my eventual career path, but I see it as connected. I loved the music of words and the economy of expression and the lapidary precision of poetry, and that stuck with me when I turned to writing nonfiction. I usually wrote poems about real experiences, but I tried to condense and intensify the writing and heighten its rhythmic pulse. I noted how poetry emphasized the pacing of sentences, the momentum that propelled the reader, the sound of language on a page. As Virginia Woolf once wrote to Vita Sackville-West, "Style is a very simple matter: it is all *rhythm*."

During college, I kept a sort of lo-fi spreadsheet that laid out the possible unfolding of my life after graduation. It included a section I called

ITEMS UNDER CONSIDERATION. One section was *What to Do/ Future Plans*, which had a subsection titled *Why I Should Go into Journalism.* The entry went on:

PRO:
Fun!
Interesting!
Writing!
Activity and excitement!
Good people (maybe)
Social value

CON:
No jobs available
Have to live in NYC for serious work on a magazine
Talent is questionable

Below this list, I did similar calculations for the only other jobs I could imagine doing. The obvious one was to get a PhD in English and then teach. The other was going to law school, which was what people graduating with English degrees in the 1970s often did. Both of those options had much shorter PRO lists, and their CONS included, most prominently, the fact that I didn't really want to do them.

After I graduated, I announced to my parents that I was not going to graduate school in English, and I wasn't going to go to law school: I was going to be a writer. My mother was tickled. She was happy because I was happy. My father, though, raked me with a hard glance and then said he thought I should go to law school. He didn't object to me trying to become a writer, but he said I needed something to fall back on. In his mind, writing was a sheer wall you might be able to scrabble up, but it was so precarious that you needed the cushion of a law degree at the base for when you inevitably fell. It was all about security. But I was twenty-one years old, frothy with confidence. I said that I didn't plan on falling back. This was long before my father confessed his thwarted desire to be a writer, so I had no idea that the financial insecurities of writing had boxed him out of the profession when he was my age. I thought he wanted me to go to law school because he had gone to law school.

He was so worried about my determination to be a writer that he took me to test-drive a car I liked, and at the end of the test drive, he said he would buy it for me if I went to law school right away. I counteroffered the proposal that I'd go in a year, and he said the offer stood only if I went to law school that fall. I really wanted the car. Somehow, though, I was stubborn enough, strong enough, to resist the temptation, and told him I would have to decline the car.

We finally agreed that I would take a year off and then go to law school. I secretly planned to use the year to become a writer. In truth, I never intended to go to law school. For decades thereafter, my father continued to press me to reconsider. Even after I'd published several books, he told me that it wasn't too late for me to apply. After *The Orchid Thief* came out, he told me once again that it wasn't too late for law school, but I finally convinced him that it was.

So here is the situation: I had a year to become a writer or face the wrath of my father. It's 1977. I finished my four years at Michigan and I immersed myself in Faulkner and Joyce and Hemingway, but I had no marketable skills. My college boyfriend, a rakish playboy with a winning smile named John Culver, was moving to Portland, Oregon, to attend law school at Lewis & Clark. My sister, Debbie, lived in Portland, so that was an added attraction. After graduation, I packed my pickle-green Camaro and followed John to Portland. I told my parents that I would look for a paralegal job once I arrived. Instead, I got a job waiting tables at a midrange, cheerful seafood restaurant in Portland, where the kitchen ceilings were freckled with grease from the spattering skillets of fried clams. I loved working in the restaurant, so I wasn't unhappy, but I was aware that it wasn't rocketing me into my chosen profession.

At that moment, narrative nonfiction—what some people like to call "new journalism" or creative nonfiction—was in high season. Joan Didion, Truman Capote, Gay Talese, Norman Mailer, Hunter S. Thompson, and John McPhee, among others, were writing long pieces about street kids in Haight-Ashbury and farm families in Kansas, in prose that was sometimes blunt and other times filigreed but always hypnotically immersive. These writers were as dogged as investigative reporters even if their subjects were disarmingly simple. They sculpted their sentences with precision and flash. Once I had put my finger on what I wanted to do, I had plenty of role models. When I read Tom Wolfe for the first time, I became so obsessed that I carried around my copy of *The Electric Kool-Aid Acid Test* for a year and read sections at random over and over, tattering the pages of my cheap paperback. For me, the book was proof that you could write at length about people who were not politicians or celebrities, and that you could write factual stories with as much wit and audacity and inventiveness as I associated with fiction.

I began nurturing a fantasy that one day I would write for *The New Yorker*—a fantasy that seemed completely unattainable. At that time, the magazine was as impenetrable as the Kremlin. It had no masthead and no "About the Author" section; bylines were in ant-size type at the end of stories, as if they were meant to be a secret. I renewed my subscription again and again. I was a seafood waitress in Portland, a law school dodger with the time running out on my stolen year, but reading *The New Yorker* gave me a destination to aim for.

One day a friend told me about a small magazine starting up in Portland. I applied immediately and, a few days later, got a call about the job. I was so excited that I was trembling. The night before my interview, I realized that I should bring writing samples with me, but my options were measly.

Michigan had a robust journalism program. The student paper, *The Michigan Daily*, was so good that many people in Ann Arbor unaffiliated with the university subscribed to it. But I hadn't been interested in majoring in journalism. I enrolled in one class because I thought I should, but the course, a history of network news, was so boring that I dropped out after a week. A lot of my friends majored in journalism. They were newspaper kids, the ink-stained version of theater kids. They were staff writers at the *Daily* and had summer internships at *The New York Times* and *Newsweek* and *Time*. They elbowed one another to break stories and reveled in knowing things before the public did. It seemed like fun, because there was always something dramatic happening in the newsroom of the *Daily*, and someone was always racing off to an important interview or yelling about big stories coming over the wire. My problem was that I didn't care about knowing things early or having an inside edge. I could never muster the passion for news that they had.

The one story I wrote for the *Daily* was a book review of *A Clockwork Orange*, so that was the only college-era clip I could bring to my interview in Portland. I had written stories for my high school newspaper. I also had been the editor of my high school yearbook. I convinced myself that the yearbook would demonstrate my potential, so I grabbed a copy along with my thin pile of clips and bundled off to try to start my career.

Now and then I try to imagine what it might have seemed like to the people interviewing me when I whipped out my high school yearbook. No one laughed at me, although they would have been well within their rights. Nor did they laugh when I announced that they absolutely had to hire me. I insisted. I declared. And I believed it. Working for this magazine was exactly what I wanted to do, and even though I didn't have a clue how to write a magazine story, I was sure I would figure it out because I was confident it was what I was meant to do. This wasn't bravado or bluster. It was the cast-iron feeling that this was my calling, this was where I belonged. It's like walking into a house that's for sale and knowing instantly that it's the place you should live, based not on a rational assessment of the house but on some intense, almost chemical reaction you have to it. That's how I felt about writing.

To my astonishment, I got the job. At first, I fumbled and stumbled and struggled, because I really didn't know how to write for a magazine. I didn't know how to develop a story idea, or how to research it, or how to structure the material once I gathered it. The job wasn't an apprenticeship. We were the writing staff of the magazine, which was romantically named *Paper Rose*. Everyone on staff was almost as inexperienced as I was, but we were all merrily game. The six or so of us were assigned to come up with stories and then report and write them, as if we were veterans. It was wonderful but also worrying, since none of us knew what we were doing.

Writers are always advised to "write what you know." But I was twenty-two, and I didn't know anything. How could I? I hadn't had much experience of the world. What I did know, though, was that I didn't mind thinking of something I wanted to learn about and chasing it down. I liked writing about what I didn't know. I never worried about whether the subject seemed "important." All I needed was to feel my own curiosity rumbling. I always liked being a student, and I loved telling people when I learned something intriguing, so that was my stance. I looked around me, saw something I was curious about, figured out how to find out about it, and when I felt I had learned it thoroughly, I told readers what I had learned.

I was new to Portland, so everything felt fresh to me. I treated writing like a process of transmission: I went out and did this or learned that so the reader didn't need to, then I reported back about what I saw or did. Years later, when I was researching *The Orchid Thief*, I researched early orchid hunters who were commissioned by aristocrats to explore the globe and bring back exotic plants as tokens of their travel. The aristocrats could taste a bit of the adventure that way, without ever leaving home. That's what writing felt like. I was a version of an orchid hunter, dispatched by readers to retrieve stories from the outer world, then return with them to be examined and appreciated. Four decades after my job at *Paper Rose*, I still write that way. I choose things I am entranced by and plunge in, and when I feel confident that I understand the subject, I write the story so I can show readers what I've learned. Even then, I knew that the challenge was deceptively simple: to write what I really thought, not what I *thought* I should think and not what I hoped it would mean; to write what was authentic and true.

I didn't appreciate it at first, but eventually, I understood that the engine of my stories was the drive from ignorance to knowledge. That was the narrative movement within each story, even if it wasn't obvious or explicit. Without a grounding in an overarching principle, a philosophy, writing can seem like a shapeless endeavor.

That was the intellectual part of it, the drive to learn and then teach. There was another element that animated me, which was much more based in the handicraft of writing: I simply loved to write. I loved the musicality of language, and I delighted in creating a tone and rhythm that sparked the reader, even subconsciously, firing them forward in the piece. I loved plucking quotes out of my long interviews that made my subjects bounce onto the page, flesh and blood, loud and lively, as if you had met them face to face. I loved cooking up sentences and producing them, fresh out of the oven, and then making the next one. It made me happy seeing them on the page.

At *Paper Rose,* I wrote about teen pregnancy counseling and girls' basketball teams and fashion and immigrants and music and food. I wrote a profile of an architect who left her practice to become a puppeteer, and a profile of a local inventor, and a story about one of Buckminster Fuller's geodesic domes at the University of Portland. I began each story with the sensation of floundering because I always started from zero—in other words, I really was floundering. I never returned to a subject, so I never began any story as an expert. I was the perpetual beginner. But if I worked hard, I emerged victoriously, breathless, exhilarated, brandishing my story as if I had been bobbing for apples and gotten one.

Paper Rose lasted only a year, and then we were all out of work. I had spent my supposed year off before law school, and I worried that if I was unemployed for long, my father would renew his insistence on me applying. I started scouring the classifieds. A local country-and-western radio station was looking for someone to do public relations. It wasn't what I hoped for, but when I went for the interview, the station manager promised the job would entail mainly writing. It seemed like a decent stopgap until I could find another writing job closer to my heart.

What I really did at the radio station was type letters and reports, and answer phones when the other secretaries were on break. The head secretary was a martinet with a steely smile and a brittle manner who teetered through the office wearing six-inch stilettos and a bondage skirt, and she bossed me around and acted personally offended by my mediocre secretarial skills. She was annoyed that I came to work in jeans and no makeup, since she and the other secretaries took pains with their looks, with their sharp-shouldered blazers and lacquered hair. I was completely out of my element. My only friend at the station was a hulking, rumpled DJ with a gentle sense of humor and bipolar disorder. One night he had a psychotic break on the air and began jabbering manically and scribbling page after page of incoherent text in tiny script. Security hustled him off to inpatient care, and he never returned to work. After he left, my hatred of the job heated up. I was a terrible employee. I often showed up late on purpose or called in sick when I was only mildly under the weather. One day the station manager summoned me to his office and fired me. Obviously, I had it coming, but my ego was so affronted that I fought back, accusing him of having misdescribed the job on purpose. Somehow I managed to talk him out of canning me. After my near-firing, I bucked up briefly and answered the phones and typed letters with a little more pep, but I knew I had to leave as soon as possible.

JOYRIDE

I wanted to write for Portland's alternative newsweekly, *Willamette Week,* and when at last I heard of an opening there, I applied. After a round of interviews, I was offered the job. I packed up my desk at the radio station and fled.

I became a real writer at *Willamette Week*. At first, my job was modest. I wrote the music listings for the weekly calendar and edited a monthly music section. But I was in the door. I loved music and I liked writing about it, but I didn't want to do it indefinitely. I was too restless and inquisitive to want to write only about one subject, even one I liked. Being an expert in something didn't appeal to me. I wasn't good at writing criticism. I didn't want a beat. I preferred diving into a new world and then scrambling to understand it. I sometimes pictured myself on an Outward Bound adventure, equipped with only a piece of rope and a few matchsticks (or, rather, a notebook and a pen), airdropped into a new world. It felt vital to how I wrote and why I wrote, that experience of clawing my way to understanding. But for now, writing about music was an on-ramp I felt lucky to have.

The late 1970s were a great time to live in Portland. Back then, it was a drowsy port town, scruffy and friendly and comfortably uncool, dotted with strip clubs and bowling alleys and old saloons. Everything, including rent, was cheap as dirt, so it was easy to live on a meager writing salary. My writer friends who were living in pricey cities like New York and San Francisco had to wait tables and do temp work while trying to get published, so it felt luxurious that I could support myself on writing alone.

Everyone at *Willamette Week* was around my age and as ambitious and enthusiastic about writing as I was. We believed, with pride, that we could write circles around the stodgy dailies, *The Oregonian* and *The Oregon Journal.* The editor in chief of *Willamette Week,* Ron Buel, was a former political consultant who schooled us in the ethics of writing. He preached that no matter how small or narrow its focus, every story was meaningful.

Choosing to write about something needed to be a principled act, because in choosing it, you were implying that the subject merited attention. He insisted that the process of writing had three parts: reporting, then thinking, and *then* writing. Thinking might seem like an obvious step, but including it as an instruction, a specific phase of the writing process, felt revelatory. Ron believed you shouldn't begin to write until you had thoroughly absorbed what you had learned through research. Even now, when I'm stuck on a piece, I think back to this maxim and realize that the component I'm most likely missing is thinking and, sometimes, reporting. What feels like a block to writing is rarely a writing problem: It's either that I haven't done enough research or that I don't know yet what I'm trying to say because I haven't thought about it enough. Three simple steps: Report, then think, then write. No observation about the craft of writing has ever rung more true, or guided me more steadily, than that.

Ron believed we should aim for fairness and truthfulness rather than strict objectivity. What's the distinction? There is no such thing as true objectivity once you add the human element to the process, so it's disingenuous to claim it as your goal. Journalism is a living example of the uncertainty principle. Observing something alters it, even if only subtly. As a result, we can never know absolute truth; we know only the altered truth we can see. Absolute truth, in the sense of a flawless capture of information, doesn't need to be the goal. Imperfect recollection is the best we can do, and it's valuable even with its flaws and limitations. In fact, those limitations are part of every story, since they are part of the real human experience—the mess, the misinterpretation, the variation and imperfectible nature of perception. Our lives are always interpretive versions of reality. What matters in a piece of writing is to acknowledge the fingerprints the writer leaves on the story. That is what makes a piece of writing true. I never had formal training as a journalist, but what I learned from Ron made up for that.

* * *

The staff at *Willamette Week* formed a single-cell unit very quickly. We rolled from long, loud days at the office to drinks after work to dinner at some Vietnamese restaurant or pasta joint and then more drinks at a tiki bar or a club. We went camping on the weekends. We hiked to hot springs in the mountains and went whitewater rafting together; we accidentally set up tents in the middle of a rattlesnake breeding ground in eastern Oregon and bonded over the experience. We saw Mount Saint Helens erupt and drizzle ash on Portland. Within our ranks, we found best friends and, often enough, lovers. Before long, I broke up with my college boyfriend John. One reason was his enthusiasm for drinking, which seemed merely spirited in college but started to seem much less fun and a lot more dysfunctional once we were in Portland. Things were weightier in that post-college time, especially bad things, as if the gravitational pull of adulthood suddenly and seriously clicked in. In no time, I fell in love with a doe-eyed Minnesotan named Tony Bianco, who covered business for *Willamette Week*. He wore a dress shirt and tie when he wrote, at a time when no one I knew owned a tie, let alone wore one. He wrote about business when most of us didn't even consider business a significant subject.

Tony thought I was wild because I was, in fact, pretty wild. I loved to dance like a maniac, and to scream at the top of my lungs while I was dancing, and I loved staying out until dawn. The sound of a cashier ringing out for the night accompanied by the vacuum mumbling across the floor of a bar as it closed was my favorite melody. I threw huge parties and often barely knew most of the people who showed up. There were drugs everywhere in large quantities. I think most of Portland's economy in the 1980s was bolstered by cocaine sales, and at parties there was always a platter of cocaine even if the host hadn't bothered to provide food. I found coke boring, but I did a lot of it because it was always present, and eventually, it ate away enough of my nasal membrane that I had to get my nose cauterized to stop it from bleeding, which embarrassed me to no end. When I went for the cauterization, I told my doctor that I thought

I'd been using Kleenex too aggressively, but he was no idiot and carried on with the procedure without saying a word. Despite this dip into debauchery, I never lost track of myself and the fact that I wanted to be a writer, writing what I wanted to write about. Even when I was raging at a party at midnight, it was never far from my mind.

Has anyone ever analyzed the significance of those first post-college years? It's so enormous. I remember once reading how the music you hear when you're in your early teens has an outsize impact on your sense of what is good musically: It brands you deeply, imprinting the way no subsequent music ever will, and you measure all music thereafter by how much it does or doesn't deviate from that music of your teens. The first years after college seem to have that same disproportionate impact—they loom larger than any years that follow, they form you more, they linger in your soul more permanently. I lived in Portland only four years, but I lived a lifetime in them. It was the first time I had a real job; the first time I set up a home; the first time I bought furniture. It was the first time I took myself seriously. It was the first time I dared call myself a writer.

I was tethered to *Willamette Week*'s music section, but after a while I wheedled assignments for front-section features and kept asking for more. Ron finally agreed to let me hand off the music section to someone else and start writing features full-time. In exchange, he wanted me to cover a beat. What he offered me was the arid topic of county government. It was perhaps the worst assignment I could have imagined, but I accepted because I wanted so badly to do features. I intended to keep my word and cover county government, but I started handing in stories in which the only possible connection to the subject of county government was that the stories took place in the county. Each time I turned in one of these stories, I sheepishly explained to Ron that the subject was part of the county; after all, it *had* taken place in the county. It was the lamest defense imaginable, but it seemed to work: He let me keep going.

I wrote about the wave of new Hmong immigrants in Portland, and the boom in sales of amyl nitrite at grocery stores and gas stations. I wrote about a time-share company that had set up shop in Portland; I attended one of their sales events and got so carried away that I almost bought a time-share. I profiled performance artist Laurie Anderson and an architecture firm. I took a cheesy gambling junket to Reno, Nevada. I wrote about prostitution on one of Portland's main thoroughfares, and I posed as a high school student and attended classes for a week at Grant High School. I wrote about how the once groovy neighborhood of Old Town had lost its sizzle—the headline was IS OLD TOWN DYING?, which did not endear me to the largest commercial landlord in the area. I wrote about a horrible murder/suicide: A young woman filed for a restraining order against her abusive husband, who had been jailed for assaulting her. He made bail on one floor of the courthouse as the paperwork for the restraining order was being filed on another floor, an administrative glitch that went unnoticed. That night he ambushed her outside their house, killing her and then himself. It is the only murder story I have ever written. I was so haunted by it that I knew I could never do another.

These stories just dawned on me. They were everywhere I looked. Portland felt so ripe. I was always being surprised by something I came across, so I would take note of the surprise, and it would roll around in my head until it started to nag gently at me, demanding to be explored and then written. Often I drove around and looked, and I almost always found something that warranted further looking. I went down dirty alleys and along the wide, wavy river; I drove into the shaggy hills and walked through downtown; I picked up flyers and followed their instructions. Back then, Portland had a quality of being suspended in time, a city preserved in amber. There were taverns peopled in the early morning with saucer-eyed drunks, and there were the remnants of the timber industry and the leftover bits of a once-thriving Chinatown that had been forcibly cleared of its Chinese citizens in the 1940s; there were cavernous nightclubs on the fringes of the city, where the entertainment might be a guy with a harmonica and a drum kit and mastery of every Paul Revere & the Raiders song in the book. I loved it all. I was happiest when I was ferreting out a subculture—the more unfamiliar, the better—and forcing myself to be a quick study of it. I wasn't drawn to writing about people who were like me, inhabiting my socioeconomic slice, probably because it didn't offer me the opportunity for that wakening plunge into the unknown. I never minded being the stranger who had to ask about everything. I began to feel that the willingness to acknowledge my ignorance was my greatest virtue as a reporter. I discovered, fast, that people enjoy explaining themselves and teaching others what they are passionate about, and I was happy asking them to do that. I had no shame in being the newcomer who didn't know.

I usually went into interviews without a plan or notes or questions or foreknowledge. This forced me into the humble position of having to ask to have things explained to me. Journalism professors who preach the importance of advance research might be distressed by my approach. A small percentage of my style of unpreparedness might be attributable to laziness, but most of it rose out of my conviction that being a reporter was no different from being a student. You wouldn't study chemistry to prepare for taking chemistry: You'd throw yourself into it blind, beg for answers, thrash around until you understood it, and finally, the result would be that you'd learned chemistry, and perhaps if you learned it well enough, you could teach it to someone else. That process felt natural to me, even when I found myself forced to ask the most basic questions. Fighting my way to understanding felt vital to the story. It informed the way I wrote, because I had gone through exactly what the reader would go through, in the sense that I started with nothing but curiosity and had to earn my way to understanding, which is what reading a story feels like, too. You plunge in; you learn; you emerge with that sharp sense of clarity.

I also believed it was important to tip the balance of power away from me to make my stories work. I was drawn to writing about people who were rarely written about. Approaching them with my notebook and the imprimatur of my job put me in a position of authority, looming over them, a scientist scrutinizing a lab sample. That equation was a hindrance if I hoped to get close to them. I wanted my subjects to know that they were granting me something valuable by allowing me access to their worlds and explaining who they were and how they lived. The keenest example of this approach was a story I worked on much later, in 1995. I set out to write about a Black gospel group, the Jackson Southernaires, who performed on the small-town gospel circuit in the South. Before I went on the trip, someone at *The New Yorker* asked if I had read the definitive academic history of gospel music. Quite intentionally, I had not. For me, the point of the story was exploring this extraordinary subculture, and I wanted to dive into it without equipping myself with book knowledge. I wanted to learn about it from the people who lived it, not from scholars who studied it. I knew I might surprise the Southernaires with my naivete and ignorance, but that was reality. I knew nothing about their world and wanted to learn about it by visiting it. They were the experts. I was the visitor, asking them to let me in. I didn't mind if they thought I was a little obtuse.

The biggest surprise of my life was discovering that I am good at running a business. Did this come from watching my dad build his? That probably accounts for some of it, and maybe my determination to get where I wanted to go powered me to one place and then the next without my exactly knowing how. I did have the capacity to knuckle into a job, figure out how to make myself useful, and calculate where it might lead me next. Even when I was in Portland, brand-new to being a writer, I was already anticipating my next step. I was impatient with people who claimed they wanted to write but didn't seem to seize—or make—the opportunity to do it. Being a writer is an entrepreneurial undertaking, and you are the product, the management, the publicity department, the stock boy, the jobber, the racker, and the janitor. This unromantic fact about being a writer—the business of it—never diminished the art of writing, the enchantment of it, for me. I didn't mind the reality of the enterprise of getting published. I never expected to have things simply happen to me. I expected that I had to set them in motion deliberately, establish myself, capture my customers, service my accounts. I had no model to work from, since I had never observed someone creating a career as a nonfiction writer, so I sort of made it up on instinct and was happy to discover it came naturally.

In addition to working at *Willamette Week,* I wanted to get a toehold in a bigger publication, so one day I cold-called the San Francisco bureau chief of *Newsweek* and asked if he wanted a Portland correspondent. It turned out he did, and that was that. I dignify it too much by even calling it a "position"—it was a very informal relationship that consisted of the magazine calling me very occasionally to gather a quote or two for a story. It never turned into much, but it demonstrated to me that if you ask for an opportunity, you might get it. I had no real business being a *Newsweek* correspondent, but I was raring to go, and it didn't cost them anything to engage me as a resource, so they said yes.

I used to think my appetite for taking initiative, as with *Newsweek,* existed entirely separate from my ability as a writer, but they're completely entwined. Being a writer of nonfiction requires enormous resourcefulness: You must figure out what you want to learn, track down the people who can explain it to you, ask strangers to talk to you, fashion your material into something a reader is compelled to notice. You are building something out of fresh lumber every time you write a story. If that isn't entrepreneurial, I don't know what is.

THREE

In 1980, an Indian spiritual leader named Bhagwan Shree Rajneesh paid $6 million for the Big Muddy, a high, dry ranch of sixty-four thousand acres in eastern Oregon. Almost half of the money for the purchase—the equivalent of about $22 million in today's dollars—was donated by Bhagwan's ardent followers. Before coming to Oregon, Bhagwan had been an All-India debate champion, a philosophy professor, and the leader of an ashram in Pune, India. He left Pune in a rush. It was rumored that he had a tax problem; another rumor was that he conducted sessions at the ashram verging on sexual assault. In either case, it's easy to see why the Oregon ranch appealed to him. It was in the middle of nowhere, surrounded by nothing. The nearest town, a flyspeck called Antelope, had a total population of forty, and the neighboring communities of Biggs, Wasco, and Grass Valley were even smaller. Bhagwan had a big presence. By the time he arrived in Oregon, he had published a million words' worth of his musings in more than three hundred books, including *Don't Bite My Finger—Look Where I Am Pointing*; *Zen: Zest, Zip, Zap, and Zing*; and *I May Be the First Person Who Has Accepted Women Totally*. His books had been translated into seventeen languages, winning him tens of thousands of followers around the world. Bhagwan was small and wide-eyed, jolly and sly. He was pro-capitalism, pro-sex. His sermons were irreverent and merry and touchy-feely, a stylish mixture of a Catskills comic and Baba Ram Dass. He promised his disciples enlightenment without anguish. To be a follower of Bhagwan, a sannyasin, you didn't have to give up anything. You could smoke and drink and fornicate and be rich. Bhagwan requested only that you dress in "sun colors" like yellow and orange; wear a wooden amulet featuring his portrait; and heed his urging to "be aware," which you could define however you saw fit. Among the era's many cult leaders and gurus, Bhagwan seemed like the easiest to follow and the most fun.

Accompanied by three hundred sannyasins, Bhagwan arrived in Oregon in 1980 and began building a community for his followers, which he named Rajneeshpuram. The residents of Oregon set to work trying to figure out if Bhagwan was a good guy or a bad guy. In that era, especially on the West Coast, everyone knew someone who had been sucked into the Moonies or Scientology or some other group that promised utopia but served up something more sinister. Portland was a cult hotbed. In a landmark case, a deprogrammer named Ted Patrick, who had been hired by a set of parents to wrench their daughter away from Scientology, was tried on kidnapping charges in Portland (*Willamette Week* covered it extensively, and most of us on the staff perfected an impersonation of Patrick testifying about Scientology leader L. Ron Hubbard: "He's a snake! He's *Satan*!").

Was Bhagwan a wise soul establishing a model utopian community on this parched, ramshackle property, or was he, to quote Ted Patrick, a snake? Tapping into Oregon's storied tolerance for individuality and pioneer spirit, Bhagwan received a warm welcome at first. But after construction at Rajneeshpuram began and thousands of his followers gathered in Oregon for a festival, the reception chilled.

I loved writing about subcultures, and the celebration at Rajneeshpuram seemed like a perfect peg for a story about Bhagwan. I valued my job at *Willamette Week,* but I hoped to write for national magazines, too. Most of the stories I came across in Portland were too local to interest a national publication. Bhagwan, though, was different. He was known internationally; cults were a high-value topic; and I knew something about eastern Oregon, where the ranch was located. It all seemed promising.

The question was how to get the assignment. By coincidence, the Association of Alternative Newsweeklies was holding its annual meeting in Portland that year. The keynote speaker was Cynthia Crossen, the editor in chief of *The Village Voice*. I had a slight relationship with the *Voice*: The previous year, the music editor had invited me to take part in a critics' poll for the best music of the year. "All I got was a thank-you," I wrote to my parents at the time, "but it was a real honor to be invited since most of the other voters are the cream of the music writing crop. I also hope it'll give me an 'in' if I ask to sell them a story. We'll see." I wrote to Cynthia and asked if she would meet with me when she was in town. I didn't mention Bhagwan or anything about an assignment. I thought I would have a better chance if we met in person and I could plead my case.

At the conference's opening reception, I found Cynthia in the crowd and introduced myself, and she suggested that we go for coffee when the reception ended. I'm not sure if my letter was persuasive or whether it was that she was alone at a conference and happy to have company, but either way, we headed to a coffee shop nearby. Sometime during our conversation, I raised the idea of her sending me to write about Bhagwan. And—she said yes.

Back then, *The Village Voice* was revered. Founded by a group of writers including Norman Mailer, it featured heroes of mine such as Robert Christgau and Ellen Willis and Peter Schjeldahl and Nat Hentoff. Even though it was based in New York, the *Voice* had a national presence, and everyone I knew read it. I was ecstatic about getting the assignment.

A few days after the conference, I begged for a few days off from *Willamette Week*, packed a bag, and left for Rajneeshpuram. My plan was to nose around, attend the festival, and then write a piece about the experience. I drove two hundred miles east of Portland—two hundred miles of yawning fields, rimrock, coyotes, and cows—past a final forlorn sign saying OREGON IS JESUS COUNTRY, past a checkpoint manned by Bhagwan disciples and an enormous American flag snapping in the wind, and at last arrived at the marble signposts marking the entrance to Rancho Rajneesh.

Bhagwan's plans for the new development were ambitious, but not much had been built yet. The dusty pastures, grazed to the bone by generations of cattle, were cluttered with bulldozers and backhoes. A few roads were scratched into the powdery dirt. On a large, flat field, eighteen hundred nylon tents had been erected for the weeklong festival. As I parked, a guard with a German shepherd approached and said that the dog needed to inspect my car. I thought the dog was looking for drugs, but the guard said he was making sure I didn't have any meat or fish in the car, because the Rajneeshis were vegetarian. Everywhere I glanced, I could see sannyasins dressed in red and orange and ocher and peach, each one a bright burst against the ashy blankness of the high desert.

Once I got the dog's approval, I made my way to the press table. A woman there introduced herself as Ma Prem Sunshine. She checked my name on a list and then smiled drowsily. "This is Swami Deva Wolfgang,"

Me sporting an oversized Bhagwan-approved press pass

she said, motioning to a young man standing near the table. "He'll show you around."

Swami Deva Wolfgang was lean and handsome and had an abstracted, sleepy air. He was wearing low-slung orange pants and a tissue-thin red shirt and red sandals that looked perilous when you considered the rocky ground, but he moved nimbly, as if skimming over the lumps and pebbles. Right away I made my first mistake in covering cults—that is, I didn't realize I was being paired up and courted to distract me from noticing if anything was amiss. I immediately fell a little in love with Swami Wolfgang, which was the point. We wandered around the ranch together for an hour. He seemed to recognize everyone we passed. At one point, he introduced me to a sannyasin, who I learned later was Shannon Jo Ryan, the daughter of the late congressman Leo Ryan, who had been ambushed and killed when investigating Jim Jones and the Peoples Temple at Jonestown. Swami Wolfgang pointed out the future dining hall and the future community center and explained that Rajneeshpuram operated cooperatively, kibbutz-style. It sounded idyllic. Everyone in their cheery red and orange outfits was good-looking and fit, an army of healthy hippies, and in that moment, romanced by everything I was hearing, I felt this might really be the best place on earth.

I didn't yet understand how reporting can slop over so easily into something less objective. This is the enduring, hard problem of reporting. Doing it well requires that you keep an open mind and gather details with gusto, embracing where you are and whom you're talking to. But at the same time, you must maintain some sort of barrier, because without that barrier, things can begin to blur in your mind. This balance sometimes feels unachievable. How do you connect deeply with a subject but stay removed from it? Is that even possible? If you're truly open, it's easy to fall in love with your subject—or at the very least begin to find it uncomfortable to write something that might make your subject unhappy. Whenever I do a story, I always get smitten with whoever and whatever I'm writing about. I get swept up, swept away. I don't think I could do what I do without that happening—without feeling that kind of transference, that intimacy. Is this the result of overly identifying with a subject? Maybe, but can you get close to something without really getting close? Journalists who write the way I do—at length, up close, sympathetically—struggle with this constantly. Janet Malcolm wrote a book about it (*The Journalist and the Murderer*) and Joan Didion puzzled over it repeatedly. Sometimes, depending on the story, infatuation with your subject is harmless. When I write a travel story, I often become convinced that I want to move to wherever I'm visiting, but that's almost the point, isn't it? When I write about people who are obsessed with something, I often get a bit obsessed with it, too; in that case, it helps me to adopt their state of mind and begin seeing the allure of their obsession. Could I write the way I do without going through this entanglement? I don't think so. The danger arises when you're writing a story about something fraught, like Rajneeshpuram, where objectivity is essential, and part of the point of the story is to see past the dazzling surface and figure out what's really going on. But off the bat, rambling around the ranch with Swami Wolfgang, I was bewitched. The only saving grace was that I knew my objectivity was being tugged hard, and I realized I had to step back.

One of the few ranch buildings already completed was the hotel. It was reserved during the festival for the press; the seven thousand visiting sannyasins would be quartered in the perky little tents, arrayed in "sleeping fields" named Socrates, Zarathustra, and Buddha. Everything at Rajneeshpuram had a name. Even the hotel rooms didn't have numbers; the rooms on my hall were named Commune, Enlightenment, Surrender, Greed, and Beyond Greed. I was beyond Beyond Greed, in a room called Disciplehood. Clean and bright, still tangy with the smell of fresh paint and raw wood, Disciplehood was furnished with vaguely Scandinavian chairs and a queen bed. I put down my backpack and stepped into the bathroom. On the counter was a lineup of Hotel Rajneesh toiletries, which included hand soap, Q-tips, and a large box of condoms. The television had four operable channels. One was playing a Jane Fonda movie. The other three had videos of Bhagwan addressing his followers.

The next morning, I got dressed and left the hotel, walking down Yoga Road to Nirvana Road on my way to the main festival tent. Nirvana Road was lined with sannyasins. One of them explained that they had gathered to see Bhagwan as he was driven around the ranch. Bhagwan liked cars: He owned twenty-two Rolls-Royces and rode in a different one every day. When his car passed—a milky white Silver Shadow—I could see him peering out the window with a shy, delighted expression. He looked like a child with a beard. Above us, an Air Rajneesh plane buzzed by and dropped thousands of rose petals that drifted down like ticker-tape confetti. The sannyasins began singing "Yes, Bhagwan, yes" on repeat. After the car disappeared down the road, we headed to breakfast. It was a limited menu: white rice and Rajneeshpuram fortune cookies containing slips of paper with quotes from Bhagwan, such as ELEPHANTS ALWAYS DREAM ABOUT FLYING and JUST TRY BEING A HUMAN BEING.

On my way out of the dining hall, I stopped in the gift shop, always my favorite activity when reporting. There were Bhagwan-emblazoned Frisbees, baseball caps, and lighters; a pillowcase with a life-size silk-screen portrait of Bhagwan's face; more condoms; a wristwatch with a photo of Bhagwan's face for the dial; tapes of Bhagwan's lectures (one, which retailed for $150, was called "I Love Soap Bubbles"); tote bags printed with a Bhagwan portrait and the slogan I AM HAPPENING TO YOU; bumper stickers that said BE A JOKE UNTO YOURSELF. I stood in line at the cashier to buy the JOKE bumper sticker. The young man in front of me put a three-pack of condoms on the counter. "Come on, Swami," the cashier said to him with a playful toss of his head, "think positive!" Swami grinned and traded the three-pack for a twelve-pack.

The day's main event was an initiation ceremony for new followers. Bhagwan preached that we should be happy and not feel guilty about guilt-inducing things, and his easy philosophy had a silky pull. Every day, carloads arrived at Rajneeshpuram filled with newcomers ready to pledge their allegiance. The enormous tent for the initiation was packed.

Bhagwan's second in command, Ma Anand Sheela, stood near the tent entrance. Wiry and fierce, without the slightest flicker of maternal warmth, Sheela was nevertheless called "Mom" by most of the sannyasins. "We love money," she was saying as I passed. The reporters around her scribbled. She continued, "Bhagwan has an answer for the poor, which is 'Get off your fat ass and start working.'" Sheela enjoyed riling the public. Right before the festival, she referred to the mayor of a nearby town as "Miss Piggy" and called Oregon "part of the Soviet Union." A pop song called "Shut Up, Sheela" was getting a lot of play on Oregon radio. I took some notes and then noticed a television cameraman whom I had met the previous day. He was packing his camera, which surprised me, since the main event was yet to begin. I asked him what he was up to.

"I'm getting ready for the initiation," he said as he unscrewed a lens. He paused and looked up at me, then added, "I've joined."

"Ha," I said half-heartedly, because I hoped it was a joke but suspected it wasn't.

"You should think about it," he said. "I just love this place. The whole philosophy is really cool." He continued packing his equipment. I stood there dumbfounded. Granted, I had been a little seduced, too. The promise of a utopian commune was seductive, and everyone here seemed so happy. I yearned to feel like I belonged, but anyone might if they were near a bonded unit like Bhagwan's people; that's the regular ache you experience as a writer, as someone who writes about groups but is an outsider. Joining for real, though? Subcultures and communities attract me, and I see how belonging to something larger than yourself is alluring.

But I could never stomach the part of belonging that involves surrender, of having your sense of identity subsumed by a group. I'm not sure if I resist it so strongly because I'm a writer and need to stay one foot out of the circle to observe well, or whether I became a writer because that arm's-length posture comes naturally to me. All I know is I'm drawn to write about these tight knots of humanity but can't imagine being part of one and losing track of myself.

I was rattled by the cameraman's conversion. He was supposed to maintain this skepticism and distance, too, wasn't he? Yet somehow Bhagwan had punched through that barrier and grabbed him. For the first time since I'd arrived in Rajneeshpuram, I felt uneasy. Was it contagious? Was joining inevitable? Was I about to be gobbled up?

I hurried to find Cathy Cheney, the photographer on the story with me. To my relief, the bewitching power of Rajneeshpuram hadn't affected her at all. She thought the Rajneeshis were sketchy. She was convinced that our hotel room was bugged because the Rajneeshi press people knew exactly what we had discussed the night before in the room. At first, I had thought she was overreacting; I hoped that this place was largely benign. But it turned out that her skepticism was justified. Years later, after Rajneeshpuram had sputtered, I learned that the hotel rooms were indeed bugged. A lot worse was going on than I had imagined, including the Rajneeshis' efforts to poison some of their critics. When I watched *Wild Wild Country,* the 2018 documentary about Bhagwan, I finally took the full measure of how naive I had been.

One technique that disarms reporters is to make them believe they are being given access to something other reporters haven't gotten. It feeds our competitiveness (the drive to get the best story) and our need to feel special (that we somehow forged a more authentic bond with our subject than other writers did). The Rajneeshis perfected this technique. On my second day in Rajneeshpuram, Ma Prem Sunshine invited me to one of Bhagwan's private audiences. In 1981, Bhagwan had taken a vow of silence. For more than one thousand days, he spoke only to Ma Anand Sheela; the one exception he made was when the Immigration and Naturalization Service threatened to deport him if he didn't speak at his visa hearing. Eventually, he began to hold occasional private audiences in the living room of his modest Rajneeshpuram ranch house. Ma Anand Sheela told me that no more than thirty people were invited to these rare gatherings. "I have my own criteria for choosing," she said. "I look for whichever disciple religiously needs to come." I took the invitation as a sign that I had been elevated above the pack, that I was the most special of the many writers there, and that I had forged a better relationship with the Rajneeshis.

Bhagwan was severely allergic to almost all fragrances and many chemicals, so anyone attending the audience had to be entirely clean of allergens. Ma Prem Sunshine gave me special soap and shampoo and told me to scrub myself head to toe prior to the audience. As an additional condition for entering the room, one of Bhagwan's lieutenants would sniff me to make sure I emitted no scent that might afflict him.

I felt privileged because I had been chosen to attend, but I was also racked by paranoia. I studied the soap and shampoo for several minutes. I wondered if they might contain something weird. Didn't the Nazis tell people to shower when they were about to be gassed with Zyklon B? I knew this was a crazy thought, but I felt increasingly disengaged from logic. The heat, the sheer vacant acres here, the riot of color, the rustling whispers of the converted, the metallic cheerfulness of everyone I encountered, the drumbeat of repetition—Bhagwan, Bhagwan, Bhagwan, in every sentence, every conversation. It unnerved me. Earlier in the day, Ma Prem Sunshine had said to me with evident pride, "We've accomplished a psychological takeover. We took over the city and the county and the state, psychologically. There isn't one person in Oregon who isn't saying over and over again, 'Rajneesh, Rajneesh, Rajneesh.'" I began to mistrust my ability to determine what was good and what was dicey. I didn't have much time before Bhagwan's talk. I cranked on the hot water and stepped into the shower, soaping myself gingerly at first. When nothing horrible happened, I scrubbed myself up and down.

At the reception area, I submitted to being sniffed by a lean young man in a turban, which was exactly as awkward as you might imagine, and then entered a warm, dim room. A few dozen sannyasins were lounging on cushions, chatting quietly. Some were meditating. As far as I could tell, I was the only outsider there. After a few minutes, the low rumble of chatter stopped, and a door at the back of the room cracked open. Bhagwan stepped in and made his way to a throne-like wicker chair. He was wearing a diaphanous white robe, tan socks, chunky sandals, and a huge, glittering diamond Rolex. His tangled, wavy hair hung to the middle of his chest. He was so tiny that his feet dangled from the chair.

Everyone leaned forward, pulled like magnets. It was as if the room had tilted toward Bhagwan's critical mass. After a moment, a sound like grass rustling in a breeze arose from him, although I couldn't see his mouth moving because of his beard. I found myself leaning forward, too, because I sensed that something was being said, but I couldn't quite make out the shape of the words. It didn't seem like language. It was more like a sound you'd encounter in the woods, something clicking and whirring and buzzing. I looked around to see if anyone else was struggling to understand what Bhagwan was saying, but everyone was rapt, drinking him in. I strained harder to hear. As my ears got accustomed to the sound, I understood a few words now and then and a sentence or two on occasion, but nothing that I could string together as a narrative except for a few snippets. "Who will the pope be when there is no God?" Bhagwan said at one point, laughing, raising his voice slightly. "That *Polack* will have to go back to Poland, and Poland is Communist now!" A few minutes later he said, "Jesus proved to be the biggest business deal in the world, and the Jews can never forgive him for that!" I kept checking the faces around me, but no one else seemed confounded. At regular intervals, people nodded vigorously, or clasped their hands in delight, or squeezed their eyes shut in a sort of appreciative wince.

After forty-five minutes, Bhagwan stood up and left as suddenly as he had entered the room. His departure had the effect of breaking a vacuum seal. The audience members began gushing with exclamations. The talk evidently had been a big hit, yet I hadn't managed to make sense of most of what he'd said. What I had heard was a susurration, a muttering, whispery, unintelligible wafting of words, as buoyant and insubstantial as a gust of air. At that moment, I understood that everyone there wanted to have heard something different, something brilliant and edifying, and that's what they heard.

I whipsawed the whole time I was in Rajneeshpuram, one minute skeptical and suspicious, and the next, a little giddy and credulous. It was oddly uncomfortable, but it was exactly what the circumstances demanded. My goal with the story wasn't to recommend Bhagwan or advise against him. I wanted to sink into his peculiar, constricted universe and see what it felt like, and allow myself to experience its seductiveness. I don't believe a writer can truly be only an observer, an unblinking recording eye. People, knowing they're being studied, perform for you, or shape what they say to what they think you want to hear, or don't tell you what they really think, or don't behave the way they usually behave. You can only hope to see something close to natural.

I worked around that limitation by acknowledging my presence in the story, so the reader was aware of the filters through which the story had passed. I wasn't the main character in the story; I was the Virgil leading the reader through it. Teetering between knowing whether this was the worst place in the world or the best place, as I had teetered, was the point. The fantasy of Rajneeshpuram was splendid; the reality implausible; the backstory impenetrable. There would be lots of excellent investigative journalism later that revealed how corrupt Bhagwan's world really was (in particular, the machinations of Ma Anand Sheela, who was behind that unsuccessful conspiracy to poison an entire town in Oregon, among other misdeeds). But for the moment, my ambition was to observe and report back. I banged out the story fast. It was such a vivid experience that it came easily. "The fact is, if you really love Bhagwan, you don't wear deodorant," I wrote.

> Everybody here, of course, really loves Bhagwan. To see him, they've come from Japan, England, Holland, Germany, and from all over the USA; paid $350; driven through the unsympathetic Oregon towns of Biggs, Wasco, Moro, Grass Valley, and Kent; crept past the creepy ghost town of Shaniko; coasted into the most unsympathetic town of Antelope; then headed down twenty twisted miles of washboard country road through hills best suited to rattlesnakes and coyotes; and finally passed through three public safety checkpoints to get to the First Annual World Celebration in Bhagwan's new city of Rajneeshpuram. Thus committed, no one would dare risk getting booted out of the *satsang* or *darshon* ceremonies by one of the official sniffers up by the stage. Let them catch a whiff of perfume or Ban Roll-On on you, and you're out: Bhagwan may be enlightened, but he's also terrifically allergic. So the sannyasins—his followers—are asked please to cut the asthmatic Great Master some slack and leave the scented stuff at home.

The *Voice* ran the piece as the cover story of the August 3, 1982, issue. As luck would have it, that issue was the first time the *Voice* ever printed in color, so in addition to being the cover, my Bhagwan piece was illustrated with a large color photo of souvenirs from the Rajneeshpuram gift shop. The image got a great deal of attention because of its novelty; the story got attention because it was snappy and revealing. Within a few days, editors from magazines in New York like *Glamour* and *Vogue* and *GQ* called to talk about me writing for them. My foray into a national publication had jump-started me more vigorously than I could have imagined.

The experience taught me many lessons that I abide by to this day. The first and most important one was to take a chance and ask, even when what you're asking seems a little bit impossible. The story in the *Voice* and subsequent assignments at magazines wouldn't have happened if I hadn't dared. I knew that Rajneeshpuram was a great story, and I could see no reason I shouldn't ask to do it. That was nervy and maybe unduly confident, but what was the alternative? At worst, I would have been turned down, but besides disappointment and light bruising to my ego, it wouldn't have been so bad. What would have been terrible was not making the effort to see if maybe it was meant to be.

It also made me appreciate how important it is for writers to cultivate story ideas. Over the course of my career, I have sometimes been assigned stories—that is, an editor comes up with an idea and sends me off to do it. But every significant move forward for me has occurred because I developed ideas for myself. Story ideas are *everything*. They are the raw material you trade in; they're the currency you can offer to editors and publishers. If I want to do bespoke stories that fit me perfectly, I need to find them and fit them to myself. I've always had an evangelical zeal about doing a certain kind of story—in particular, the reveal of hidden worlds or the reexamination of a familiar one. It isn't always easy to persuade editors that those stories are important to do, so it is up to me to agitate for them, or they will never happen. I have to figure out what I care about, find those stories, and then adamantly and excitedly lobby an editor to let me do them.

The wealth you need to acquire as a writer is a wealth of ideas—it's even more important than a thick stack of good clips. Those ideas are what make you a writer. Knowing how to craft a beautiful sentence is critical, but what is that sentence about? Your task begins *there*, at the earliest stage of thinking about what you want to learn about; it doesn't start when you're at your keyboard. It's maddening that we don't get trained to come up with story ideas, considering how vital it is to being a writer. My technique for coming up with ideas is simple and elemental: If there is something that interests me, something I want to understand, it feels like a story to me. Where do I find things to be interested in? That's a long list. The newspaper (usually the story that is tucked somewhere in the back). The radio. Notices on bulletin boards. Community news sites. Conversations with anyone and everyone (neighbors, cabdrivers, colleagues, anyone). Walking through unfamiliar neighborhoods. Thinking of the backstory of a big story. Reconsidering something I thought I knew. Everywhere, anything that catches my attention could lead to something that could bloom into a story. I am always looking. This means that I have lots of ideas, and many of them will never see the light of day. When I was preparing for my first meeting with Richard Pine, who became my book agent, he told me to bring a few book ideas to the meeting. I'm sure he expected me to bring two or three. I brought twelve. Some would have made terrible books, and some were impractical, and others never would have found a publisher, but it was a good sign that I was already letting myself conjure such an unruly pile of possibilities.

Bhagwan had been in the local news nonstop since he'd arrived in Oregon, so my story was not one of those ideas that I found hidden in a haystack. Recognizing it as a story that had broad appeal, even national appeal, was what I did, and it rewarded me. Sometimes great story ideas aren't secreted away. Sometimes it's the story that's right in front of you, but you begin to think about it in a fresher way.

Not long after my Bhagwan story was published, I got a call from a wonderful writer for *Rolling Stone* named Mikal Gilmore. He grew up in Portland, and he still read the local papers even though he had moved to Los Angeles. Besides keeping tabs on his hometown, he liked to look for Portland writers he thought had potential for *Rolling Stone*. When I got his call, I reacted with what probably looked like a cartoon of someone banging the phone on the desk and saying, "Excuse me, I'm having trouble hearing. I could swear you said you thought I should be writing for *Rolling Stone!*" Once I settled down, I told Mikal that I would pretty much die to write for *Rolling Stone*. He suggested I review an upcoming performance of a Portland band called Johnny and the Distractions. At that time, I had trouble believing I was a writer, afflicted as I was by that familiar devil, impostor syndrome. But with calls like this, I was gathering outside proof that was harder and harder to dismiss.

I need to stop for a moment here and talk to you about luck. Without a doubt, I am very, very lucky. I was born into a comfortable home with a loving family. I am a member of a race that is afforded infinite privilege. Even at my most broke, I have never been desperately broke, just temporarily disadvantaged. I am sound of limb; sound of mind. In addition, I have been drenched by the rain of good fortune. The color photo with my Bhagwan story. The fact that Mikal Gilmore read *Willamette Week*. Other lucky accidents, little geysers of auspiciousness, have met me along the way. But I have also used the explanation of luck to shield me from my constant worry that what goes well for me will somehow turn back on me in a painful way. Many of my friends are writers. We are dear to one another but rather like a litter of puppies, nipping and snapping, unsure if there's enough kibble to go around—because really, there isn't enough. Writing can be a mean business, breaking your heart at the drop of a hat. Disappointment and frustration are a constant. Most writers yearn for approval and acclaim, so among them you are guaranteed to encounter competitiveness and jealousy. Being a writer requires having the confidence to think you have something to say, but it is almost always linked with the neediness of wanting an audience to hear and approve of it. That mix can be brutal.

Writing is an unforgiving enterprise, and it's a shrinking one. I hate thinking about all the magazines and newsweeklies and newspapers that have shuddered to a halt since I began working. But I have had a golden run, which makes me feel very fortunate, and also a little vulnerable. Sometimes people have been annoyed that things have gone my way. When I was young, I was baffled and hurt when certain friends didn't celebrate if something good happened for me. Then I got older, and I learned not to expect so much celebration, and to be careful, and to shield myself from jealousy by attributing some of these good things to dumb luck, as if most of my life's turns were as accidental as a lightning strike, no credit to me, don't blame me, above all, don't blame me.

When I read the great writer E. B. White's book *Here Is New York* for the first time, I was struck by the line "No one should come to New York to live unless he is willing to be lucky." His book was about the charmed nature of living in the city, but his insight reverberated for me in a more general way. I felt he was saying that it's up to you to prepare a soft bed for luck to land in, regardless of where you are. Reading that line changed me. I realized that I have made that soft bed. I have always been ready to be lucky. I've been good at that bed-making all my life. Whenever luck happened, I was there to welcome it.

Other than waitressing and my radio station stint, all I've ever done is write. On a bad writing day, I forget the enjoyment of making sentences and how pleasing it can be when it's going well. When that happens, I try to remind myself of the delight gotten from tacking a series of words in place that feels right. Reminding myself of that pleasure is medicinal when the more exasperating stuff crowds in (the sentence that won't comply, the source who won't call you back, the deadline that is causing you to panic, the editor who nitpicks). What can be better than building sentences into sturdy little structures? What could be better than getting to do the thing you love?

I write because I think it's important. There are a million different kinds of writing, but this belief applies to all of them. Writing in all its forms is the essence of human interaction. It's the most essential unit of exchange. It is the way we organize the world and the information that floats through it, the churning experience of being alive; it is the gesture we use to make ourselves known and to know others. We write to make a mark on the world. We write to express the whirring in our heads, the thousand thoughts and impressions that are private, internal, invisible, until they spill out into being, made present through language. Talking does that, and writing does it, in a more permanent way. The Internet, which we all believed would be the end of writing, has instead made us write all the time, probably more than we ever have. If we're not tweeting, we're texting, or we're posting on social media. Being able to communicate through writing is sorcery. Little scratches on a page or screen, delivering knowledge and emotion and mystery—it's astonishing. To make those little scratches on the page for a living is a miracle.

To be empowered to write, to feel entitled to broadcast your thoughts to the world, is an honor, so I choose what I write about with a lot of deliberation. Picking a topic is a significant act; you elevate a subject when you light it up with attention. You are declaring that it matters. I have done plenty of writing that doesn't strive to be morally meaningful, too. I have done my share of celebrity profiles and fizzy stories that existed to entertain and little more. But once I was given the opportunity to choose my own subjects, I began to appreciate the weight of those selections. If I can write about anything, what do I pick to write about? What does it mean to profile an African king who drives a taxi in New York? What does it mean to tell the story of a burned library?

What's the value of wondering why I write? Everyone benefits from stepping back and considering what and why they do what they do, whatever it is that they do. But it's particularly essential for writers to ask and answer that question. Writing is *hard*. It can be discouraging, exhausting, frustrating, depleting. It's easy to forget why it's so compelling; why it's satisfying; why it's important; why and how it can feel good. Taking a moment to do that reboots the part of me that wants to write with passion and drive and a sense of delight. I want to write with a burning desire to do it. I want to write with urgency, with the feeling that I *must* do it. Readers can sense that, just as they can sense when someone is merely shuffling words around without feeling fired up. I like to picture myself bubbling over with my story, as if I simply can't contain it; I must share it *or else*. When I can lock into that emotion while I'm working, I can respond to the question of why I write with a very simple answer: I write because I must.

In 1982, my boyfriend, Peter Sistrom, and I decided to move east. Peter and I met at *Willamette Week*. He was a brilliant guy, an intellectual, an ice climber, a passionate cook, and a depressive, with a square jaw, blue eyes, and unruly brown hair. We liked the same music, the same jokes, the same movies. We thrilled each other. Our relationship started on the sly when both of us had other partners—a hint of what was to come—but eventually we broke up with those other partners, and very quickly—too quickly, probably—moved in together. I was mad about him and, at least initially, he was clearly mad about me.

Peter was a fantastic editor, but he hated the hustling he knew would be required to get ahead in journalism, so he decided to make a shift. He toyed with the idea of going to graduate school in anthropology. The prospect of being a faculty wife filled me with horror, so I voted for his other thought, which was law school. He applied to a few schools, all on the East Coast. Moving east suited me because it put me closer to the magazines and newspapers I hoped to write for. By the time we moved, I was contributing regularly to *Rolling Stone* and had assignments from *Glamour* and *Vogue*. Peter got accepted to law school at Northeastern University, and he and I went to Boston that summer to find an apartment for the fall.

Before the trip, I wrote to *The Boston Phoenix* and *The Boston Globe* and set up meetings with editors. The *Globe* editor, a fussbudget in a bow tie, clucked his tongue and warned me that the *Globe* rarely hired writers from alternative newsweeklies because, he said, those kinds of writers didn't have a work ethic. He was sniffy and arrogant, and clearly uninterested in my clips.

My interview at the *Phoenix* was much more successful. An alternative newsweekly like *Willamette Week*, the *Phoenix* had become a well-regarded publication, and people were willing to overlook the fact that most of its income came from ads for sex services. The *Phoenix* prided itself as the anti–*Boston Globe*, more tuned in to street culture and the arts; funnier, looser, cooler. Many of its alumnae, including Janet Maslin and Charles Pierce, went on to publications like *The New York Times* and *Vanity Fair*, and one of its writers, Lloyd Schwartz, had won a Pulitzer Prize for Criticism. The editor, Richard Gaines, was rangy and intense. He liked my clips, and at the end of our meeting, he offered me a job. A few weeks later, Peter and I packed our belongings and drove a bone-shaking secondhand pickup truck across the country to our new apartment, the ground floor of a clapboard duplex in a neighborhood called Jamaica Plain. Back then, Jamaica Plain was cheap, diverse, and run-down—full of students who were relieved, like we were, to find somewhere affordable to rent.

The *Phoenix* offices were in Boston's Back Bay, in a ratty old building at the end of the otherwise glamorous Newbury Street. I don't mean ratty in a figurative sense, either: Rat traps were set in the office's corners and nooks, and they were often full. The office had the disarray of a yard sale five minutes after closing time. The staff was young and shaggy. As one would expect in a workplace of young people, there were a million desperate romances and personal dramas and the like, but everyone was serious about their work.

I didn't know the first thing about Boston, but that didn't bother me. As I had in my early days in Portland, I used my unfamiliarity with the city as my entry point. I treated each story like a guided expedition into my new world. The stories reflected that effort of discovery and my attempt to answer the question of what Boston felt like, what the character of the place was.

I began to be braver about allowing that reflex to propel my writing. My stories had a primary layer, the nominal subject. But there was always a bigger subject or purpose or quest that transcended the immediate.

Who are we? Why do we do what we do? How do we make meaning in our lives? Why do we live the way we do? Could a story about a photographer who documented a dying Massachusetts mill town really be that profound? I was sure it could be.

My first piece in the *Phoenix*, though, was an oddly ill-tempered essay about how Oregon wasn't as progressive as it purported to be. At that time, Oregon was synonymous with tolerance and liberal thought, but I had found a surprising amount of rigidity and conformity, too. The story was a strange way to announce my arrival in Boston. Maybe I was wallowing in homesickness for Portland and was trying to convince myself that I was glad to have left. What I remember most was that when the issue came out and I galloped to a newsstand to see my first *Phoenix* byline, I made the unpleasant discovery that my byline was in fact missing. I was crushed. I called Gaines in tears. We finally figured out that the little strip of paper with my name on it had fallen off the pasted-up layout page—remember, this was several years before desktop publishing, and the paper was produced by literally pasting pieces of text on a board and submitting that to the printer.

After that jolt, I settled in. I wrote stories that were sturdy but uninspired: a survey of Boston's next generation of arts patrons; a story about an overpass that was too low and caused countless truck crashes; the new system of using state lottery money for arts funding. I also had fun. I covered a reggae festival in Jamaica; I wrote about how Miami was being reborn, as embodied by *Miami Vice*; about Ginsu knives; about a janitor at Wellesley College who created amazing outsider art from discarded Styrofoam.

I made a lot of friends at the *Phoenix*. I was closest to Stephen Schiff, the film critic, who was on the brink of leaving for a job at *Vanity Fair*. Even though we overlapped only briefly, he mentored me, instructing me in ways that were large—such as strategies for moving up and out of the

Phoenix—and very small. At the time, I used "Susan C. Orlean" as my byline. Growing up, everyone had called me Susie, but I wanted a byline that seemed more adult, and beginning with *Paper Rose*, I signed my stories as "Susan." But I hankered for more gravitas. Many writers at *The New York Times* used their middle initials, so with that in mind, I added the "C" for my middle name, Carol. At our first lunch, Stephen said he had several pieces of advice for me. The first one, he said, was to drop my middle initial because it was pretentious. Once he pointed it out, I was mortified, and from then on, I banished the "C."

I had been at the *Phoenix* for a few months when I somehow learned—to this day I can't remember how—that a male writer about my same age and experience, who had been hired when I was, was being paid one and a half times my salary. I was livid, even more so when Gaines sloughed off my complaint by telling me I hadn't negotiated as well as this other writer had. In a fury, I told him that I was quitting, and if he wanted to rehire me, he could call me at home. Where did I get the nerve? I was so outraged that I didn't hesitate, even though I was walking out of a job I really liked. At that time, there was no employment protection or law against discrimination based on gender. I was on my own. I felt sick to my stomach when the full weight of what I'd done settled on me. I was unemployed. Luckily, Gaines called me the next day, and this time I negotiated for the same salary my male colleague was getting. My tactic had been successful, but I was angry that I had to use it to get a fair shake.

In 1983, the summer after our first year in Boston, Peter and I got married at my parents' country club in Cleveland. I wore a silk chiffon wedding gown from Priscilla of Boston because I imagined that was what a real adult would wear, but with ballet slippers. I didn't own, nor would I have been willing to own, a pair of high heels. I was impatient to get married because my father was recovering from colon cancer and I believed, foolishly, that it would cheer up my parents in that cheerless time if one of their children had a wedding. I shouldn't have done it, although I was deeply in love with Peter. We had a buoyant, playful, passionate rapport and I thought he was unbelievably attractive. But he could be clam-like and darkly secretive. I tried to overlook it by telling myself that maybe I was too much of a revealer. He was terrible with money, but I blamed it on his tightfisted parents. He had a chilly relationship with his family—only his mother came to our wedding—but I convinced myself it didn't matter. He deflected me anytime I wanted to understand him more, or learn about his past, or ask him about his mood. We were a canoe balanced on a hair, but I persuaded myself we were on solid ground.

By the time we got married, my wishful portrait of our relationship was starting to crack. I was uneasy. It felt like Peter resented how quickly my career was moving forward, almost as if I had elbowed him out of the way. I don't think he liked that I was happy and that people were telling me I was good at my job. He became even more passive and evasive, which made me clingy, wary. Even before our wedding, I began to suspect that he was cheating on me. Our relationship had far too many wobbles to justify making it permanent, but my impulse to be the child who made things right for her family propelled me to get married anyway.

A year or so after I started at the *Phoenix*, I got a call from Ande Zellman, the editor of the *Boston Globe* Sunday magazine, a glossy publication that had space to run long features, like many Sunday magazines in that fertile era. I was getting restless at the *Phoenix*, so her invitation to write for the magazine came at the right moment. She said she would publish as much as I could write. I left the *Phoenix* and focused on *Globe* stories full-time. Working with Ande was wonderful. She encouraged me to think as adventurously as I could, and she was willing to take a chance on almost all my ideas. I wrote about the artist Christo's *Surrounded Islands* project in Miami (I worked on one of the building crews), and about epidemiologists tracking cancer clusters in Boston, and about the vicious rivalry between Persian cat and Siamese cat fanciers, and beyond.

This was the first time in my life that I was working for myself, which was both thrilling and terrifying. I set up shop in our living room. My desk was an old door laid across a set of sawhorses, with a view of our little Jamaica Plains backyard. At *Paper Rose* and *Willamette Week* and the *Phoenix*, I'd had a desk in the newsroom. Even though my real work took place when I was out reporting, I came to those offices every day, docking to them hungrily, sustained by feeling part of a community. I went to the office so I could see friends, and to see people who weren't close friends but whom I knew well enough to gossip to or gossip about; they were part of the social padding that made me feel like I fit somewhere.

Now, though, I was completely on my own. Peter left for school in the morning, and I rattled around our apartment trying to figure out where to start and what to do. Every effort seemed both not enough and too much. I looked forward to errands to get out of the house, to chat with the clerk at the post office and the grocery store cashier; at least that made me feel purposeful. My loneliness was different from any I had ever experienced. I felt unmoored. The only thing that snapped me back to being productive was the need to earn money. Since Peter was in school, we relied on my income. Immersing myself in a story had the tonic effect of giving me, at least temporarily, a universe I felt part of.

One of my *Globe* stories ended up becoming particularly important to me. By chance, I had met a law clerk who was training for the Ironman competition in Hawaii. He had a crazy life; he ran fifteen miles to work every day and then poured a gallon of water over his head as a makeshift shower before he went into his office. At the time, the mid-1980s, triathlons were a novelty. The Ironman competition was brand-new. My story idea was to follow a few people as they prepared for the Ironman. That law clerk was one of them; another was a woman he introduced me to, a heavy smoker—and nonexerciser—who was doing the Ironman on a dare from her dad. The story examined a subject I've returned to again and again: what it's like to be passionate about something, and how we shape our lives around our obsessions, how a focus can make sense of life, and how a singular goal can bring together the most unlikely people. We are usually defined by how we differ from one another, so this commonality fascinated me, especially when it attracted people who never would have met otherwise.

While I was working on the story, I had lunch with a friend from Oregon named Mark Christensen. Mark was the first of my friends to write a book—he had published *The Sweeps: Behind the Scenes in Network TV* in 1984. To me, writing a book seemed impossibly glamorous. Mark saw it as merely pragmatic. He said a book was a two-pound business card that proved you could sustain a story for a few hundred pages.

Until that conversation, I hadn't thought about writing a book. I didn't feel ready for it, and I didn't think I had any ideas that were book-worthy. Writing a book seemed like something *real* writers did, and I didn't yet believe I was a real writer. Mark insisted that I was more than ready, and he encouraged me to talk to his agent, Richard Pine. I waved Mark off, but over the next few weeks, I kept turning it over in my mind. Could I really write a book? I finally decided that talking to Richard was worth doing, no matter how doubtful I was. Never say no. Richard encouraged me to come to New York and meet with him.

I always had a lot of ideas, but I didn't know how to judge how big they were, whether any of them had the heft to fill a book. At that point, my longest story was perhaps five thousand words. Books are usually at least a hundred thousand. But I got excited as my meeting with Richard approached, and I composed a long list, which included "Travel for a year with someone who sells things at flea markets" and "Write about a year living in Rajneeshpuram" and "Follow three people training for the Ironman"—an expanded version of my *Globe* story.

Richard and I got along right off the bat. We were the same age, although he seemed much wiser and was more seasoned by far. His father, Arthur, was a longtime, beloved literary agent, so Richard had the self-assurance of someone who'd grown up in the publishing world and knew how it worked. He seemed unfazed by my crazy gush of ideas, even though most were barely marketable and sure to scare off many publishers. He told me that the triathlon idea was the strongest of my lot. He gave me a book proposal from another of his clients to use as a model— a gesture that was extremely helpful, because I had no idea how to write one. I was about to learn.

FOUR

ULTRA-ATHLETICS: THE LIFE AND TIMES OF SUPER-ENDURANCE ATHLETES BY SUSAN ORLEAN.

Introduction:

Forget the Bhagwan. Ignore Reverend Moon. Stop wondering about Krishna, EST, and otherwise.

The real cult of the '80s is emerging: its adherents can be identified by their aerodynamic nylon vestments, their fear of fats, the arthroscopic surgery scars on their knees, and their determination to see how far and fast they can go.

They are the ultra-athletes—the triathletes, ultramarathoners, and distance swimmers—and they, to turn William Faulkner's phrase on its head, "prevail to endure." . . . like all extreme subsets of society, endurance athletes are a microcosm. In prying open this microcosm, *Ultra-athletics* will reveal a lot about athletics, a lot about the business of fitness, something about the sweetness of success, and mostly, a lot about the way we choose to live. I will cover the Ironman competition. But rather than just recording who crossed the finish line, I will go to Kona at least three weeks before the race to watch the competitors. Expect such chapters as A Day in the Life / The Gym Generation / How to Succeed in Business Without Really Tri-ing / Building Strong Bodies Twelve Ways / The TriAthlete, Body and Soul / Back on the Train Gang / Agony and Ecstasy: Ultramarathoning / The Metalmen / To Tri or Not to Tri / The History of the Ironman / The Week That Was: Seven Days Before the Ironman.

On it went for forty-four feverish pages, concluding with a short bio that began, "Susan Orlean was born 29 years ago in a suburb of Cleveland, Ohio. In spite of that, she had a happy childhood . . . Her nagging interest in endurance athletes began as a story about triathletes . . . Only an armchair athlete (she will run if chased), the fascination parallels her earlier coverage of cults (EST, Bhagwan Shree Rajneesh) and kooks (acupressurists, cat fanciers). Orlean lives in Boston with her husband, her dog Molly, her priceless collection of syrup pitchers, and an exercycle she found at the Salvation Army."

The tone of the proposal was much sassier than it should have been, but I was so excited to be writing it that I couldn't help myself. What had seemed plainly impossible a few months earlier—the idea of me writing a book—was starting to feel a little bit plausible.

Because I was a book-writing rookie, Richard said I'd have a better chance of selling my proposal if I met with publishers and showed them in person how keen and determined I was. He set up meetings in New York with editors and publishers from a number of major publishing houses. What followed was an exhilarating, hectic week of warm welcomes and glasses of sparkling water with lime slices and gentle querying about what *exactly* I had in mind for *Ultra-Athletics*. I tried to hide my dewiness and incredulity, to not let on that I could not believe I was sitting in a publisher's office talking about *me writing a book*. I chattered about how I would spend time with these athletes and how their stories would be aspirational and inspirational and literary and journalistic and sociological all rolled into one, and I believed it.

Then I waited. Over the next week, the rejections tiptoed in, tender in their tone. We aren't crazy about the topic, McGraw Hill noted, but "Susan Orlean is a terrific writer. Does she have any other ideas we could get together on?" No thank you from Crown, but "if she has other ideas she'd like to discuss I'd love to get together with her when she has the chance—she sounds like a winner!" No thanks from Morrow, Simon & Schuster, Viking, Times Books, Little, Brown, and Putnam. At last, as my confidence was buckling, Richard got a call from Joni Evans, who ran an imprint at Simon & Schuster called Linden Press, saying she was interested. She called me late the next afternoon and said that she and her deputy, Marjorie Williams, wanted to publish a book with me. Then she asked if *Ultra-Athletics* was really the book I wanted to write.

Without thinking, I blurted out that it wasn't. I knew ultra-athletics was a solid idea, but it didn't thrill me. What did I really want to write about? I told Joni that I wanted to write a book about Saturday night in America. I jabbered for a few minutes about how Saturday night was a cultural touchstone and a great common denominator and I wanted to document a swath of the American experience through that one lens, and I didn't think anyone had looked at popular culture this way before, and I was dying to do it.

Perfect, she said. I'll send a contract to you.

Years later, when I tried to parse the end of my marriage, I realized with a jolt that I have no memory of celebrating with Peter when I got my book contract for *Saturday Night*, even though it was such a thunderclap moment in my life. Obviously, I told him about it immediately, but then the memory goes dark. I don't recall him buying me flowers or exclaiming excitedly on my behalf. I remember him asking me sourly what the book would actually be about, that "Saturday night" sounded awfully vague. It was a legitimate question, but it wasn't cushioned by an expression of pride or gladness. It sounded accusatory, like he intended to deflate me.

A few months earlier, Peter had been awarded a highly sought-after clerkship with a federal judge. I was so happy that I called everyone I knew to crow about it, to brag about *him*. I'm not a saint, nor am I selfless, but it was easy to feel happy about something good happening for him, to bask in it; it felt like it was happening for us together, even though it was solely his achievement. I assumed he would feel that about something good happening for me. But Peter saw happiness as a zero-sum game, and he must have felt that anyone else having some of it meant there was less available for him. I felt punished. When I managed to tell him how hurt I was that he didn't seem happy for me, he told me I was demanding and then shut down. There was nothing more I could do.

Once, during college, I found an old pair of my jeans in the back of a closet. I shoved my hands in the pockets and found two hundred dollars' worth of unused travelers checks I had forgotten about. That's what coming up with the idea for *Saturday Night* felt like. I had never articulated the concept before my conversation with Joni Evans, but evidently, it was there all along. When I was prompted, it spilled out of me. Like that money in my pocket, it was a lovely, abundant surprise, a marvelous discovery, but I wasn't sure what to do with it. Never mind. Richard and Joni conferred, and in short order, I had a contract to write *Saturday Night in America* and a modest but respectable advance of $25,000 (equivalent to about $70,000 today). *Saturday Night in America* was the original title of the book; it was shortened to *Saturday Night* before it was published, because my editor thought that looked better on the cover.

I loved the idea of writing it. As much as I surprised myself with it as a book topic, I knew exactly why Saturday night captivated me. Instead of a travel book about a place—a summer in Provence, a trip to the Azores—I would travel through a temporal window. I would voyage through an idea. I would take a frame and place it around a wide variety of circumstances and people and settings. To write a book about random places in the United States could seem haphazard, but illustrating a universal concept like Saturday night gave me the freedom to look at almost anything. The concept was what held the separate pieces together. My curiosity was genuine. I did want to see what Saturday night meant to a range of people. I wanted to show how similarly or, more often, how differently Americans celebrated it.

As convinced as I was of the idea, I was also truly, deeply scared. I had never written anything close to a book, and here I was, starting with one that was conceptually difficult. The subject didn't have a built-in chronology, or characters, or a dramatic turn. I would have to provide those. Many years later, Tina Brown, then the editor of *The New Yorker*, cautioned me that my stories were all "tightrope acts"; any misstep would send them, and presumably me, plunging. Conventional ideas give the writer firm footing. By contrast, my stories are built on slender supports, such as time-traveling through the United States on a Saturday night. "Your stories all depend on execution," Brown said. "If they're not written well, they fall apart." I knew I had to muster everything I had to make this work.

Where do you begin with an idea as big as Saturday night? In the summer of 1985, I wrote "Saturday Night" across the cover of a blank reporter's notebook, and then I started compiling a list of questions I wanted to answer.

> *How many weddings are there?*
> *Do people buy clothes Saturday afternoon for Saturday night?*
> *Who has to work*
> *Are there any towns called Saturday*
> *Do people use more drugs on Saturday night*
> *What about Sunday letdown?*
> *Don't terrorists avoid acting on SN because of low news coverage?*

Look at surveys about leisure
Murder. Why are guns called Saturday-night specials
Call Vidal Sassoon and ask him about hairdressers
Have there been surveys done about Saturday night?
The difference on SN for married vs. single people
Being lonely

    I began thinking of places or kinds of people I wanted to include. To make sure I had an assortment, I drew a chart and plotted each possible subject along it, noting the region of the country they were in, the socioeconomic position of the people I might meet, their age, and every other variable I could think of. It was hard to choose when there were so many choices. The point the book would make was that Saturday night means something to everyone, and that bold, broad assertion made it nearly impossible for me to figure out how to illustrate it. The universal stems from the specific and vice versa. But every choice seemed too specific, and yet this needed to be a book of specifics. I listed appealing possibilities and then kept narrowing and narrowing until I came up with ideas that clicked. For instance, I wanted at least one chapter about people who work on Saturday night. Since going out to dinner is a typical Saturday-night ritual, writing about restaurant workers seemed ideal. But which restaurant, of the millions of possible restaurants? The busiest one in the United States was the Hilltop Steak House, outside of Boston; why not choose that, the Goliath of restaurants? The Hilltop went on my list. Other ideas were more happenstance. One day a friend mentioned that there was a polka parlor called Blob's Park near his house in Maryland. I swooned at the name "Blob's"—so delicious that it alone was almost enough to make me want to write about it. I associated polka with Saturday night because, when I was a kid, the most popular Saturday-night television program was *The Lawrence Welk Show,* led by accordionist and bandleader Lawrence Welk. I hated the show and its stodgy mix of polka and waltzes, but my sister and brother and I often watched it because there was nothing else on. It turned out, quite fortunately, that Blob's Park was open only on the weekends, and it was busiest on Saturday night, so it was a perfect candidate for the book.

I made my first *Saturday Night* reporting trip to Blob's. I had no plan other than to go and watch and listen. I didn't know how I was going to shape the book overall, or how I'd shape any individual chapter. I didn't know what I was looking for or how I would tell the story, and I definitely didn't know how I would stitch these separate chunks of reporting into a bigger book-length idea. But I had to start somewhere. I hoped that once I gathered enough stories, some connective tissue would reveal itself to me.

Except for confirming that Blob's would be open the weekend I visited, I didn't do any preparation. I simply showed up. I went alone, as I almost always did when working on a story, and I looked for the cheapest way possible to make the trip, since I needed to stretch my advance to cover a lot of travel. I didn't think I could afford to go to any destination more than once, so I had one shot to make it work. I didn't do advance reconnaissance. I wanted to experience Blob's the way any newcomer would. In principle, I always advocate this method of reporting, this seat-of-your-pants approach, but the reality of doing it is pure, naked panic. Imagine showing up somewhere that is new to you, full of people you don't know who have attitudes and customs and social systems you aren't familiar with. Add the pressure of feeling you have limited time to figure out the story. That, in a nutshell, is what I do. That is what I did. I assumed the patrons of Blob's would be friendly, but I also knew they would be preoccupied with one another and not with me, an unknown, and that I would have to pry and wheedle to get inside their world.

Images of water always come to me when I'm reporting. I am standing on the edge of a pool and I must enter it, but I have nothing to cling to, nothing that will lift me above the water's surface. I'm alone. I don't know what I'm looking for except I don't want to sink. I tamp down the instinct to thrash, to paddle madly and leave. I must calm myself and try to find buoyancy. Someone drifts into view, glances at me. I reach out, and in an instant, they decide whether to take my hand or turn away. I'm a stranger here, I say, and I might drown; help me.

I wandered around the dance floor at Blob's, doing my best to look both busy and approachable and anything but desperate, even though desperate was how I felt. A few days earlier, I had gone to the library to see if I could find any hard research that applied to Saturday night. I discovered a Gallup poll asking adults to name their greatest fears. The fear cited most often was swimming. The second was going to a party of strangers. I read the poll and barked with laughter, realizing that writing nonfiction could easily be described as a nonstop experience of going to parties of strangers, and *Saturday Night* would be the ultimate version of that. I would be spending many Saturday nights at parties with people I didn't know, on my own.

How do I endure the sometimes excruciating experience of being the odd one, the outsider? In part, it's a performance. To do this kind of reporting, you must develop a resting face that looks neither too detached nor too engaged, friendly but not clingy, vulnerable but not needy. You learn to perform some activity or gesture or adopt a stance that makes you look a little bit occupied, so you don't seem to be staring in an anxious way at nothing. You defy the most deeply human emotion of hating to approach strangers; instead, you walk up to them—not too fast, so you don't look aggressive—and toss out a soft question to begin the conversation, something as bland as where the restroom is or how late the place is open, even the proverbial "Come here often?" and then you introduce yourself and explain that you have never been here before and are curious about it. You feel out the atmosphere, a toe in the tide, and then ride it, tentatively at first, until someone finds it interesting that a newcomer is here, at Blob's, how did you hear about Blob's all the way up in—where did you say you live? Boston, goodness, that *is* far. Come, let me introduce you to Cecelia, she knows everything there is to know.

Every writer dreams of finding someone like Cecelia. She was a regular at Blob's, an eighty-two-year-old pistol who had dominated the dance floor almost every Saturday night for twenty-nine years. Saturday nights at Blob's were the high point of her week. She was small, bright, chatty, and, most importantly, she loved to explain things. She wanted to teach me everything about Blob's, everything about polka, and everything about the way she dressed for Saturday nights. She told me she had three hundred and thirty-five polka outfits. The night we met, she was wearing a ruffled white blouse, black bell-bottoms, a silver vinyl belt, silver high heels, a gold chain with walnut-size links, and a side-vented, back-belted, zipper-front vest made of Chinese satin and artificial pony fur. She wanted me dancing with her all night long, but I took breaks from doing the polka so I could take notes. Cecelia was that ideal subject, the person who is not at all distracted by your notebook and is delighted by the challenge of explaining the ins and outs of her life. As soon as we were introduced, I was whisked into her world, and for that time, in my eagerness to hear Cecelia's story, I forgot the fact that I wasn't sure what my book was about.

Meeting Cecelia gave me the intoxicating rush that keeps me doing what I do. For a moment I was able to see myself in the setting as if I were observing it from afar, and I could appreciate, with deep astonishment, that I had shown up somewhere I had never known about and probably never would have come across otherwise, and I was talking and dancing with total strangers, and it was as if I had blasted out of my life into an astounding, unfamiliar one; I had slipped into a new skin. Anyone could do it. Anyone could show up at Blob's, but most likely they wouldn't.

Being a writer means having an excuse, a kind of permission, to be there and savor these places and then return to testify about what you've seen. It is a way of engaging in life fully, freely. As included in the "Instructions for Living a Life" set out by poet Mary Oliver, pay attention; be astonished; tell about it.

I wasn't sure how I was going to shape my reporting into a book, but I soldiered on, making a trip every few months to one of the places that I had chosen. The advance was enough to be serious but not enough to really support me, so I kept writing magazine pieces to earn money. But each magazine piece slowed me down and made the completion of the book recede even further. Book advances are doled out in portions. Typically, the writer might receive half of it up front, and a portion of the remaining half when the book is accepted by the publisher, and the rest when the book is actually released. I had gotten a payment of about $12,500, minus fifteen percent for my agent, when I signed my contract. I wouldn't get more until I finished the manuscript.

When I traveled for the book, I pinched every available penny. I had met some club kids in Los Angeles and decided to write about their Saturday nights for the book. Airfare to Los Angeles from Boston wasn't much back then, but it was enough to make me keep putting it off, worried about stretching my advance too thin. Finally, I decided I had to go. I booked the flight. Paying for a Los Angeles hotel was out of the question, so I asked my father's cousin Gerri if I could stay with her. Gerri was my father's age and clearly thought I was doing the equivalent of a school project with painted macaroni and cotton balls. She was happy to have me stay with her and insisted that she would drive me around to my appointments so I wouldn't have to rent a car. No one had driven me anywhere in decades, but I was so worried about money that I agreed.

The first time Gerri drove me to an interview and sat in the car while I met with my subject, I felt like a ten-year-old being taken to her piano lesson. It was so infantilizing that I decided no matter the cost, I had to have my own transportation. I called Rent-A-Wreck and arranged for their lowest-priced car, which turned out to be a battered yellow Pinto that looked like it had been used in a regional skirmish. I guess Rent-A-Wreck took the "wreck" part of its name very seriously. After securing the Pinto, my first meeting was with a movie producer whom I was interviewing about theater attendance on Saturday nights. He suggested we meet for breakfast at the Beverly Hills Hotel, as swanky an address as you can find in Los Angeles. When I pulled in, weaving through a lineup of Porsches and Bentleys, I took the full measure of my car's shabbiness. I tossed my key to the valet, who stared at me with piteous disdain, and said, "Do. Not. Dent. It."

I was making sluggish progress on the book. I had completed the research for a few chapters but not nearly enough. Moreover, I hadn't begun writing. I rarely start writing before I've done all my research. I can't know what I will say on any particular page until the entire story has settled in my mind. I might be able to anticipate discrete chunks of story, and often those are intact in my head before I write them, but without knowing what has come before or what will come after, I don't know how I want to tell it. It's my writerly metabolism; it always has been, and I suspect it always will be. I know it might take a long time before I write anything, but it's unnerving. A year, two years, even three years might slide past, and I won't have a single word on the page. I know I've got lots of material and some jellylike concoction of a story in my head, but until it sets up and holds its form, I can't start.

In the meantime, there were changes afoot at my publisher. Soon after I signed the contract, I met with my editor, Marjorie Williams, whom I liked immediately. She and Joni Evans had been the progenitors of my project; their enthusiasm for me was the reason I had a book contract. A few months after signing, though, Marjorie announced that she was leaving Linden Press to focus on her own writing. I was dismayed, but Joni assured me all was well and that she would edit the book herself. A few months after that, though, Joni was appointed editor in chief of Simon & Schuster. Good news for her, but it meant that Linden Press would be absorbed into Simon & Schuster and cease to exist on its own.

Then more change. Because Joni would be running Simon & Schuster, she no longer had time to edit my book. She assured me that everything was fine, and she assigned me to a jolly, bald Shakespeare scholar named Herman Gollob who had previously edited writers such as Richard Price, Dan Jenkins, and James Clavell. Herman and I seemed like an unlikely match, but he said he loved the idea of *Saturday Night*. Simon & Schuster flew me from Boston to New York so we'd have a chance to meet face-to-face, and I reported to Joni that we had gotten along well. She wrote back, "I'm delighted that you like Herman—I love him! Don't forget, you'll always be my baby."

I did like Herman, but it's never ideal to go from an editor who helped you conceive of your book to the duty nurse who is called in once you're already in labor. But I settled in. A few months later, Herman called to say he was leaving Simon & Schuster for a job at Doubleday. I was jostled. I felt like each editor to whom I was assigned was a little less invested in the book and a little less interested in me. If I'd been a veteran author or writing something easier to unwind than *Saturday Night,* I might have weathered it. Instead, it made me even more reluctant to pour myself into the work and more daunted by what I had taken on. When Herman left, Joni assigned me to Fred Hills, a tall, dour veteran editor who I suspect had agreed to the task as a favor to Joni rather than out of any affection for the project. I was two years into *Saturday Night,* and I was already on my fourth editor and second publisher. And I still didn't quite know what the book was about.

I chugged along. I kept taking magazine assignments, not only because I needed a paycheck but because I had begun to worry that if I didn't have anything published for the duration of work on the book, I would vanish professionally. Long stories interfered too much with the book, so I started a weekly column for the *Globe* magazine called "Primer." Each week I dissected a different distinct feature of New England, such as the Boston accent, or the faded brick-colored pants called Nantucket Reds that WASPs wore as a proud statement of shabbiness, or the rotaries that governed many intersections. I liked the orderliness of having a column, each week slotting a new subject into the concept.

Meanwhile, I kept plugging away on chapters. In Houston, I attended a zydeco dance, which provided a regular Saturday-night reunion for a group of Creole people who had moved there from Louisiana. Returning to the subject of people who work on Saturday night, I hung out with a second-rate lounge band in Portland, Oregon, and spent Saturday night with a teenage suburban babysitter in Pleasantville, New York. I heard about the tradition of quinceañeras—the celebration of a girl's fifteenth birthday that is central to Mexican and Latin American cultures. I started poking around for one to attend in the Southwest, which led me to the discovery of Azteca Wedding Plaza, the biggest formal-wear shopping center in the world—a complex of forty thousand square feet in Phoenix that included a florist, an invitation shop, a tuxedo annex, a bridesmaid wing, a veil wing, parking for two hundred cars, and a wedding-gown center the size of a suburban roller rink. They did a brisk business in quinceañera gowns. When I called, the manager told me about the city's most exclusive quinceañera, featuring sixteen young women from prominent Phoenix families, so I went to Phoenix for those festivities. Even though I was not yet sure how to tie it all together, I was fascinated by what I was learning about Saturday night. The book was starting to make sense to me, even in its disjointed way.

Near the end of his clerkship, Peter began looking for a permanent job. He wanted to move to Washington, D.C. I worried that I'd feel like a novelty act there—the one writer in Washington who didn't cover politics. I was itching to move to New York, to be in the thick of the magazine and publishing worlds. I knew that this was a rare opening in time, a scene shift, and if we didn't move to New York when we were young and didn't have kids, we would never do it. I also felt like it was my turn to set our course. We had moved to Boston for Peter to go to law school and then stayed an extra year for his clerkship. I didn't hate Boston, but we were there on his behalf, and now I wanted to choose. It was a fraught, uneasy time. We never said it out loud, but it was a standoff. Peter had been offered jobs in both New York and Washington, but he wanted to accept the one from a prominent firm in DC. I wanted to write for a variety of magazines, and I knew that wasn't going to come in the form of a job: It would happen if I was in New York and made myself known. I felt it was the golden moment for me to be in New York; I knew it.

I agreed to look at Washington one more time. We went for a few days, and I had a friendly interview with the Style section of *The Washington Post*. Maybe if they had offered me a job, I would have taken it, but they didn't have any openings. Peter and I had to decide. I stood my ground—it's *my turn*—and finally, Peter accepted an offer from Paul Weiss Rifkind Wharton & Garrison, a prestigious firm with offices in midtown Manhattan. It was a lavishly compensated and intellectually challenging job, but moving to New York vexed him, and he held the move against me for the rest of our marriage.

We found a pretty two-bedroom apartment in a prewar building on the Upper West Side. Our first week in New York City was a sitcom of blunders and rookie mistakes, of not knowing where to stash our car, of not being sure whether to talk to people on elevators or assiduously avoid making eye contact, of hoping our dog, a leggy Irish setter named Molly, would adjust to the sidewalks and city sounds, of hauling groceries back from the store and ending up in our apartment winded and sore, mystified that anyone lived this way. But it was also intoxicating. I went to two book parties that first week, and I remember how excited I was. I felt like fate was telling me this had been the right move, even if my husband sulked and glowered and was building a case against me. I was jazzed, electrified. I had enough old friends in New York to feel I had a bit of a toehold already, so the enormity of the city didn't make me feel lost. I have always imagined how plumbers might feel at a plumbers' convention: that satisfying sizzle of recognition, the buzz of connection, of being known and understood by fellow plumbers, people who understand immediately the stuff that fills their everyday. In New York, I felt like I was at an ongoing writers' convention, communing with my brethren and sistren, and I loved it.

My friend David Blum, a writer for *Esquire,* asked if I wanted to share some office space. This would be a chance to reclaim a little of the communal spirit I missed so much from my time at *Willamette Week* and the *Phoenix.* He knew of a large room in a building above the lone gas station on the Upper West Side. Down the hall was our friend Don Katz, who also wrote for *Esquire* and later went on to found Audible. The space was humble and drafty and cheap. David and I christened it the Exxon Building in homage to the gas station downstairs. To make it work for the two of us, we put a partition down the middle of the space that gave us privacy but allowed us to talk to each other as we were working. Every morning, I walked the few blocks from my apartment on West End Avenue and Seventy-second Street to the Exxon Building, stopping along the way at a bodega for a greasy, gargantuan corn muffin and cup of muddy coffee. Being in the office made me feel like I was a real writer at last.

I was busy with assignments. For *Rolling Stone,* I profiled Andie MacDowell and Tom Hanks and the Bangles and the mall sensation Tiffany. For *Vogue,* where I had begun contributing regularly, I profiled Donna

Karan; explored the history of Lycra; explained how legs became the focus of 1980s fashion; examined the sudden ubiquity of ponytails. I loved writing about fashion as a sociological event, even though my own wardrobe remained a time capsule of my college years: jeans; wild hair; vintage cardigans. Every time I went to the *Vogue* offices, I was struck by how even the lowliest staff person looked sleek and sophisticated. Occasionally, I ran into the editor in chief, Anna Wintour, in the hallway, and I could tell she was taking stock of my appearance and finding me wanting. I knew there was a shoe closet—all heels—and an accessories stash that contributors and staffers could borrow from if we had a meeting that required us to upgrade our look; it was a sort of fashion lending library. I used it when I went to interview Donna Karan, signing out a Prada handbag to use instead of my backpack, but otherwise the contents were too elegant for my taste.

One day I mentioned to an editor at the magazine how much I loved giving parties, and she encouraged me to write an essay about it. After I submitted the piece, she told me that Anna wanted to illustrate the story with a photograph of me in hostess mode. I was stunned. A photograph of me in *Vogue* was never something I'd anticipated happening when I decided to become a writer, and I was surprised that *Vogue* would want a picture of me alongside their usual supermodels. Curious, I agreed to do it.

A few days later, the editor in charge of the shoot, Phyllis Posnick, asked if I would consider getting a haircut for it. I liked the idea of a free haircut. The next day, late in the afternoon, I showed up per her instructions at an Upper East Side salon called Bruno Pittini—a fancy place I never would have visited on my own. At that hour, the salon was empty except for me, Phyllis, and Bruno Pittini himself, an elegant Frenchman with thick eyebrows and a puckish smile whose clientele included Catherine Deneuve and Brigitte Bardot. He and Phyllis guided me to a sink, and then they stepped away, conversing out of earshot. A young woman materialized beside the sink, shampooed me, and led me to Pittini's chair. After a moment, he came up behind me and ran his fingers through my dripping hair. He murmured that he would trim here and there unless I would consider—just a thought!—taking a little more off. He smiled into the mirror in front of me, leaning in so I could catch a whiff of cologne. Well, why not take a little more? Okay, I said, let's do it. He began snipping in earnest. I believe champagne was served. I couldn't help giggling at the absurdity of the scene, me at an Upper East Side salon having a private audience with its namesake. This was hardly what I pictured journalism to be, but what the hell? When Pittini was done, I had lost at least three inches of hair. Purring, he asked if I would consider letting him blow-dry my hair. At that point in my life, I had never used a blow-dryer: I let my hair dry naturally, a mane of ringlets and waves. Again, I thought, what the hell, use the blow-dryer. Fifteen minutes later, my hair looked like copper satin. I was speechless. "Voilà," Pittini said, spinning the chair. "Magnifique."

Bruno Pittini's handiwork, for my story in Vogue

*   *   *

Working for *Vogue* was more girlish fun than anywhere I've worked. Every few weeks, word would circulate that there was a shoe grab, which meant the editors took all the shoes that had been sent to them for reviews or photo shoots and piled them on a bench in the hall, and everyone took whatever they fancied. We got notified of sample sales, when designers offered their best stuff for a song, several days before they were open to the public. I had never dabbled in designer clothes, but *Vogue* got me hooked, and I used the sample sales to build a great wardrobe, above my pay scale, for very little money.

I also had some wonderful assignments. One day my editor told me that an upcoming issue would focus on body types. A writer of one body type would be paired with someone well-known of that same body type, and they'd have a conversation about the impact it had had on their lives. I wasn't interested in the subject until my editor told me she wanted to pair me with Joan Didion. I immediately said yes. I had never met Didion, but I idolized her. She was famously thin, almost fragile. She had written that her stature made people underestimate her, which allowed her to get close to them because they imagined her to be harmless and mouselike. Compared to Didion, I felt like a giant, but Anna considered us compatible size-wise for the purposes of the issue. Coincidentally, Didion began her career at *Vogue*, writing for the magazine from 1956 to 1964, and she was quietly, determinedly fashion-conscious. She wasn't precisely beautiful, but she was incredibly cool and had an effortless stylishness. Several photographs of her—in particular, the one in which she is dangling a cigarette and leaning against her convertible—have become iconic. In her later years, she modeled for a few brands.

The best outcome of meeting a hero is finding them friendlier than you imagined and as glittering as you hoped. That was my experience with Didion. She invited me to her Upper East Side apartment for the interview. After she made tea, she introduced me to her husband, John

Gregory Dunne, who was shuffling around the kitchen, and then we retired to her library and talked about New York and writing and a few mutual friends. Finally, I awkwardly raised the subject of my visit—the perils and privileges of being small. To my relief, she talked about it enthusiastically. She said she used it as a tool in her reporting, and was well aware of how she took up space—or, more to the point, didn't—in the world. She treated me like a colleague, which made me feel proud, and happy once again that I had said yes to a challenge.

I liked working for *Vogue* and *Rolling Stone*, and they seemed eager for me to continue. In 1986, in fact, I got a letter from Bob Wallace, the editor of *Rolling Stone*, saying he wanted more of my work in the magazine. I kept looking for more places to be published—I had a restless desire to expand my options and a constant yearning to be recognized, approved, acknowledged. My office mate, David, and his wife, Terri Minsky, worked with an editor at *New York* magazine and suggested I contact him. Maybe I was getting cocky, but I simply assumed I would be welcomed there, too. Instead, I got a snippy note from him saying, "Dear Susan Orlean, I read through your clips, and though you handle the topics you write about well, I just don't hear a distinctive voice yet. I don't mean to discourage you, but we're extremely selective about making assignments, and at the moment, I just wouldn't feel comfortable asking you to write for us." I was outraged. *I just don't hear a distinctive voice?* Who the hell did he think he was? I was smarting, furious, and, more privately, unnerved: Maybe he was right, and maybe I didn't have a distinctive voice. Believing you are a writer is mind over matter, an act of sheer confidence. It's like balancing a huge stack of plates on your head, and the minute someone suggests you can't really balance that many plates, you quaver and drop them. I restacked my plates and thought: Fuck him, fuck *New York* magazine and their selective assignments, blah blah blah.

Around the time that I was being spurned by *New York*, I had my first *Rolling Stone* cover story, a profile of the band Bon Jovi, with whom I had traveled on tour for several days, dodging the balled-up underpants teenage girls hurled at them onstage every night. I wasn't a Bon Jovi fan. That's what made me want to write about them. They were incredibly popular, and I wanted to understand what millions of people saw in them that I didn't. There it was again, that impulse to puzzle out a mystery. I didn't want to write about the bands I loved. I wanted to save the pleasure of listening to them and not know too much about them. But I couldn't resist writing about anything whose appeal I didn't understand. It was a theme that I revisited again and again.

In the fall of 1986, I was in the office at my desk, and David was on his side of the partition. We could hear each other typing and talking. It formed an indistinct murmur of sound, more like white noise than anything. But at some point, my ear snagged on something specific. I heard David on the phone, saying "*The New Yorker*? Really?" *The New Yorker* was uncharted territory. Since I'd moved to New York, I'd met people who worked for *The New York Times, Esquire, Vogue*—really, almost every publication around—but I hadn't met a single person who wrote for *The New Yorker*. Its unknowability was by design. There was no masthead, and Talk of the Town had no bylines at all. These omissions implied that the magazine was somewhere you either already belonged, or you didn't belong. I harbored my fantasy of writing there, but it seemed like a keyless lock, unopenable.

When David finished his call, I peered over the partition and asked what he'd been talking about. He said that *The New Yorker* was looking for new Talk of the Town writers. This was shocking. It was as if the Vatican had put a listing for cardinals on Craigslist. I didn't feel ready to take a shot at the magazine. I wanted to wait until I had a collection of really, really good clips, and a lot of fantastic story ideas, and I didn't think I was there yet. But this was like a solar eclipse, an occasion so rare that you couldn't question it or propose an alternate date. I started photocopying my favorite stories and girding myself.

The reason for the unusual opening was turmoil at *The New Yorker*. In 1985, the magazine had been sold by its original owners, the Fleischmann family, to publishing magnate S. I. Newhouse. At the time of the sale, the magazine's editor was William Shawn. He had run the magazine since 1952, after its founding editor, Harold Ross, died. Shawn had a Buddha-like presence. He was quiet, single-minded, and beloved, nearly deified. The magazine reflected his taste and tone, channeled through his writers. But two years after the Newhouse acquisition, in a move that surprised everyone, Shawn was fired and replaced with Knopf editor in chief Robert Gottlieb. In protest, a number of writers, including Jamaica Kincaid and Jonathan Schell, quit *The New Yorker*, and Talk of the Town, in particular, was suddenly shorthanded. Perhaps for the first time in its history, the magazine peeked out into the wide world and actively looked for new contributors.

I scoured my clips for anything that seemed Talk-like—short, observational, lively, wry. To my mind, I'd been writing Talk pieces for years. My arts column for the *Phoenix* was a direct homage. My Primer column for the *Globe* was a little more explanatory, but I had looked to Talk when crafting it. The question was whether *The New Yorker* would see that I had been warming up in the bullpen all these years. I called the main number listed for the magazine and explained to the receptionist that I had heard the magazine was looking for writers. She responded frostily and suggested I mail my clips to the attention of an editor named Charles McGrath. I immediately pictured a manila envelope landing in a vast mailbox and settling with a sigh into a moldering pile, never to be retrieved. This would not do. I decided to deliver my package by hand.

I had a fantasy in mind. I would show up at the *New Yorker* offices, and I would be warmly welcomed and escorted to the big, open, sunny newsroom, and I'd explain how much I wanted to work there, and somehow, through sheer will, through wishing, I would make it so. Instead, I took the subway to midtown, found the building on West Forty-third Street, rode the elevator up to the office, and opened a door onto the sort of dreary foyer you might find at a failing accounting firm. A slim, doe-eyed, dark-haired woman sat behind a glass window and didn't look up when I walked in. I leaned up to the window and explained that I was bringing my clips for Mr. McGrath, as I had been instructed on the phone. Without glancing up, she indicated that I should push my envelope through the slot at the bottom of the window. I stammered something about handing them to him directly, but she didn't respond, so I did as I was told. It was about as ceremonious as exchanging foreign currency.

The envelope containing my precious photocopied collection of clips now lay on the counter in front of the receptionist, as flat and bland as a flounder. She did not invite me to wait while she delivered it to Mr. McGrath; she did not assure me that my envelope would shortly be on its way to its destination. After a moment, I realized that there was nothing more to do. I ached with disappointment. I felt like I had one shot at *The New Yorker*, and I had misfired, and now it would be even harder, or perhaps impossible, to try again. I was so blue when I stepped out of the building that I decided to walk home rather than ride the subway, so I could air out my head and perhaps sweat off my disappointment.

I trudged uptown, past the clanging, flashing tourist shops with window displays of cameras and pagers and Statue of Liberty snow globes, and then wound around the clumps of hagglers by the diamond shops, with their sparkling rows of twinkling wedding bands and tennis bracelets. It was close to rush hour. The traffic clotted and then surged, clotted and surged. It was a long way home, over two miles, and I wanted to go slowly, as if I could walk off and wait out my defeat. I knew what was at home: my dog, and a book project that intimidated me, and an empty apartment, since Peter worked late every night and some weekends, too. He had been assigned to the securities fraud case of financier Michael Milken, and the team cranked out legal briefs day and night. I scarcely saw him, and when I did, he seemed more aloof than ever. I crossed

Central Park South and entered the park, joining the flow of joggers and baby strollers and horse carriages, and peeled off at Seventy-second Street, heading west to my apartment.

From a distance, my building looked strangely dark. The sconces at the entrance were off, and the usual patchwork of lit windows was dim. When I arrived, the doorman explained that the power was out, so I clambered up the seven flights of stairs to my apartment. Molly was sleeping. I dropped my bag in the front hall and went into the kitchen. Back then, everyone had an answering machine, and every time you got home, you immediately cast an eye to see if the machine's jolly red light was flashing, signaling that you had messages. With the power out, the machine sat dark on the kitchen counter, a dumb box. I took off my shoes and rubbed my feet for a few minutes, trying to decide what to do for dinner. Suddenly, the power came back on and the whole building seemed to jump, as if it had been reanimated. The lights I'd left on when I'd headed to midtown sputtered back to life, and then the answering machine clicked and screeched, and the red light blazed. I had a message. Before the power had gone out, McGrath had called, saying he was interested in discussing the possibility of me writing for Talk of the Town, if by chance I was available the next day at eleven.

FIVE

Of course I remember what I wore. At the time, my favorite outfit was a short-sleeved camp shirt and matching pleated skirt made of fabric printed to look like cowhide. It was a little loud and a little juvenile, but I loved it, and believed it had magical powers, that it could bring me good luck, like a rabbit's foot. I couldn't have chosen anything to wear that was less in keeping with the *New Yorker* staff aesthetic, which leaned more toward beige cardigans and beige slacks and beige shoes or, as Tom Wolfe famously wrote in his 1965 parody of the magazine, "Tiny Mummies! The True Story of the Ruler of 43rd Street's Land of the Walking Dead!" "button-up sweaters and black basket-weave sack coats . . . the tweedy, thatchy, humble style of dress."

Before I headed to midtown for my meeting with McGrath, I made a list of a dozen Talk of the Town ideas. They sprang to mind easily. I was so new to New York; everything felt like material to me. I scribbled notes: "Benetton. Shower curtains. Gray's Papaya. Citarella Fish."

It felt momentous to splurge on a cab to midtown—these were subway days for me. Was I nervous? I was more electrified than nervous: keyed up, jittery, but good jittery, feeling I might be on the brink of something. The cab felt like it took forever, and it probably did; as I got more accustomed to Manhattan living, I came to understand that no one in a hurry takes a cab to midtown at midday. I got out of the taxi a block away from the building because traffic had congealed into a solid metal mass.

I was met at reception by the same chilly woman who had taken my clips the day before, and she wearily called McGrath to announce that I had arrived. After a minute, he appeared behind the window and signaled for me to follow him. He was lanky and long-legged, with a scramble of light brown hair and the same horn-rimmed eyeglasses as Peter's. He led me down a hall to his office and took a seat at his desk, peering at me over a pile of books and stacks of paper. I flopped into a chair, fussing with my tote bag to steady my nerves.

After a quiet moment, McGrath asked how long I had lived in New York. I began babbling, saying that I had gotten to the city a few months earlier, and before New York I had lived in Boston, and I liked Boston but I was happy to leave because it was clannish and insular and mean-spirited and I had come to realize that Boston was a really racist city, and oh, where was he from?

"Boston," he said.

I caught my breath.

"I have a bunch of Talk ideas," I said weakly. I started reading from my list: The rebirth of American nudism. The dispute between the two Moroccan brothers who founded Jordache jeans. The use of Playmate coolers to transport donor organs (was Playmate aware of this? Did they have a specific organ transplant department?). How Benetton stores trained their staff to fold sweaters so precisely. The artist Roger Henry, who specialized in creating the longest paintings in the world. The Miniature Art of the Month Club.

McGrath listened without reacting. Out loud, my ideas seemed so . . . what? Odd? Twee? Peculiar? Dumb?

After a moment, he told me to pick three or four of my ideas and focus on them. He suggested starting with my idea about Benetton. I was so surprised by his encouragement that I hardly responded. I didn't ask when the story was due, or how long it should be, or what I would get paid. I must have levitated my way out of the office. I don't think I've ever been more excited in my life. I made my way to the Benetton in midtown as soon as it opened the next day.

FOLDING

"Once you know how to fold, you always know how to fold," Robin Pinkowitz, the manager of the Benetton at Fifth Avenue and Fifty-third Street, told us one afternoon last week. But the folding they do at Benetton is more than just folding. When Afra and Tobia Scarpa designed the Benetton stores, in 1967, they said they wanted the sweater shelves to look as if they were holding wooly accordions, and at Fifth and Fifty-third the sweaters are creased so neatly they're like origami. Once stacked, they're as much a part of the architecture as the lighting fixtures. Of course, folding like this doesn't come about naturally, Ms. Pinkowitz said. Benetton folders are made, not born. They're trained on the job (for the moment, but there's talk of establishing a university of folding at the Benetton headquarters, in Italy), and then they maintain a standard so rigorous and inspiring that it could permanently elevate the expectations that mothers have for their children *in re* closets and drawers.

"When I started with the company, I didn't know how to fold," Ms. Pinkowitz went on. She herself was wearing a long black cotton V-neck sweater. "They put me on the floor with a pile of T-shirts and told me to fold them. I folded them. I folded that pile twenty times. That's how I learned. Now I think our display looks really nice. That's one of the reasons for design folding. Well, there's not a real name for what we do, but that's what we call it. Or creative folding." She pulled a purple-and-green Argyle cardigan off a stack, slapped it onto the standard-issue Benetton folding table, and, without a hitch, smoothed it, eyed it for size, folded the sleeves in, halved it, flipped it over for final molding, and laid it gently back on the shelf. "I can airfold, too," she said, "but my tablefolding is better. Everyone has a forte. Mine is slacks. Richard, who used to be the manager of the store at Fifth and Forty-eighth, can fold things starting with the bottom at the top. I can't. Look at this pile, though." She pointed to some orange-and-beige plaid seersucker slacks stacked on a shelf. "That's a good pile. Not a perfect pile, but still a beautiful pile." She poked a bulge to flatten it and straightened the pair of slacks on top. "Folding is really like artwork," she said. "Part of it is what the company tells us, but a lot of it is the folder's personality. If somebody is a blah person, you could probably see it in her folding."

When Ms. Pinkowitz hires a new employee, she tells that person five things. First of all, working at Benetton means living, breathing, eating, and sleeping folding. Second, fold your Argyles on the diamond. Third, fold your cardigans with a button showing on the shelf edge. Fourth, when you make your first fold the sleeve should nest approximately a quarter of an inch from the edge of the sweater. And fifth, you can't yell at the customers if they mess up one of your piles, even if it's a really good pile. Because Benetton is a store, she explains, there are customers around a lot of the time, and there are those among them who will thoughtlessly finger, and even unfold, sweaters. Then they fold them up, ineptly, and put them back. Some employees take this harder than others.

"You don't know how awful that is—you just don't know!" said Carolyn Rothkin, who was stacking some pink sweatshirts. "It's so upsetting. You feel like crying. It's heartbreaking. But you know you have to get used to it. I just had to learn. Some folders are better than others, by the way. There are people—I don't know if I should mention their names—that I really look up to. I just look at their stuff and I go 'Ohhhh.'"

Michael Fox, who prepped at the Gap but has done graduate work in folding since he switched to Benetton, a year ago, can airfold as well as tablefold. He is the recognized sweater expert at Fifth and Fifty-third, and we found him looking over his section. He's a slim young man with a sculpted flattop, and he was wearing a navy cotton cardigan. "If you fold too, too well, you can scare the customers," he said. "But there really is a mastery to it. And now that I've mastered it, I'm very pleased with myself. I find myself folding at home. I fold my own clothes. I fold my mom's clothes. I fold my dad's clothes. My parents are kind of worried about me because I'm folding everything in sight." He said he wasn't sure, though, whether his interest in folding would stick with him beyond next fall, when he would be leaving for pre-dentistry at Columbia. "Look what happened to Lisa Lisa, of Lisa Lisa and Cult Jam," he added. "She used to work at Benetton and was known in her day as one of the best folders we had. Now that she's a big recording star, her folding talent has taken a back seat."

When the store closes each day, every one of the several thousand items in it—including socks, shirts, and sweatsuits—has to be folded perfectly and shelved for the night. "You look up close and it means nothing," Ms. Pinkowitz said. "But you stand back and it's like a great flow." She lowered her voice. "Of course, sometimes at home I get rebellious and just throw everything into my closet."

My Benetton piece ran in the May 25, 1987, issue of *The New Yorker*. The issue also included a story by Lawrence Weschler about Brazil, and a review by William Maxwell of Marie Vassiltchikov's *Berlin Diaries, 1940–1945*. I wrote the piece fast. I had so many great quotes from the salespeople that it came together very naturally; my intuition that there was a company ethos about folding had been borne out. But when I turned it in, I was horribly nervous. Did it work? Would they accept it? I delivered the manuscript in person and paced to calm myself down. After McGrath called to tell me they would run it, I jumped up and down shrieking. I returned to the office the next day to review his editing suggestions. Most of the changes were minor: simplifying language, cleaning up sentences that meandered. The major change he made was lopping off the final paragraph. I was wounded because I thought I'd written a bravado last paragraph, but he said I had written a better ending already in the second to last paragraph. It was an editing gesture he repeated for the next half-dozen or so pieces I wrote for him, until I learned my lesson. Stories don't need a "conclusion," a flourish of finality. It's better to leave readers falling forward, tumbling through the piece and beyond it, finishing the tune in their heads.

In those days, *The New Yorker* edited on physical copies of stories and reprinted the pages as each set of corrections was made. I'm sure most writers at the magazine tossed the printouts when the new versions were ready, but I was so astounded to see my work in the *New Yorker* typeface that I hung each set of galleys on the wall until they lined my entire office. I truly couldn't believe I was going to be published in *The New Yorker*. I wouldn't have a byline, since it was an uncredited Talk of the Town piece, but I would know it was mine, and that was all that mattered. When I was at the office going over the fact-checking corrections, I wandered into the production room, where the galleys for the entire issue were pinned to a work wall. At that stage, the Talk pieces had the authors' names written in pencil on the galleys—probably for keeping track of who was doing the editing. I noticed that a piece about Peace Corps volunteers running next to mine had been written by John Updike. *John freaking Updike!* I truly was in the land of giants. I wasn't sure I belonged, but I was intoxicated by the opportunity to even have a toe in it.

Everyone called Charles McGrath "Chip," but I didn't feel like I had the right to assume that familiarity, so I continued calling him "Mr. McGrath" in a shy mumble, and wondered if that would ever change. I mustered any excuse I could to come to the office, hoping to ease my acute awkwardness and sense of being a fifth or tenth or hundredth wheel. I didn't know anyone who worked for the magazine, so my visits were precise and targeted: into McGrath's office for editing and then out, past the unsmiling receptionist and the occasional person hurrying down the hall without glancing. The place felt dim, insular, ingrained. Most people had come to the magazine right out of college. Even the younger staff people had been there for years. As Tom Wolfe wrote in that acidly funny essay, "One went to work [at *The New Yorker*] and one—how does one explain it?—began to get a kind of . . . *religious* feeling about the place. There were already a lot of . . . *traditions*." Wolfe skewered the "happy-shabby, baked-apple gentility" of the office, which was exquisitely accurate. I felt like an interloper more there than at any other place I'd worked, like it was a cellular body I couldn't penetrate. But my optimism was so sturdy that I kept showing up, hoping to crack the code.

Once "Folding" was published, McGrath asked what I was going to write next. I proposed writing about a shower curtain printed with a map of the world that I'd started seeing in bathrooms around the city. I didn't really expect him to approve of it. There was a squeamishness at *The New Yorker* that I assumed would recoil at a story about bathroom decor. But he was game, and I was game, and the shower curtain story, called "The World," ran a few weeks after "Folding." I then immediately started on a piece about the display windows at a fishmonger on Broadway called Citarella, which featured tableaus made entirely of fish and an occasional prop such as a plastic Godzilla, assembled by a young man named Fernando Lara who worked behind the counter.

I was having the best time. The magazine accepted all of my stories and seemed primed for whatever I came up with next. I continued to feel like an outsider, but I had begun to meet a few writers on my many trips to the office: Roger Angell, whom I had always venerated; Alec Wilkinson, whose book *Big Sugar* was one of the models I looked to for the best nonfiction writing; Mark Singer, whose piece "Supers" had made me want to write literary journalism; Calvin Trillin, who had just published his amazing collection *Killings* (I had almost worn out my copy already).

I saw Robert Gottlieb frequently. His office, decorated with his collection of vintage women's handbags, was next to McGrath's, and he often roamed over to say hello. He was owlish, skinny, giggly, teasing. Maybe because he was something of an outsider, too, he welcomed me in a way few other people at the magazine did. This emboldened me. One day I dared to ask him if I could formalize my relationship with the magazine. What I had in mind was a contract, a title, perhaps a workspace. "Of course!" Gottlieb answered merrily. "We will get a pair of golden rings, one for you and one for me, and we will toss them into the sea together!" Not what I'd hoped for, but at least I had spoken my mind.

On December 7, 1987, I published my tenth Talk of the Town piece—about the hilarious display signs at Fairway Market—and I felt on top of the world. I loved writing these pieces, and the more I wrote, the more confident I felt. I had become friends with a few people at the magazine, including the frosty receptionist, who turned out to be a gloriously eccentric and gifted writer named Alison Rose. As Tom Wolfe would have noted, I was getting "religious" about *The New Yorker*. I couldn't stop thinking of stories I wanted to do, and I was gearing up to ask whether I could write a full-length feature. I dreamed all the time of bypassing that golden ring ceremony Gottlieb had teasingly proposed and getting some kind of promise, some sign, that I was part of the magazine. I had even eased my way into calling Charles McGrath by his nickname, Chip.

Was this evangelical excitement what made me oblivious to the rest of my life? Peter was rarely around. He claimed that he had to work weekends and had to stay late at the office almost every night. And yet when I called the office, he never answered his phone. If I asked his secretary to page him, he didn't answer. When I quizzed him about his elusiveness, he clouded up and said nothing or said that it was unpleasant to come home because I met him at the door scowling. But I was scowling because he was never home and never answered the phone. Round and round we'd go. I burrowed into my other friendships and tried to ignore how unsettled I felt, how unloved. Occasionally, we ended up in howling, shrieking, grappling fights that went in tight, suffocating circles, never leading anywhere, ending with us both exhausted and weepy. I didn't understand who he was anymore, and I barely recognized myself.

On December 15, I got a letter from Fred Hills, my editor at Simon & Schuster. I hadn't talked to him in a while, and when I did, I assured him that *Saturday Night* was coming along. Was it coming along? My foray into the world of *The New Yorker* had completely distracted me. I had also lost sight of my advance. I'd deposited it into our bank account when I'd received it, so it had melted into the rest of our money. Instead of being drawn out of an account set up for the purpose, every book expense felt painful, subtracted from our general funds.

I had no excuse for not working on the book. I had signed a contract and been paid. But I was a novice, and I hadn't learned to discipline myself to focus on it. Every short-term option—another Talk piece, another *Vogue* assignment—looked easier and more immediately gratifying. I continued doing research and reporting trips for the book, but I was stumped by how to weave them together and always found it a relief to turn to something closer at hand.

Hills's letter was stern. "Dear Susan, the extended delivery date of December 31, 1987 . . . is fast approaching and I'll need to know if you are going to be able to meet it. S&S has been very patient and supportive about this project, but I'm doubtful they will wait any longer. Can you bring me up to date on your progress?"

An anvil dropped on your head would perhaps feel like what it felt to read this letter. I was mortified, panicked, unable to catch my breath. But I was also a little indignant: I was flailing, and Fred Hills had never offered me any help at all. I certainly couldn't finish the book by the

December deadline, and the letter made it clear that Simon & Schuster wasn't likely to give me an extension on the contract. What was worse, not long after she assigned me to Fred Hills, Joni Evans had left Simon & Schuster. She had been my champion there, and now it was clear I was on my own.

An advance is essentially a loan against your likely earnings. It's not a fee or a grant or an honorarium: It's a sum subtracted from the royalties you will theoretically earn once your book is published. In other words, the publisher doesn't owe you more until your royalties exceed your advance. Publishers aren't "giving" you anything. They are simply advancing you your own hypothetical earnings. Most books never "earn out" their advance, meaning they don't sell enough copies and generate enough royalties to zero out the advance, because the publisher's bet on how well the book would sell was too optimistic.

There was a time when publishers tolerated—and forgave—people who frittered away their advances or drank them away and never produced the promised book. Depending on the state of the economy or the importance of the writer or the size of the advance, publishers often treated these advances as a lost cause, a necessary condition of the business, and that would be that. But by the time *Saturday Night* was due, the mood had changed. If you signed a contract and took an advance and didn't complete the book, you were expected—and legally obligated—to pay back what you'd already received. The thought of my contract being canceled and having to find more than twelve thousand dollars to pay back to Simon & Schuster made me sick to my stomach.

The root of my problem was more intractable than finding the money. I hadn't yet figured out what the book should be. Or maybe that's not quite it. The truth was that I didn't have the confidence to write it in the way that felt natural to me—namely, as a loose collection of inquiries and answers to the question of what Saturday night looked like and meant to a variety of Americans. There was no grander purpose, nor did there need to be, but I wasn't bold enough to believe that was enough.

Richard Pine consoled me after I got Hills's letter and assured me that we would make it through this mess and that canceled book contracts happened all the time. Without my knowledge, he began talking to other publishers he thought might be interested in acquiring *Saturday Night*. I was in a different position than I had been when I'd pitched *Ultra-Athletics* to no avail. I now wrote regularly for *The New Yorker*, and I had written an introductory chapter for *Saturday Night* that made a pretty strong case for my idea. Even though I was so downhearted by my situation with Simon & Schuster, I knew I had something worth showing around. And I wasn't wrong. Not long ago, I reread a note that an editor at William Morrow, Tom Congdon, had sent to one of his colleagues about *Saturday Night*: "Jim, I'm recommending we set a $100,000 floor. We'll certainly be in competition with other houses, so I hope you can take an early look. (You'll be glad you did.) This is TERRIFIC. Susan Orlean, 32-year-old redhead, Talk of the Town regular, is the next great American humorist/chronicler . . . soon to be up there with Tom Wolfe and the rest, I do believe, and we've got a shot at getting her for Morrow."

After Richard began distributing my *Saturday Night* material to publishers, he told me that Sonny Mehta, the publisher of Knopf, wanted to meet with me. This was astounding news. Knopf was an elite publishing house, and Mehta was revered, having published six Nobel literature laureates and countless other critically acclaimed writers since he had taken over Knopf after Bob Gottlieb left for *The New Yorker*. I scrambled to set up the meeting for the following afternoon.

I knew it would be a demanding encounter. I had to convince Mehta that *Saturday Night* was a great idea at the very moment I was wobbling. Mehta was slight, with glossy black hair, an imperturbable air, and the ability to stare at you without blinking far longer than seemed humanly possible. When I arrived at his midtown office, he was sitting behind a desk in a huge chair that extended above his head, like a Herman Miller Aeron throne. We sat for a few deadly minutes. Finally, he said, "Tell me about your book." I explained what I had in mind and what I had done so far and why I thought it was a good idea—no, a *great* idea. He didn't respond. I kept talking. The sunlight, slanting through the windows, slowly paled and finally disappeared. The room went gray and then black, the candy-colored shimmer of midtown below us the only lights visible. Mehta made no move to turn on a light or end the conversation, so I kept talking to the dark outline of his face.

At last, he said he wanted me to accompany him to Bloomingdale's to buy a gift for his wife. Was this a test? I grabbed my coat and followed him to Bloomingdale's linen department, helping him choose a set of napkins. What the hell? When we were done shopping, he headed out the door. Something in his posture implied that he expected me to follow, so I did. We ended up in his apartment. His wife was somewhere upstairs, and we sat in a dark library that smelled of leather and cigarette smoke. He poured us each a Scotch in a heavy crystal glass, and I choked it down, trying to figure out when the test was over, as we talked about literature and New York and mortality and napkins.

I must have done my best talking ever, because the next day, Richard told me that Knopf wanted *Saturday Night* and were offering an advance of a hundred thousand dollars—four times my original advance. I could pay back Simon & Schuster out of the first slug of the Knopf advance, so the transaction would be seamless. Jane Amsterdam, a veteran magazine editor who had just joined Knopf, would be my hands-on editor. I simply couldn't believe it, any of it, all of it. If there ever was a time when I felt ready to be lucky, this was it.

In the summer of 1988, I noticed a small story in *The New York Times* about a Ghanaian tribe called Ashanti, and a cabdriver named Kwabena Oppong who had recently been named king of the Ashantis who were living in the United States. I liked the idea of a king in America, and I thought a story about Oppong would make a good Talk of the Town piece, so I tracked him down. He said he would be happy to talk to me if the members of his council of elders agreed, and he invited me to his apartment in the South Bronx to meet them.

As I headed there, in a cab whose driver was very annoyed at having to go to the Bronx, I felt a clutched, ecstatic, almost tearful sensation of amazement and gratitude that this was how I was living my life. This snippet of a story had caught my attention, and just like that, I was off on an adventure, going somewhere I never would have gone otherwise, to meet people I never would have met otherwise. It felt like joy.

Oppong lived in Co-op City, a cluster of faded brick towers overlooking the freeway in the Bronx. His apartment was plain and small, dominated by a beautiful wooden throne that sat in the center of his living room. He was soft-spoken and bright-eyed, courteous and even-tempered except when his young son climbed on the throne after being told it was off-limits. The phone rang ceaselessly. The calls were from his subjects, asking him to help resolve problems—how to ship the body of a dead relative back to Ghana, how to smooth out a rocky marriage, how to apply for health insurance. The contradictions in his life fascinated me. He was a working-class man with the usual headaches (rowdy kids, a stretched budget, tight living quarters), but at the same time, he was an elevated being—the king of a large group of people who turned to him for advice and counsel and treated him as royalty.

By the time I left Oppong's apartment, I had gotten the council's approval and was convinced that this was more than a short Talk of the Town piece. The next day, I asked Chip if I could write it as a feature, and to my delight, he approved. I asked him when the story was due. "When it's finished," he said, Sphinx-like. Would I have an expense budget? "Spend what you think is necessary." Should I go to Ghana with Mr. Oppong? "If you think you should, then you should." And finally, could he give me an idea of what I would be paid? He paused and then said, "It will be sufficient."

And so I set off on my first *New Yorker* feature assignment, a blank check of a task, arranged by a brief enigmatic conversation. I probably don't need to tell you that magazines don't work that way anymore, and most of them never did, but this was the way *The New Yorker* worked back then. I spent the next two months following Kwabena Oppong as he bounced between the everyday demands of his life as a cabdriver and a husband and father, and his royal duties—ceremonies, community gatherings, dispute resolution. I knew I had a lot at stake. This would be my first byline in the magazine, my first full-length assignment. But I was so fascinated by the story that it carried me along without worry.

The lede dawned on me immediately. I wanted to telegraph the incongruities that made his life so interesting, so I began there, with that first image I had of his apartment:

> Kwabena Oppong, who is the king and supreme ruler of the African Ashanti tribespeople living in the United States of America, has a throne in his living room . . . The Ghanaian king [of the Ashantis] is royally born, richly rewarded, divinely inspired, and holds his office for life. The American Ashanti king is elected every two years from the ranks of an Ashanti social and cultural organization. The first Stateside king, Kwadwo Tuffuor, was a plumber. The second, Kusi Appouh, repaired air-conditioners and refrigerators. Kwabena Oppong is the third king; he drives a cab.

I had grown much more confident as a writer over those months of writing for *The New Yorker*. I shed some of the curlicues and flourishes that I had relied on to fancy up my writing, trusting instead in the richness of what I had observed and the punch of the facts I'd dug up. My new preoccupation was on the sonic quality of my writing—the rhythm and tone of the sentences. I began reading all my work out loud, listening for places that lagged and dragged, that didn't sparkle. I knew it was unlikely that anyone else was reading my stories out loud, but I was convinced that you do "hear" writing in your head as you read, and this pushes you (or stalls you) through the piece. I wanted the music—that is, this subconscious tonal effect—to match the subject. I always loved including lists in my pieces. They had a scenic quality, encouraging the reader to visualize, and I appreciated how they changed up the pacing of a story, almost like a montage in a film. I had wonderful material from my time with the Oppong family, more than enough for a long feature, so I devoted myself to crafting it metrically, to keep readers committed, carried along by the pulsing and swinging of the words.

As absorbed as I was working on the piece, I hadn't forgotten my near-death experience with *Saturday Night,* so between reporting on the Ashantis, I made several trips for the book. I spent a Saturday night with frat boys at Georgia Tech, watching them ransack their own fraternity house after a football game. I spent a Saturday night underground in a nuclear missile silo in Cheyenne, Wyoming. To give you an idea of how innocent the world was in 1987, let me tell you how I managed to get access to that silo: I wrote a letter to someone in the press office of the Pentagon, explaining that I was working on my first book and that I wanted to see what Saturday night was like in a nuclear silo. In short order, I received a letter giving me permission and providing me a date for the visit and directions to the silo in Wyoming. I don't remember being subjected to any security clearances at all. I wasn't searched when I got to the silo, and I was ushered in (and down) with as much (or as little, really) scrutiny as I would have received if I'd been attending a real estate open house. I didn't have a Pentagon official with me while I was underground with the crew of three young men—so young that they looked like they'd just gotten their first shaving kits—who were on duty that night. (They whiled away the night watching *WarGames* on video.) I'm sure the Pentagon no longer allows outsiders to camp out in their nuclear installations, certainly not without rigorous security processing. No one seemed concerned that a young female reporter was alone, without a way to communicate to the outside world, with a crew of men (no one, that is, including me; I felt completely at ease).

So many aspects of my reporting on *Saturday Night* now seem like they took place in another world—a guileless, unguarded one. I was an unknown writer approaching people I didn't know, and they all agreed to let me observe them in their private moments. The more official settings, like the missile silo, were governed by the most half-hearted rules. On occasion, it verged into lackadaisical. Toward the end of work on the book, I decided to write about Saturday night in a prison. I didn't expect or want to spend a Saturday night incarcerated, but I hoped to talk to prisoners to learn whether they treated the night as something special, even behind bars. I contacted the warden of Arthur Kill Correctional Facility, a medium-security prison on Staten Island, and asked if he could gather a few inmates for me to interview. He readily agreed.

Getting into the prison was difficult—I had to leave all my possessions in a locker and beg to be allowed to bring a pen and notepad, since pens are usually forbidden. The assistant warden walked me down a long hall to a room where six men awaited me. He then wished me luck and left. On one hand, I was glad to have the chance to talk to the men without an authority figure lurking in the background, but I was astonished that I was left alone, with no way to call for help if something went wrong. I had a shiver of nerves, then soothed myself with the thought that perhaps these men had committed nonviolent crimes—tax fraud, maybe.

I began by asking them how they had ended up in Arthur Kill. Four of the six said they were serving time for manslaughter or murder but they were innocent or, as one of them put it, the death "was the result of a misunderstanding." We talked for an hour or so, and I found the men likable, thoughtful, and generous with their anecdotes. One of them mentioned that he was going to be released soon, and for reasons I honestly can't understand except the optimistic flush of the moment, I gave him my phone number, in case he wanted to call me when he was released. I usually think I'm careful and savvy when I'm out reporting, but this was plainly stupid; I marvel at how dumb I was.

The inmate never called me—thank goodness. A few months later, I saw a news story about a convicted murderer and drug dealer suspected of killing a Drug Enforcement Administration agent—it was headline news because it was the first such murder in thirty years. The entire New York City police force and the DEA were trying to track down the suspect. I glanced at the newspaper photo, and it hit me in the gut: It was the guy I'd given my phone number to. His name was Gus Farace. I did some research and discovered that, as charming as he was when I interviewed him, he was a genuine monster, convicted of killing a young male prostitute. Ten months after he killed the DEA agent, he was gunned down in what was assumed to be a Mob hit. It was a bleak story in every way, and blunt evidence of how reporting makes you feel invincible, and how the bond you form with subjects can blind you. I consider myself perceptive, attuned to personalities and moods; I couldn't do my job without having some talent for that. But this incident made me realize that my urge to connect with the people I'm writing about can muffle that instinct. I'm so hungry to empathize that I lose the edge that might make me see more clearly, especially if what I need to see is something ugly.

The toughest assignment I gave myself for *Saturday Night*, though, was the one that seemed the most privileged. I wanted to attend a dinner party with a member of the ritziest of social sets, the denizens of Manhattan's Upper East Side, for whom entertaining was a defining ritual. I decided to reach out to Nan Kempner, a socialite who was then at the peak of her powers. I asked if I could observe her organize a Saturday-night dinner party at her baronial Park Avenue apartment, and rather surprisingly, she agreed. In the book, I detailed her fastidious preparations, which climaxed in her last-minute change of heart about letting me join her guests at the table. A few minutes before they arrived, she insisted that I couldn't stay and sent me out the door via the servants' elevator. I was frustrated, but it was so predictable, considering her social milieu, that I couldn't really complain.

* * *

Was I ever afraid when I was reporting? No. I was often lonely, because I was on my own, away from home, with people I didn't know. But I was never afraid. Everyone has misgivings about doing something scary, and there's nothing scarier than, say, approaching teenage boys you don't know and saying, "Talk to me." But when I'm working on a story—versus when I'm simply living my life—I have enormous courage. It reminds me of the phenomenon of a mother being able to lift a car if it's crushing her baby: In those circumstances, fueled with adrenaline, she finds superhuman strength. I find superhuman self-confidence when I'm working on a story. The bashfulness and vulnerability that I might otherwise experience in a new setting melt away, and my desire to connect, to observe, to understand, powers me through. On occasion, this impulse has led me to places I probably would have been wise to avoid. Once, Kwabena Oppong invited me to an Ashanti party that was being held at a function hall in the South Bronx. He warned me that Ashanti parties started late and ended late. I thought I understood what "late" was, but the Ashanti clock ran hours later than that. The party started around one a.m. and was going full throttle when I petered out at four a.m.—a schedule I had previously experienced only at a Grateful Dead concert. I bade my farewells to Oppong and his wife, tucked my Mead Spell-Write notebook into my pocket, and headed out to hail a cab. Standing on that deserted street corner in an eerily quiet neighborhood, I had a mild out-of-body experience, observing myself doing what I was doing. My immediate thought—the giveaway that I was in that disassociated state of reporting—was thinking that I could never, ever tell my mother what I was doing. From that point on, that was how I measured the danger I put myself in: Was this something my mom should never know?

I was lonely, though, in a more profound way, because my relationship with Peter was strained, strange, bewildering. He fended me off whenever I asked what was going on. At the same time, he began lobbying for us to have a baby. We were either speaking different languages or not speaking. I couldn't make sense of his wishes. He would hardly be tender with me but wanted to have a child with me? I was pretty sure I wanted to have children, but did it make sense for us? I was unhappy. I felt unloved. Why did I endure it? For one thing, I had the model of my parents and their decades of tolerating their obvious unhappiness. Rather than learning from that and vowing to avoid it, maybe I found it familiar. I know I was guilty of wanting to hold on to the parts of my life with Peter that suited me; I know I preferred stability, no matter how tentative, to the prospect of starting over again. Peter was smart, attractive, charismatic. Everyone liked him. His sins were those of omission: He was absent, withholding, resistant to intimacy. I'm sure he had complaints about me, but he wouldn't tell me what they were. Dealing with his inscrutability was harder than it would have been to deal with active behavior that I disliked. It was like shadowboxing, trying to explain that what *wasn't* happening was what hurt me. I burrowed into work because I loved it but in part because it gave me what I didn't get from him—a sense of appreciation, accomplishment, satisfaction.

I was in hard denial. The clues that Peter was having an affair were scattered liberally and carelessly, poisonous little breadcrumbs, but I wished them away, believing the ridiculous explanations he provided for why he was gone so often, so late. Years later, when we were getting divorced, he admitted that he was amazed by my willingness to accept what he told me even when his lies were so clumsy. I had an easy explanation: I thought believing was what you did when you loved someone.

SIX

I finally finished writing *Saturday Night*. My battle with getting it done had been a battle with myself, convincing myself to write the book as I really pictured it: a journey through space and time, a documentary account of a social ritual. My work at *The New Yorker* bolstered me, encouraging me to trust my instincts and tell stories as I saw them. I had to fight my way to that realization, and it took a long time. No one could lead me to that self-confidence, the recognition that I was a storyteller. It dawned slowly, but then it was thunderous. I was going places anyone *could* go, but they wouldn't; I was hearing stories anyone might have been able to hear, but they were not there to do so. I was the collector of tales and visions, a proxy for anyone who was curious about the world, and when I was filled up with a story, I couldn't wait to have it spill out of me for other people to hear.

I sustained yet another editor disruption before I was done with the book. When I met Jane Amsterdam, I told her about my repeated changes of editors at Simon & Schuster. I'd become self-sufficient out of necessity, but I felt like a feral author, raised by wolves rather than editors. I was lucky Peter was a brilliant reader and had been reading and editing my work—something he did enthusiastically even when we were most estranged. Otherwise, I was on my own. Amsterdam, whom I liked and respected, promised me she was at Knopf for the long haul. She had just started her job, and it was arguably the best publishing house in the country.

A few months later, she called to tell me that the *New York Post* had offered her the position of editor in chief, which would make her the first woman to run a major metropolitan daily in the country. She couldn't say no. Since I was such a veteran of these upheavals, I barely flinched. After she left, Mehta assigned me to Elisabeth Sifton, a starchy, seasoned Knopf editor who had worked with Don DeLillo, William Gaddis, and Peter Matthiessen. I soldiered on. I submitted my draft manuscript to Sifton. Her editing changes were minimal. Mehta loved the book except for my working title, *Saturday Night in America*, which he thought took up too much space on a book jacket, so he truncated it, with my reluctant approval, to *Saturday Night*. Suddenly, after five years of work, I had book galleys in hand.

My experience of churning through so many editors and publishers and publishing houses was not typical. In fact, it was almost comical. Some years later, I wrote a column about it for the *New Yorker* website:

> My first book was acquired by two people I will call Editor A and Editor B, who ran a small imprint at a big publishing house. We had a great lunch to celebrate. A few months later, Editor A left book publishing to become a newspaper writer. Editor B became my primary editor. She and I had a nice lunch to talk about my book.
>
> A few months after that, Editor B was promoted to publisher of the larger house—let us call it Publisher W—that owned the small imprint. Because Editor B—that is, Editor/Publisher B—now had too many duties to edit my book, I was assigned to Editor C.
>
> Editor C and I had lunch. A few months later, he got a new job at another publishing house. I was assigned to Editor D.

Editor D and I had lunch. It was a pleasant-enough lunch, but Editor D had no actual interest in my book or me; he was just taking it on because Editor/Publisher B, now his boss, had asked him to.

A few months later, Editor/Publisher B was fired.

A few months after that, Editor D, now freed from his promise to Editor/Publisher B to oversee my project, asked me if my book was done because according to my contract, it was due.

My book was not done.

I paid back my advance to Publisher W and sold my book proposal to Publisher X. My editor at Publisher X—let's see, that would be Editor E—had been a magazine editor and was brand-new to the publishing world and full of crazy excitement about it. I was starting to get a little sensitive about all this change, and I asked Editor E if there was any chance that the publishing world would not always seem to her worthy of crazy excitement; that is, I asked Editor E if she thought she would ever leave. Editor E assured me that this was simply not possible.

Editor E and I had lunch. A few months later, she called me and said an incredible opportunity had presented itself in the newspaper world and she was leaving.

I was assigned to Editor F. I was very scared of Editor F, and I don't think we had lunch. I finished my book. I had the longest acknowledgments section in the history of the written word.

I could go on, about how I left Publishing House X for Publishing House Y because I was still scared of Editor F, and how at Publishing House Y I managed to get three books written there working with Editor G—who assured me that he would never leave, and this was almost true, except for a brief period when he did, in fact, leave, but then he came back—and then the head of Publisher Y got fired, and eventually I left and then Editor F left, and then I was working with Publisher Z, and then the head of Publisher Z left, and then I left Publisher Z to go back to Publisher W, because the person now running it was an old friend from the magazine world, who I knew would never leave, but you might think I was exaggerating. But I'm not.

Anyway, the head of Publishing House W and I had lunch to celebrate my return to Publisher W. A few months later, he got fired.

My new publisher, at Publishing House W, is Editor G, who left Publishing House Y for the job. As some great philosopher once said, it's like déjà vu all over again. This time, though, I am going to suggest we skip the lunch.

Even though it usually takes a year to prepare a manuscript for publication, there are so many tasks along the way that the time flies by and abruptly, like a summoning, the bound galleys appear. Then you're at the final stages of the process—choosing the cover and asking other writers for blurbs to festoon it. My wish list for blurbs was absurdly aspirational: Calvin Trillin, Ian Frazier, Garrison Keillor, Paul Theroux, Nora Ephron, John McPhee, Hunter S. Thompson, John Irving, Tracy Kidder. Some of them never responded to my note asking for a blurb. A few sent back a polite refusal, saying they didn't have time to read the book. John Irving wrote a long note praising *Saturday Night* but asked that we not use his comments because he had a rule against blurbing books. As I was despairing, Mehta announced that he didn't want blurbs on the back cover; he wanted a large photograph of me. I didn't love the idea, but I was tired of the fruitless chase for blurbs, so I agreed.

We sent the manuscript to magazines and newspapers, hoping to place a few excerpts, and the reception was a wonderful surprise. *The New Yorker* wanted to run my chapter on quinceañeras. *Spy* wanted my account of Nan Kempner's Park Avenue dinner party. *The Boston Globe* wanted nuclear missile silos. *The Washington Post* wanted Blob's Park. And most surprisingly, *The New York Times Magazine* wanted to adapt the introduction.

Most books yield one excerpt or at most two. Any more than that would probably cover too much of the same ground. But because each chapter stood alone, *Saturday Night* was excerpt-friendly. I knew I couldn't expect huge book sales. It was a quirky subject, and in 1990, I didn't have a reputation that would drive people to a bookstore. But having so many excerpts would bring the book a lot of welcome attention.

In the back of my mind, I was surprised that both *The New Yorker* and *The New York Times* were running excerpts. While the two publications are so different, they viewed each other with rivalrous jealousy. One of the few conditions of writers' contracts at *The New Yorker* has always been that they can't contribute to the *Times*. Apparently, though, they were in harmony about *Saturday Night*, or so it seemed. My quinceañera chapter was set in type at *The New Yorker* while I worked on my *Times* excerpt with my editor there. How lucky could I be?

Not quite lucky enough, it turned out. Somehow, the magazines caught wind of the fact that they were both running *Saturday Night* excerpts. In a flurry of phone calls, the editor at the *Times* told Richard Pine that they were canceling because they didn't want to run a section from the same book as *The New Yorker*. On another call, Gottlieb told Richard that *The New Yorker* was going to cancel my excerpt for the same reason; plus, he didn't want to print an excerpt that would appear twenty-four hours later than the *Times*'s. (The *Times* excerpt was supposed to appear in the Sunday magazine; *The New Yorker* came out on Mondays.) I was crushed. I called Gottlieb and pleaded with him to reconsider for my sake. Then I called my editor at the *Times*, whom I barely knew, and begged him to relent. Somehow a compromise was reached. The *Times* excerpt would appear on Sunday. *The New Yorker* would publish theirs on Monday, but back then, *The New Yorker* sent a courier around on Sunday to deliver the new issue to its most important subscribers. Gottlieb pointed to this as evidence that the *Times* had not beaten *The New Yorker*. The people who mattered would get the two excerpts of *Saturday Night* on the same day.

I had forgotten that publishing a book means getting reviewed, and as

Holding the finished draft of Saturday Night

Saturday Night, *done at last*

we approached the official publication date, I was terrified. If you write a magazine piece that doesn't soar, you don't experience any consequences. Sales of the magazine don't drop, and no one is likely to review the piece savagely. But a book was real nakedness. Would it sell? Would it get good reviews? Would it get reviewed at all? In a panic, I called Elisabeth Sifton and asked if it was too late to cancel the book. Yes, she explained to me, it was too late. I busied myself—distracted myself—by planning my book party with a group of friends who had offered to host it.

The party was on a Friday. That morning, Christopher Lehmann-Haupt reviewed the book in *The New York Times*, calling it "An unusual and entertaining cultural profile . . . with the drollness of her prose, the sharpness of her ear and eye, and her breadth of curiosity . . . Enlightening." To even get a review in the daily paper was amazing, but to get a great review from the lead critic? I was beside myself, jigging around our apartment in delight. There was also a review in the *San Francisco Examiner*, calling it "scrupulously researched" and "elegantly written."

Peter was quieter than usual. As he was getting dressed for work, he stopped and sat on the edge of our bed. I couldn't decipher his mood. He clearly wasn't celebrating my reviews, which was the type of withholding I'd come to expect from him, but this was something more, some heaviness, some portent. After a moment, he asked me if I respected him. The question was startling, odd; his delivery even odder. I didn't know how to answer, which I realize now was a kind of answer itself. Finally, I managed a weak "yes" and then, flustered, tried to talk around the question. He sat for a few minutes, his eyes fixed on the floor, and then finished dressing and left for work. The incident hung in the air like the aftermath of a bell ringing—a disturbance in the air, not quite audible, but I could feel it in my bones.

I spent the day fussing around, getting ready for the book party and fielding congratulatory phone calls from friends. Midday, Peter called. His voice sounded thin. He stammered and then stopped. I felt my heart thud so hard that my skin pulsed. "I've been seeing someone," he said.

Now the thudding was rising through my body. I asked what he meant. And for how long. And whom. A paralegal. At his law firm. For a year. My breath came so fast that I felt winded. He asked if he could come home. Nothing made sense. Yes, come home. Or don't come home? I don't know. I have to go.

The only thing that I could think to do in that moment was to call an out-of-town friend we had planned to visit that weekend. It felt urgent to let her know that Peter was having an affair, therefore we would not be visiting her that weekend. I moved like an automaton responding to offstage commands. Okay, I have canceled the weekend plans. Now I must make up the bed in the guest room because I can't sleep in our room until I buy a new mattress; he admitted he had slept there with his lover when I was out of town. Now I must get dressed for my book party. Now I must answer a phone call from the lover herself, who informed me that Peter had told her he and I were getting divorced. When he'd hedged and stalled, she'd warned him she would tell me about their relationship herself. Thus, it dawned on me that Peter hadn't confessed to the affair because he felt remorseful and wanted to reconcile. He'd told me because she had threatened to do it first. I slammed down the phone.

Every betrayal is unique, but they all have a pattern, a wave form, a surging and crashing that sucks you below the waterline and then pitches you, breathless and wet with tears, onto the sand. Some people find their footing and dash away before the next wave reaches them. I was the other sort of person, so dazed that I had to let the wave hit me again and again, churning me and spitting me out repeatedly. In that moment, I knew only that I had to gather myself and go to my book party, my celebration of the culmination of five difficult years of work, even as I gagged and spun and seized up again, sobbing. When Peter got home, I was shocked to see how haggard he looked, how beaten. I began quizzing him insistently, in a rage. Tell me more about her. Did you travel together, buy things together, make plans together. You owe it to me to tell me. Don't tell me—I don't want to know. Tell me or I'll kill myself. All the while, in the next room, I could hear my answering machine broadcasting calls—Richard reporting more enthusiastic reviews of the book, sweet messages from friends—but it all rolled off me. I was slippery with sadness.

I think I had fun at my party; I don't really remember. I do remember feeling like I was bleeding. Peter was there, hovering out of sight most of the time, chatting with friends as if nothing had happened, although there was a grayness to his face, a saucered sinking under his eyes. That night, when the party was over, I heaved myself onto our foldout couch and lay awake, the bony slats of the frame rasping against my spine. I didn't have a good night's sleep for months.

Why didn't I leave? You are right to ask. I ask myself. Even now, many years later, I continue to wonder, the way you might wonder how you hadn't noticed a suspicious growth that ended up nearly killing you. Why didn't I take my measure and find myself worth more than what this marriage felt like? I've come to think it was like driving a tire over a nail. The nail makes a deep, punishing puncture. If you leave it in, the tire seals around the wound, and at least you can keep driving. The tire might even look like it has healed, but it's merely survival. If you pull the nail out, your tire will go flat. I didn't realize that going flat was the better option, the one that would get rid of the nail forever, even if it hurt at first. I wanted to keep driving, keep going, no matter what.

I did a book tour for *Saturday Night*, which was busy enough to be a good distraction. It's a wonder I was able to do the tour. Since I was a kid, I had traveled without any problem, but right before the book was published, I developed an intense fear of flying. My phobia had gotten so severe that I started canceling trips. When I flew, I stumbled off the plane, shattered by the stress and strain. I had to do something about it, or I wouldn't be able to go on tour. A friend who didn't know what was going on with Peter suggested that my kind of sudden-onset fear often meant you had an unresolved problem in your life. I felt uneasy, caught out, when she said it. For some reason, Peter's infidelity embarrassed me; I didn't want anyone to know my husband found someone else more appealing than me, as if I'd gotten a terrible review from the most important critic in my life.

Another friend suggested I try hypnotism; she had used it to quit smoking, and she thought it might work for flying. She called her hypnotherapist—I'll call him Dr. Alexei—and he said he would be happy to work with me.

Dr. Alexei was wiry and tall, with a shiny cap of oily hair, a heavy brow, and a throaty Russian accent. He waved me through the door and motioned for me to sit. He asked why I had come.

"I'm afraid to fly," I said.

"That's your first mistake," he said, tapping his pencil on the pad. He did it very rhythmically—tap, tap, tap, tap. "Do not say that, ever. Say, 'I used to have a fear of flying.'"

"I used to have a fear of flying," I stammered. He nodded, looking pleased.

For five weeks, I came to his office once a week, settled on the lounger, and then listened as he walked me through visualizing my body parts and had me describe an ordinary week of my life in plodding detail. I alternated between paying attention and carrying on an internal conversation about what a waste of time it was. After three sessions, Dr. Alexei hadn't mentioned flying. I sometimes wondered if he had forgotten why I was there. Finally, during my fourth session, he told me to imagine packing a suitcase. At last we're getting somewhere, I thought. I battled the urge to leave and the conviction that I was not hypnotized. But I never got up and left, even when I posed it as a test to myself.

Around this time, I began running regularly. Often, in the middle of a run, it dawned on me that I could simply stop. I could hold that thought but never act on it, even though I was exhausted and the idea of stopping was very appealing. It occurred to me that I might be hypnotizing myself while running. I decided to train for the 1992 New York City Marathon, and my long runs felt like meditations, as if I weren't fully conscious. My sessions with Dr. Alexei were the only other time I'd experienced this odd duality of thinking one thing and doing another, of having my thoughts feel both unconnected to my body and intensely connected.

The day before my last hypnotism session, my publisher called to go over my tour schedule. I nervously agreed to the plans, even though I felt no closer to being able to do the tour. The next day, I stomped over to Dr. Alexei's office, planning to complain that I wasn't getting results, but I ended up on the lounger, as usual, thinking about my toes and ankles. The session started where we'd left off last time—with my packed suitcase—and then, in Dr. Alexei's narration, I got into an imaginary taxi, which drove me to the imaginary airport. He talked me through the entire experience of a flight. When he finished, and the imaginary plane landed, I opened my eyes. "That's it?" I asked.

"That's it."

Had anything happened to me besides having five expensive naps on a lumpy lounger? I had no way to tell, but with the book tour looming on my calendar, I decided to test myself. I booked a flight to Boston to visit a friend. On past flights, I was too busy clawing the seat to conduct a conversation, but this time I greeted the man seated next to me. We talked about the weather and our mutual dislike of Boston traffic. Without me noticing, the plane whipped down the runway and tilted into the air. The sky opened wide beside us.

I turned to my seatmate and said, "I'm thinking of getting a pilot's license."

"Really?" he said, sounding impressed.

What had Dr. Alexei done to me? As we leveled at thirty thousand feet, I added, "I think it would be really fun to fly a plane."

And then I flew and I flew and I flew. I became one of the people I used to find so bewildering, those who approached flying with nonchalance, who read the newspaper during rough air without glancing up, who napped during takeoff and landing. I never really considered getting a pilot's license and never will. I think the desire to fly a plane was specific only to that first post-hypnosis flight. (Or maybe it was an Easter egg planted by Dr. Alexei?) All I knew was that somehow my circuit of anxiety had been disrupted. It was as if an overactive loose nerve had been sealed. I wondered how hypnosis worked, but I was nervous that examining it too closely might undo it, as if it had been a spell. Seeing myself change so dramatically was heady but also mystifying, so I was mostly happy to let it be.

By all rights, I should have been ecstatic. The book was selling surprisingly well, and it had gotten almost all good reviews. I started toying with a follow-up. My working title was *The House in My Head*. I pictured it structured like *Saturday Night*—each chapter would examine one person's home and how it had come to be, why the person had created the kind of home they had. I liked the idea of learning how and why people had put together their living quarters, how they'd chosen to live where they lived, and then, on a more intimate scale, how they'd made it look the way it did. I started a file and scribbled down a few ideas.

In those pre-Internet days, agents and publishers paid services to gather reviews from newspapers around the country. That was the only way to keep track of them. I asked Richard to forward only the good *Saturday Night* reviews because, given my state of mind, I couldn't bear seeing bad ones. Fortunately, there weren't many. As unconventional a concept as the book was, readers and reviewers seemed to understand it and embrace it. Before long, Propaganda Films, a company run by esteemed Hollywood producer Steve Golin, optioned the book to turn it into a documentary television series. They hired a great young director, Mark Pellington, and put me on staff as a writer, and we toiled away for a few exciting months, figuring out how to translate the book for television. So many wonderful things were happening, but they didn't sink in. My ruptured marriage had ruined me. I couldn't stop thinking about Peter with this other woman. I couldn't sleep without Trazodone. I had no appetite. I lost close to twenty pounds, worrying it away and then becoming sickly fascinated by watching it happen. I probably hadn't weighed myself in years, but I began weighing myself throughout the day, marveling at how little I could eat and how fast I was shrinking.

Peter and I went into counseling. For a brief, raving moment, I convinced myself that the affair had been a *good thing* because it had brought us closer and helped us appreciate how much we meant to each other. I think Peter scared himself with his callousness and dishonesty and perhaps was frightened, seeing how devastated I was. We were like trench buddies, bonded by living through disaster together. We bought a new mattress, decided to have a baby, felt the giddy rush of nearly drowning but clawing to shore just in time, shocked by the glimpse of catastrophe.

I was too thin to get pregnant. For months, my body fat was so low that I didn't get my period. And yet I increased my running, looping the Central Park Reservoir until my toes were raw. I ran in the rain. I ran at dusk, wondering and almost savoring how guilty Peter would feel if I were murdered. I began an affair with a friend, defiantly, wretchedly. He was staggeringly smart—a MacArthur Genius, in fact—and far kinder than Peter. I was crazy about him and would have left Peter for him in a wounded minute, but he wasn't interested in anything permanent. I felt like an idiot having an affair, but I was so shattered and confused that I simply followed whatever instinct seized me. I ran the New York City Marathon and then a half-marathon and a whole calendar of races. I went to cooking school. I cut my hair. Peter discovered my affair after it had ended, and his outrage was fresh and furious, as if he had never done the same.

I began a *New Yorker* profile of Fab 5 Freddy, the hip-hop pioneer and artist, who was then the host of *Yo! MTV Raps.* As I was working on that piece, I sat down with Bob Gottlieb. My contract at *Vogue* was about to expire, and they wanted to renew it, which would bind me to a steady stream of *Vogue* assignments. I preferred to be officially at *The New Yorker.* I told Gottlieb that unless he could give me some assurance of my status at the magazine, I would renew my contract at *Vogue.* "All right, all right," he said, chuckling and waving at me as if I were a pesty bird trying to grab his lunch. "You can be a staff writer! You can have an office! Just stop bugging me! Stop bugging me!" Thus, with no flourish, no ceremony, no golden rings, I became a staff writer at *The New Yorker.* For bookkeeping reasons, the arrangement would begin formally in September, a few months away. I was incredibly, buoyantly happy, at least about work. I used those few months to finish out my *Vogue* assignments and to write "The American Man, Age Ten" for *Esquire.* After such a miserable period in my personal life, this finally seemed like the change that would break the spell.

At the beginning of August 1992, I wrote a Talk piece about the Girl Scouts, who were moving to new headquarters. It would be the last piece I would write for the Gottlieb-era *New Yorker.* As soon as I finished the piece, Peter and I left for two weeks on Cape Cod. While we were packing, I got a call from Alison Rose, telling me that Gottlieb had been fired and was being replaced by Tina Brown, the editor of *Vanity Fair.* This was a double-barreled shock. No one expected Gottlieb to get fired, and no one could imagine what Tina, who had loaded *Vanity Fair* with celebrity news, true crime, and reporting on the new rich, would do to *The New Yorker.*

I was frantic. What would happen to my arrangement with Gottlieb—my staff job, my office, my contract? The agreement was not on paper. Even if it had been, would Tina honor it? I had never written for *Vanity Fair* and didn't know Tina at all. I called everyone I knew at *The New*

Yorker, but no one had any more information. Peter and I had rented a bare-bones cabin on the beach near Wellfleet. It didn't have a phone, and this was many years before cell phones were available. There was a pay phone down the hill from the cabin, and I hiked to it several times a day to call Alison and other *New Yorker* writers who knew Tina, primarily Adam Gopnik and Stephen Schiff, to see if they knew what was going on. There were scraps of information but nothing, of course, about my particular situation.

By this time, Peter had left his job at Paul Weiss Rifkind Wharton & Garrison. During his annual review, he had been told that he would not make partner, perhaps in part because it was known around the firm that he'd had a relationship with a subordinate. He landed a job as a special deputy counsel to New York governor Mario Cuomo, which required being in Albany during the week. On weekends, I went to Albany, or Peter came back to the city. Being together so little was a relief, but it was a false relief: We got along better because we didn't have to get along very much.

I remained shattered by what had transpired, broken. I felt like the cliché of a betrayed spouse: suspicious, needy, vengeful, fragile. I played a tape in my head about the affair over and over, almost compulsively. I tasted it, explored the pain, the way you stick your tongue in a sore tooth even though it hurts. Peter swore that he loved me and said he regretted what he'd done, but I didn't trust him, and not trusting your partner is poisonous. Living apart, now that he spent most of his time in Albany, made the possibility of cheating almost too easy. What was this all about, anyway? Was it an accident that he'd told me about his affair the day of my book party, or was it purposeful, meant to puncture my happiness at that specific celebratory moment? Many of my friends insisted that he was jealous and competitive, but I refused to believe he was that petty, that stingy with emotions. Yet he was. Amid the upheaval at the magazine and my legitimate worry that my position there might evaporate, he was impassive.

What was I doing? Why did I tolerate this? I can't tell you. I can say only that I came to understand the mysterious magnetism of cruelty, that making a mark on someone, emotional or otherwise, seems like it should be repellent but often has the terrible effect of forming a bond, as if the scar tissue is adhesive.

Everyone at *The New Yorker* was so alarmed by the change of editors that any shred of news, true or imaginary, spread fast and furiously: Tina is firing so-and-so, hiring so-and-so, changing such-and-such, closing the magazine. The only information I gathered about myself was distressing. Apparently, in a meeting with the advertising staff, Tina cited two stories as examples of what her version of *The New Yorker* would *not* be publishing: One was E. J. Kahn Jr.'s multipart treatise on grain. The other was a story I had written a few months earlier about a supermarket in Queens.

The bitter irony was that the supermarket story was especially dear to me. It was an example of what I had come to think of as "hiding in plain sight" subjects, those aspects of life that are so familiar we no longer really see them, and we assume we know more about them than we actually do. These are among my favorite types of stories to write.

It also represented a writing breakthrough for me. In the past, I had used first person here and there but always sparingly and somewhat apologetically. I wrestled with the supermarket story, trying to figure out how to move the reader around the store and in and out of the anecdotes I was writing. Everything I tried was awkward. Finally, I remembered how long it had taken me to write *Saturday Night* and how, at the end of the day, the solution to what hampered me was to write it as naturally as I could, stepping into the story when it was necessary for moving the reader through. I didn't make myself the central character; I let myself inhabit the story the way I inhabited it in real life—as an observer and a guide and the person whose curiosity was guiding the tale. I let myself be present, the reader's friendly chaperone. It was a tone best embodied by John McPhee, one of my heroes, who was always present in his pieces without requiring your focus to be on him. While I was working on the grocery store piece—"All Mixed Up"—I tried to imagine how McPhee might have approached it. The writing then fell together organically, authentically. When I wanted to write about something I had observed in the meat department, I wrote that I had gone to the meat department. I didn't need to contort the narrative to move the reader there; I could take them with me, direct them. It was deceptively simple and instantly felt right. I would be a gentle companion to the reader, helping point their attention to what was interesting. This allowed me to reveal the mechanics of the piece—explaining how it came together—so that I no longer had to struggle to put the sections together on their own. It felt so natural that it startled me.

Hearing that Tina had used the grocery store piece as an example of what she would be purging from *The New Yorker* convinced me that she wouldn't keep me on staff. On the off chance that she would, we clearly didn't agree on what or how I should write. I limped back from vacation, downhearted, and was stunned when I got a call from Tina's assistant a few days later saying she wanted to meet with me. I'm not sure how it happened. I don't know whether Gottlieb had created some paperwork documenting our agreement, or whether he or someone had told Tina about it, but I was relieved to be summoned.

A few days later, I had a brief, perfunctory meeting with Tina. She was so distracted by the whir of activity around her that I'm not certain she registered exactly who I was. All the better, in my opinion. Of course, I didn't breathe a word about grocery stores. She gave me an office across from John McPhee's and a contract to write four features that year. I knew I'd have to convince her I was a worthy addition, but at least I was being given the chance.

I assumed the magazine would continue as it always had, with story ideas bubbling up from the writers. Typically, writers developed ideas on their own and presented them for approval before starting to work on them. That's why the magazine was distinctive. At times it could also come across as indulgent because it allowed writers to pursue their own curiosities, no matter how idiosyncratic. But Tina had other plans. She intended to assign stories, and to rattle the cages of all the writers at the magazine who had staff positions but hadn't written anything in years.

One of those she planned to rattle was the legendary writer Joseph Mitchell, whose work, which included books such as *Up in the Old Hotel* and *Joe Gould's Secret*, had defined literary journalism. Mitchell joined the magazine in 1938, after spending time working on an ocean freighter. He specialized in exquisite, moody character studies and portraits of New York City subcultures that were rapidly disappearing—the longshoremen, the ticket-takers, the vagabonds. In 1964, he began work on a story about a man, Joe Gould, who claimed he was writing a nine million-word oral history of the world. In his reporting, Mitchell discovered that Gould had written only a chapter or two of this mammoth history, then spent years obsessively revising, paralyzed by writer's block and an obsessive-compulsive mania. In an instance of tragic irony, *Joe Gould's Secret* was the last major piece Mitchell wrote. He, too, suffered from a crushing case of writer's block, and some people wondered if Joe Gould might be an imaginary projection of Mitchell's own depression.

For the next twenty years, Mitchell came to his office at *The New Yorker* every day and maintained regular working hours even though he never published another piece. Rumor was that he wrote all day and threw out what he had written at the end of each day. Another rumor was that someone at the magazine collected the contents of his wastebasket every night, with the intention, someday after Mitchell's death, of publishing what he had written, but no such project has ever emerged, even though he passed away in 1996. Mitchell was slight and soft-spoken, with a buttery North Carolina accent and the custom of wearing a hat long after men stopped wearing hats, which made him look like a time-traveler from, say, 1938, who had dropped in on the modern world. I once rode the office elevator with him. He addressed me as "Miss Orlean" with a slight bow and his hand brushing the brim of his hat, and he said he had enjoyed a recently published story of mine, which left me quivering with happiness.

Apparently, Tina thought the magazine was babying Mitchell by allowing him to wallow in whatever had stifled his writing. Word went around that she called him shortly after she came to the magazine and said she would like him to profile musician Eric Clapton. Mitchell, always gentlemanly, told her it was a wonderful idea but that unfortunately he had to decline. I don't know if this story is myth or fact, nor do I know what Tina would have said to him in response, but we all saw it as a sign of what Tina Brown had in mind: a magazine directed from above, with an appetite for celebrity and little tolerance for idle genius among the staff.

Within a few days of settling into my office, Tina called and said she wanted me to profile Mark Wahlberg, then a muscle-bound hip-hop artist and Calvin Klein underwear model known as Marky Mark. I had no desire to write about Marky Mark, and I didn't see him as *New Yorker* material, but I was afraid to say no. I was finishing the last draft of "American Man," so I decided the best approach was to stall. I told Tina I could do the Wahlberg piece in a few weeks. I hoped that, in the interim, she would lose interest or assign it to someone else.

"You need to do it immediately, Susan," she said. "He's only going to be hot for about ten days."

I was impressed that she assessed celebrity so cynically and so precisely; she had a knack for understanding the metabolism of popular culture. I didn't want to do the piece, but I had to do something, obviously. I said I would do it immediately but that I thought it would work better as a Talk piece. I could stomach writing about Marky Mark for eight hundred words; I didn't think I could do it for four thousand. To my relief, Tina agreed. The story, "Brief Encounter," ran in the November 2, 1992, issue. It was my first piece for Tina Brown. It was also my first Talk piece with a byline, since Tina decided Talk pieces should no longer be nameless;

she also instituted a larger table of contents and short bios of each issue's contributors. The days of polite anonymity, of "happy-shabby, baked-apple gentility" at *The New Yorker*, were over.

I edged around Tina carefully, trying to figure out how to persuade her to let me do the kinds of stories I wanted and how to come up with ideas fast enough to fend off the assignments she had in mind. It was like playing dodgeball. I always had to be on offense, with an idea that somehow straddled her new vision for the magazine and my peculiar curiosities. The first long piece I wrote for her was a profile of Felipe López, who was then the best high school basketball player in the country. I landed on the idea in a roundabout way. One day I was browsing the sports pages in the newspaper and saw the headline CHRIST THE KING AIMS FOR REVENGE. I can't resist reading a story with that kind of headline. I quickly learned that Christ the King was the name of a Catholic high school, and the revenge planned was by its basketball team against another school that had beaten it earlier.

The story, with its language of defeat and vengeance and victory, intrigued me so much that I clipped it and hung it on my wall, figuring it might inspire me somehow. My high school, Shaker Heights High, paid scant attention to sports, so I was surprised that high school–level athletics could evoke such passion. Maybe there was a story there. I noodled around a bit and found the name of a scout hired by NBA teams and colleges to identify promising high school players. I attended a few basketball games with him and asked who he considered the best player in the country. He immediately cited López, who was a junior at Rice High School in Harlem, a few miles north of my apartment on the Upper West Side. I thought he would make a great profile. Felipe was happy to do the story, and Tina liked the idea, so I was all set.

I loved working on the piece, which was eventually titled "Shoot the Moon." For one thing, López was a delight. As I wrote in the piece, "Before I met Felipe, people told me I would find him cuddly. Everything I knew about him—that he is a *boy*, that he is a *teenage boy*, that he is a six-foot-five-teenage-boy *jock*—made this pretty hard to believe, but it turns out to be true. He is actually the sweetest person I know . . . 'Oh, my goodness' remains his favorite phrase. It is a utility expression that reveals his modesty, his manners, his ingenuousness, and his usual state of mind, which is one of pleasant and guileless surprise at the remarkable nature of his life."

I had an idea for the lede, but I was worried about it. I had been struck by how racially stratified the high school basketball scene was. Most of the players were Black, and almost all the scouts and coaches and managers were white men. Felipe, who was from the Dominican Republic, was trailed constantly by this cohort of white men—his every move analyzed, every growth spurt recorded, every muscle measured. He handled the scrutiny with great poise, but it dominated his life and invaded his privacy, even when he was years away from a possible professional career. I wanted to begin the piece there, and I wanted to land hard on the racial aspect because it was impossible to miss. I began writing:

> White men in suits follow Felipe Lopez everywhere he goes. Felipe lives in Mott Haven, in the South Bronx. He is a junior at Rice High School, which is on the corner of 124th Street and Lenox Avenue, in Harlem, and he plays guard for the school basketball team, the Rice Raiders. The white men are ubiquitous. They rarely miss one of Felipe's games or tournaments. They have absolute recall of his best minutes of play. They are authorities on his physical condition. They admire his feet, which are big and pontoon-shaped, and his wrists, which have a loose, silky motion. Not long ago, I sat with the white men at a game between Rice and All Hallows High School. My halftime entertainment was listening to a debate between two of them—a college scout and a Westchester contractor who is a high school basketball fan—about whether Felipe had

grown a half inch over Christmas break. "I know this kid," the scout said as the second half started. "A half inch is not something I would miss."

I wasn't sure if this lede—this tone, this language, and in particular the phrase "white men"—was going to pass muster at the magazine. I didn't know how to proceed. I rarely show work in progress to my editors. A snippet without context never conveys what I'm trying to do with the piece. Some of my resistance is vanity: I hate to show anyone my work until I think it's buffed and polished. But I felt like I was trying something a little risky with this lede, and I didn't want to invest too much time if it wasn't working or wouldn't be accepted.

Chip had been my editor since my first Talk piece. After a shy start, I'd settled in with him, and with each piece we worked on, I felt more of a bond between us. He was reserved, even stoic, but when he liked something, he lit up, and getting his approval felt like winning a sweepstakes. I loved hanging out in his office, shooting the breeze, and soon we got in the habit of walking out of the office together at the end of the day.

I decided to show him the Felipe López lede, even though it made me uncomfortable. Would *The New Yorker* let me call out people as "white"? Chip took my pages upstairs to his office and, after ten minutes, came down beaming. I was good to go. I started writing furiously. I had great material from my time with the team and with Felipe, so the piece fell together easily once I had navigated the lede.

Everything about doing this piece was heady. Was it because I had taken a chance with the writing and it had paid off? Was it because I got a congratulatory note from my dad, who continued to believe I had missed my chance by not going to law school, saying, "Sue! 'Shoot the Moon' is one of your best! Congrats!"? It was also my first long piece for Tina, so I was keyed up until she read it. But she loved it. This was a huge relief, in terms of the specific piece but also because it helped convince her to let me do more stories of my own devising.

Everyone at the magazine was on tenterhooks, desperate to figure out Tina and her intentions, so perhaps Chip was relieved, too, that he had shepherded a piece she liked. The night we finished editing "Shoot the Moon," Chip and I left the office together and then, at the last minute, decided to head to Cafe Un Deux Trois, a packed bistro around the corner. Sitting at the bar, we smoked cigarettes, drank martinis, and talked for hours. I was in no rush to get home—Peter was in Albany, and those days I always felt I was on my own, rattling around in the husk of a marriage, not sure where it was going. Talking to Chip was so much easier, so much more fun. Peter made me feel bad when something good came my way. I felt punished, as if I had depleted him somehow, even when those good things were something we could both savor. It was almost shocking to be around someone who seemed buoyed by my accomplishments the way Chip was. "I'm so proud of you," he said that night. "You're an artist." Nothing had ever made me feel so good. We drank and smoked and shared secrets until the bar closed. It was the first time in a long time that I felt loved.

SEVEN

Those were strange days at *The New Yorker*; strange, changeful days. The staff churned, with people being hired or fired or quitting every day, which was rare at a magazine that had been stable to the point of stultification. That was Tina's point, to shake it up, prune the deadwood, question conventions, revitalize the place; who knows what would have become of the magazine had she not done so? She brought a host of *Vanity Fair* writers to *The New Yorker* and edged out some of the people who had been at the magazine forever. She wanted to run *The New Yorker* with a strong editorial hand, but paradoxically, she also wanted to make the writers celebrities, something the old *New Yorker* avoided at all costs. In addition to putting bylines on Talk of the Town, making feature bylines much bigger, and adding a contributors' page, she hired a renowned photographer, Gasper Tringale, to shoot portraits of us for use in promotions. For a while, it was even rumored that thumbnail photos would run with our contributor bios. Nothing encapsulated the new *New Yorker* more perfectly than that. It had been a magazine that had barely run bylines; used second-person plural to obliterate attention to individual writers; and looked askance at anyone on staff becoming too prominent on their own. Yet here we were, having headshots done by a high-end photographer. We were going through the looking glass, into a new incarnation of the magazine. Tina also decided to buck the tradition of using only drawings and illustrations. *The New Yorker* had never published a photograph until 1992, when master photographer Richard Avedon joined the staff. One of his first assignments was to photograph Felipe López for my piece.

I began to develop a sense of the story ideas Tina liked. She was wary of anything too ambling; she liked stories that popped. If she began her tenure at *The New Yorker* believing I was too much of an ambler, she was at least willing to be persuaded otherwise. She liked stories that explored the ideas and conventions of class. She liked anything that felt immediate—a quality that the magazine had never pursued. Even though she and I started as the most uneasy of colleagues, we had more interests in common than it had seemed. My piece after Felipe López was a profile of a popular New York DJ, Kool DJ Red Alert, a subject I had suggested. After I finished that, Tina asked me to profile designer Bill Blass. I liked writing about fashion, and while I wouldn't have come up with the idea of Bill Blass on my own, I loved doing the story. Almost by accident, Tina and I developed a rhythm: a few of my ideas and then one of hers. After Bill Blass, I profiled a children's party clown (my idea); did a story about skater Tonya Harding's hometown (my idea); and then wrote about fading super-agent Sue Mengers (Tina's).

I had come to see my work as falling into roughly two categories. One of them was what I liked to call the "who knew?" stories—the exploration of a subject I had no idea even existed, a subculture I didn't know, a hobby that came as a complete surprise. These stories felt like discovering a new country on the map, all wonder and revelation. In that "who knew?" category: my piece on taxidermy or my profile of popular artist Thomas Kinkade.

The other sort were the stories I thought of as "hiding in plain sight"—namely, the kinds of things that were familiar, even mundane, but once examined closely, turned out to be much more unexpected and fascinating. That would include the profile I wrote of a student council president at one of Manhattan's most troubled high schools, or the phenomenon of backyard chickens. Often these kinds of stories were funny, the humor arising out of the remarks people made to me. In 2001, I did a story about tattooing in Massachusetts, where it had finally been legalized. (Massachusetts and Oklahoma were the only two states that prohibited the practice until then.) I interviewed lawyers writing regulatory language to manage tattoo and body modification within Massachusetts. Sitting beside lawyers writing policies might have seemed dry, but it turned out to be hilarious. "I need you guys to help with this subregulatory language," one of the lawyers said to her assistants. "We need to cover tongue splitting, cartilage sculpting, finger and toe and rib removal, and teeth filing."

"What about implantation of spikes and so forth?" one eager assistant replied.

"We need to spell it all out," the lawyer said. "If someone wants their neighbor to artistically amputate their leg, there might be liability issues."

Tonya Harding was a new sort of undertaking for me. At the time of my piece, Harding was a leading competitive figure skater and the first American woman to land a triple axel in a judged event. In 1994, shortly before that year's Winter Olympics, her archrival, Nancy Kerrigan, was kneecapped with a police baton. An investigation revealed that Kerrigan's assailant had been hired by Harding's ex-husband. The question was what role Harding had played in the assault. The media gobbled up the story, titillated by drama and the irresistible comparison between poised, pretty, prim Kerrigan and Harding, who was muscular and surly and working class.

In the storm of publicity, Harding had gone underground, refusing to speak to the press. I felt I could write a story even without her involvement—I would take an oblique approach to her biography, focusing on Clackamas, Oregon, where she grew up. Some newspaper stories described Harding as being from Portland, and it is true that Clackamas is not far from Portland. But because I had lived in Oregon, I knew that being from Clackamas was very different from being from Portland, and understanding the world that produced Tonya Harding was a way to begin to understand her.

By this time, Tina trusted my instincts on stories that relied on venturing out without an agenda, and when I proposed my idea to her, to write *around* Tonya Harding, she agreed. When I'd lived in Portland, I had rarely been to Clackamas, so it was new to me, a place that was a world away from the gentrification and coffee culture of Portland. In many ways, it felt like a town that belonged on the Alaskan frontier. I roamed aimlessly but attentively. I stopped in thrift stores, where I came across a surprising number of souvenirs from Alaska, and in the town mall, a bland commercial doughnut with a skating rink in the center, where I was rewarded with a sighting of Tonya, who had emerged from hiding to skate for a few hours. While watching her slice her way around the ice, I happened to meet members of the Tonya Harding Fan Club, so for the next few days I tagged along as they debated how to push back against the popular narrative that Tonya had orchestrated the attack.

I didn't have an agenda for the story besides wanting to give context to what the mainstream media was reporting—a shallow and mostly sensational account. I hate reporting that relies on coded shorthand, that doesn't really consider the nuance in a story, that supposes readers share an assumption about certain things. Saying Tonya Harding was from Portland was inaccurate and misleading. Appreciating the hardscrabble world she clawed out of, and intended to stay out of, was essential to understanding her situation. I had no intention of excusing the attack, but I wanted to portray it as part of a continuum in her fierce, unyielding life. If I had gotten the opportunity to speak to Tonya, I would have been glad, but I felt I could write about her through the context of where she lived.

I always avoided writing about anything too immediate in the news, but working on this piece woke me up to that approach. I could use the news as a departure point, an occasion to go deeper or to come at a subject sideways. It felt fresh. In April 1995, after the horrific Oklahoma City bombing, I again used this tactic. I knew I wouldn't interview Timothy McVeigh, but I ached to write something about the event. I noticed that newspaper stories about McVeigh mentioned he had lived in a trailer park, without giving any further description. There it was: shorthand meant to convey something without really spelling out what it was. I had never spent time in a trailer park, nor had anyone I knew, and yet I suspected most of us had an immediate response to the image the phrase evoked. I proposed writing a profile of a trailer park as a way of decoding the story, and Tina was game. I headed to a trailer park outside of Portland. I knew doing the story wouldn't be easy: I would have to find the heart of it once I was at the park. But I was intrigued by the challenge. I liked pushing myself to look hard at things I had made assumptions about and letting myself unlearn what I thought I knew.

I was settling into a comfortable rhythm, but the mood at the magazine was tense. People fell in and out of favor on an hourly basis, and many decisions felt capricious—what got published, what didn't. We enjoyed the fatty overindulgence that Tina had begun at *Vanity Fair:* car service home if we worked late, unlimited lunches delivered from the nicest New York restaurants, lavish travel budgets. The parties were a blast. When I first got to the magazine, in the Gottlieb era, the Christmas parties were modest homemade affairs held at the office, with a few bottles of wine and platters of cookies if anyone remembered to buy them. Tina preferred a catered event at a starry venue—a bash, a happening. She liked the idea that outsiders would wangle to get invited. The holiday parties and magazine anniversary parties became elaborate occasions. She sent individually selected Christmas gifts to the staff, and you could tell where you stood by the lavishness of your gift. One year, a friend of mine on staff got a high-end DVD player. My first Christmas gift was a pair of slingback heels.

Chip and I whiled away a few nights each week leaning on the bar at Cafe Un Deux Trois and commiserating about the magazine. He was the most important person in the world to me, and sometimes I thought I had found an odd balance at last: I had my marriage and what it offered me, and the rest I got from Chip—deep intimacy, mentoring, encouragement. Ours was a closeness deeper than almost any I had ever experienced. Working together, especially in the turbulent, intense conditions at *The New Yorker* during that time, brought us even closer.

Tina never hid the fact that she believed in keeping people off-balance. She thought it brought out people's best work. She was quick to praise stories she liked, fast to send notes complimenting a piece. At the same time, most of us felt like we might be fired any minute. Whenever my phone rang and I saw it was Tina calling, I wasn't sure if she was going to tell me I was being let go or that I was the best writer at the magazine (which she told me now and then, and I suspected she told everyone at the magazine at one time or another). I was doing some of the best work of my career, but the pressure was punishing.

In 1995, I saw a sign on a telephone pole on the Upper West Side advertising a gospel concert. I didn't know gospel music very well, but I loved what I had heard, so I got tickets. The audience was markedly different from the usual Manhattan crowd. It was almost entirely Black, middle-aged or older, and dressed to the nines. I chatted with the woman next to me, and she laughed when I expressed my surprise. She said, You know there's a whole gospel circuit, don't you? No, I sure didn't. I made a mental note to find out more.

Months passed. One day in *The New York Times*, I noticed an obituary for a gospel singer named Franklin Williams, who was so beloved in his hometown of Jackson, Mississippi, that the streets downtown were closed for his funeral procession. What struck me was that someone whose name I didn't even recognize had loomed so large in his world that he stopped traffic. I wanted to see inside that world. I tracked down one of Williams's brothers who was a singer with a group called the Jackson Southernaires.

I explained to Huey that I would like to profile the group and perhaps travel with them as they journeyed the gospel circuit the woman at the concert had mentioned to me.

Looking back, I realize how brassy my request must have seemed. *The New Yorker* meant nothing to Huey Williams. He had never read it, and being profiled in it was of no great interest to him. Also, he was shocked that a woman was asking to travel with a group of men. The Southernaires were known as "the gentlemen of the gospel circuit." Their rules list, which was fifteen pages long, included fines for cursing, for having a wrinkled uniform, and for singing the wrong note. The highest fine was for "bringing a young lady to the restaurant when the group is eating."

Huey was polite and mostly discouraging, but he agreed to raise my request with the other Southernaires and get back to me. I was a little embarrassed when I realized how my request must have struck him, a deeply religious and conservative man who was uninterested in *The New Yorker*, but I didn't mind being knocked down a few pegs. I was so used to people being awed by the magazine that I appreciated being reminded that its influence was not universal. As for breaching propriety, that was a good reminder, too. I had made my career on being skilled at reading social cues, so this was a gentle slap back to reality. After all, if the group agreed to it, I would be in the Deep South, where men and women followed traditional rules.

A few days later, Huey called and said that the group wanted to meet me in person before making a final decision. Luckily for me, those were the days when the *New Yorker* travel budget was generous, and it was possible to travel at the magazine's expense to feel out a story. I flew to New Orleans and drove an hour outside of town for lunch with the Southernaires, five middle-aged Black men who, like Huey, had been singing gospel on weekends for decades. I must have done well explaining myself and my story idea, because at the end of our meeting, they agreed that I could join them for two weekends on the road.

I returned to Jackson a few weeks later with a roller bag and a lot of blank notebooks. The Southernaires were successful enough that a few years earlier they had graduated from traveling in a convoy of cars to owning a tour bus, which had been donated to them by a fan. They spent many hours and many miles in the bus, performing in towns that were pinpoints on a map: Blytheville, Arkansas; Demopolis, Alabama; Madison, Georgia; Marianna, Florida. They slept on the bus or in roadside motels.

Once I got to Jackson, the extraordinary nature of what I was undertaking dawned on me. I was completely on my own, about to submerge myself in a world that was truly unfamiliar. I was excited but also overcome by a sense of isolation like never before. I had a few days to kill in Jackson before the first weekend's concerts. I needed the time to settle myself, feel my way around town, think through how I would approach my reporting, but I had never felt more strangely disengaged in my life. What was I doing? The un-joblike quality of my job began to feel almost surreal. It was a wild, wonderful adventure, sending me into worlds I might never have visited otherwise—Little League baseball in Cuba, bullfighting in Spain, footloose backpackers in Bangkok, the trials and tribulations of an Oregon lounge band, and now the gospel circuit in the Deep South—but it was also a free-fall leap, no net, no parachute, always a bit dumbfounding until I could find my way. I went for long runs up and down Jackson's back roads, my mind empty. I roamed around the big mall in town, looking but not seeing, just to occupy my time. I was homesick. Finally, at last, it was Friday, and I was relieved to join the Southernaires on their bus.

The oddness of the situation was plain as day. The Southernaires had never had a woman travel with them—not wives or girlfriends or female acquaintances—and I suspect they hadn't encountered many women who would travel alone, as I was, not to mention with a group of men she barely knew. They were polite and at first a little shy. I was as unusual a creature to them as they were to me. But as the hours rolled by, our conversation livened up, and we found a tempo that worked. I felt like they began to view me as part daughter, part mascot, part space oddity. They were funny and loose with one another in the way of people who have spent endless time together, who work as a team, who know one another's worst and best.

I didn't have an angle for the story. I approached it like a travel piece, hoping to capture a sense of this gospel subculture, without news or a narrative hook. That this community existed, and had been essentially unchanged and self-contained for decades, was story enough for me. Crowds met the bus in each little town, hailing the Southernaires like heroes as they clambered down the steps of the bus. When I emerged, the crowds quieted and tried to puzzle me out, until Huey introduced me as "a lady writer" who was "telling the Southernaires' story." Then they welcomed me.

I spent most of my time with Huey, the lead singer and senior statesman of the group. He had been a construction worker before he formed the Southernaires, but he said he always knew singing was his destiny. He was a tall man with deep dimples and high cheekbones and light eyes. The first time I met him, he took my chin in his hands, tilted it toward him, and said, "Take a good look at my face. Have you ever in your life seen blue eyes on a Black man?" He had a potent, knifelike tenor but could also whisper in a sulky, silken tone. I knew he was intrigued by me. We spent a lot of time together, including the days off between touring.

One day we drove across most of Mississippi to his taxidermist's, so he could pick up a bobcat he had shot that was being mounted. On the drive, he told me some very personal things. I panicked, wishing he hadn't confided in me, because now it was in my head and, for all intents and purposes, in my notebook. We were always on the record—or, rather, he did not say what he was telling me was off the record—so I was weighted with heavy pieces of information that troubled me. Huey wasn't media-savvy. Would it even have occurred to him to say, "Off the record"? What was I to do? What he told me would add fiery details to the story, but could I live with myself if I decided to use them? The reporter's dilemma: I had worked so hard to earn his trust, and now he almost trusted me too much. I stared ahead as we approached the taxidermist's, pretending I hadn't heard him. I would decide what to do when I sat down to write, but I already knew I couldn't live with myself if I used it.

Huey's interest in me started as curiosity, transitioned into friendliness, and then, I knew, began deepening in a discomfiting way. The dynamic between subject and writer is intense. A writer appears in a subject's life, tells that person they are the most interesting human on earth, and becomes the most avid, enthusiastic listener imaginable, demanding nothing in return. It is as indulgent as therapy—let's talk about *you, you, you.* This odd relationship appears out of the blue, carries no demands or reciprocity, exists in a vacuum outside the realm of ordinary life, and feels hermetically sealed, utterly contained—that is, until the writer is done with the subject and sits down to share the story with the wide world, which is the part of the process the subject often forgets. Until then, the writer-subject relationship can feel ideal, ego-nurturing, for the subject. Until Huey, I'd never had a subject fall in love with me, but I was always aware of the bond I formed with my subjects and how it mimicked the contours of a perfect one-sided romance. In this case, there was the additional element of exoticism: I was a novelty in Huey's world, an adventuring, independent woman, and I could tell that enthralled him.

I have never had to manage so many emotions while working on a piece, and I wasn't sure I knew how to do it. To chide Huey for flirting with me risked offending him; at the very least, it might chill our interaction, which would hurt my reporting. But I didn't want to encourage him; I didn't share his feelings. I also was sure that he was mistaking his enjoyment of my attention for something romantic; I knew it felt intimate, it felt like love. I dodged his affection as nimbly as I could. I decided my best defense was to joke about it, to parry his declarations with gentle humor. It was hard. It's difficult enough to have someone smitten with you when you don't feel the same under ordinary circumstances, and these were not ordinary circumstances. We were traveling together, and I needed his cooperation, and I was going to be writing about him for the world to see. One night I finally told him flatly that I knew he thought he was in love with me, but he was just enjoying the experience of me paying him undivided attention. Even that didn't dissuade him. For several months after I had finished the reporting and left Mississippi, Huey called me occasionally and asked me to meet him somewhere so we "could talk." I declined, usually blaming it on a jammed schedule, and I always hung up hoping I hadn't hurt his feelings but unsure what else I could do. One time he called and said the Southernaires were performing in Brooklyn, and I said I would come. The music was glorious, and I thought back with pleasure on the time I'd spent with the group and how fortunate I was to have had that experience. I went backstage to say hello, and as soon as I saw Huey and sensed his yearning, I realized I could never do it again.

Writing the story about the Southernaires, which was titled "Devotion Road," was a profound experience. Why did it move me so much? I was deeply affected by what I saw: faded towns that lit up with sheer joy at the arrival of the Southernaires; animated crowds dressed in their best clothes; hours of magnificent music; the ecstasy of the audience moving as one to the surging melodies; aching solos; propulsive, pulsing sound. People didn't only listen to the music. They were immersed in it, crying and shaking and reaching out for it. Every bit of cynicism in me dissolved; every cool reportorial stance softened. I was stirred beyond measure. I was reminded throughout the experience how unbelievably fortunate I was to have this entrée into such a range of communities and cultures; this is the single greatest privilege of being a writer. I was excited to bring the story to *New Yorker* readers, knowing that it would be new to most of them, too. Navigating the emotional currents of the story made it more intense than it might have been—crossing the lines of race and gender, and then, of course, dealing with the complexity of Huey's attachment to me, and juggling how much he revealed to me with what I felt comfortable including in the story. It was a lot, almost an overload.

I wrote the story over the summer, in the dining room of the little cottage Peter and I rented in the Hudson Valley. Every time I went for a drive, I listened to one of the Southernaires' albums. The urgent push of the music, its yearning, longing, soaring sound, looped through my head constantly. When I sat down to write, I found myself falling unconsciously into rhythms on the page. I felt transported. When I finished, I thought I had done the best writing of my life. I remember showing Peter a section midway through. He was always my first reader, and he looked at everything with an editor's eye, so he didn't feel that his primary purpose was to praise me, but this time he did. He was so stingy with me emotionally that I knew not to expect much. This time was different. "You did it," he said.

> At the concerts, I saw men wearing spats and women wearing hats such as I'd never seen before: a black porkpie with a turquoise veil and bow; a midshipman's white cap with little pearls sewn along the rim; a tricorne of orange faille; a green beanie; a purple derby, worn at a slant; a red saucer that had netting looped around the edge and a piece of stiff fabric shaped like a Dorito sticking straight up from the crown; a fuchsia-colored ten-gallon with an ostrich feather drooping from the hatband. The hats were on elderly ladies, who moved through the crowds like cruise ships. Teen-age girls came to the concerts, too, in flowered dresses or in jeans and tank tops, wearing their babies slung on their hips, the way hikers wear fanny packs, or jouncing them absentmindedly, like loose change.
>
> I heard people at gospel concerts call eyeglasses "helpers" and a gravel road "a dirty road," and I heard an infant called "a lap baby," and a gun called "a persuader," and dying called "making it over," and an embarrassed person described as "wanting to swallow his

teeth," and a dead person described as "someone who was having his mail delivered to him by groundhogs." Everybody talked about Jesus all the time. He was called a doctor, a lawyer, a lily of the valley, a lamb, a shepherd, joy in the morning, a rock, a road, peace in the evening, a builder, a captain, a rose of Sharon, a friend, a father, and someone who is always on time.

In December 1994, Peter and I went to the Yucatán Peninsula for a vacation. We were in a quiet stalemate, gingerly making our way forward together and starting to talk again, hesitantly, about starting a family. He was still working for Mario Cuomo and spending most of his time in Albany. Cuomo decided to run for a fourth term. Initially, he was expected to win, but a little-known Republican state senator named George Pataki pounded him on his record on crime, pointing to a murder committed by a felon who had been paroled while Cuomo was in office. Peter and I went to Cuomo's election-night party and watched in shock as the returns came in, giving Pataki a decisive win. Peter's job would end when Cuomo left office. It seemed like a good time to get out of town.

On the flight back from Mexico, I finished reading everything I'd brought with me, so I fished around in the seat pocket to see if someone on an earlier flight had left anything to read. I found the front section of the previous day's *Miami Herald*. I flipped through it, not expecting to see anything of note. Toward the back of the section, I noticed a peculiar headline: LOCAL NURSERYMAN, SEMINOLES, ARRESTED WITH RARE ORCHIDS IN STATE PRESERVE. This interested me. The story reported that a local horticulturalist named John Laroche and four Seminole men had been arrested in a state preserve called the Fakahatchee Strand with four pillowcases full of endangered orchids the men had pried from trees in the swamp. Laroche told the arresting officer that he was planning to clone the orchids. As I later wrote,

I read lots of local newspapers and particularly the shortest articles in them, and most particularly any articles that are full of words in combinations that are arresting. In the case of the orchid story I was interested to see the words "swamp" and "orchids" and "Seminoles" and "cloning" and "criminal" together in one short piece. Sometimes this kind of story turns out to be something more, some glimpse of life that expands like those Japanese paper balls you drop in water and then after a moment they bloom into flowers, and the flower is so marvelous that you can't believe there was a time when all you saw in front of you was a paper ball and a glass of water.

The click in your brain when you feel you've found a story idea is incredibly satisfying, like the rich *thunk* of an expensive car door shutting. It just fits. I knew there was something to this story, even though I couldn't really make sense of it. I didn't know that orchids grew in Florida or that they grew in the wild at all, and I didn't understand why anyone would try to propagate orchids rather than going to Home Depot and buying them. I didn't know you could clone an orchid; that sounded like science fiction. Also, what was the significance of this guy working with a group of Seminoles? The newspaper mentioned that there would be an initial hearing in Miami the following week. I was sure there was some kind of story to tell.

I worried that Tina would consider the crime too minor, but she encouraged me to go to the hearing and see what I could find out. Then she gave me what was both a compliment and a word of caution she'd told me several times before: that without the strongest, most assured writing, the kinds of stories I was drawn to—observational, loosely structured, based on a wisp of a narrative—would sputter. This orchid story fit squarely in that category. The burden to pull it off was on me.

A few days later, I headed to the courthouse in Miami and then experienced what often happens to me at the beginning of a story: utter loss of confidence that it is a story at all. I tried to calm myself: At the worst, this would be a wasted trip to Miami. The courthouse was a low, bleached building of pocked concrete south of the city. A few people were milling around the courtroom, and a few sat on the benches, chatting quietly. I recognized Laroche from his picture in the newspaper. He was a string bean of a guy, wearing wraparound sunglasses, a neon shirt, a Miami Hurricanes baseball cap, and gray trousers that inched down his skinny hips.

The judge called the court to order and read the charges. Laroche listened with a peevish, defiant look on his face. When called to testify, he made a racket as he rose from his seat, then slouched in front of the judge with his thumbs hooked in his belt loops. He recited his professional accomplishments and then, grinning, looked around the room. Finally, he turned back to the judge. "Frankly, Your Honor," he said, "I'm probably the smartest person I know."

Writers fall into two categories: There are those who have something they want to say to the world, and there are those who believe the world has something to tell them. I'm wholly of the second sort. I loved being bewildered by this story and knowing I had to learn a lot to master it. In this instance, I would have to learn about orchids; about the Seminole tribe; about Native American law; about the Fakahatchee Strand; about John Laroche. I thought I knew Florida, because I'd visited many times over the years. I'd done several stories there. But this story would take me to a Florida different from the one I knew—not tourist Florida but wild Florida, and agricultural Florida, and the Florida of cons and scams. On my first trip, I spent ten days hanging around with Laroche, who loved lecturing me about every imaginable topic, including the scheme he had devised for the poached ghost orchids. I visited several orchid greenhouses, which were ubiquitous once you ventured beyond Miami.

I came back to New York fired up, eager to keep reporting. A few weeks later, I returned to go to the Miami orchid show with Laroche and meet the Seminoles who had hired him to run their tribal nursery. My story hinged on the court case, but it was a slender hinge: It mostly provided an excuse for delving into the curious, cantankerous mind of John Laroche and unpacking the circumstances that had led him to a swamp with a Native American crew and a bag full of orchids. The details I was gathering were juicy, funny, weird. After one more reporting trip, I sat down to write. I couldn't figure out how to begin. Should I start with the Fakahatchee? I tried that, writing, "You have to want something very badly to be willing to go looking for it in the Fakahatchee Strand." *Thud*. Another try: "The Fakahatchee Strand is a preserve of sixty-three thousand coastal lowland acres in southwestern Florida, about twenty-five miles from Naples, in that part of Collier County where velvety lawns and golf courses give way to acres of wild sawgrass with edges as sharp as knives." No reader would know what the Fakahatchee was, so this didn't seem very captivating. Anyway, I had come to believe that people are less interested in reading about places than they are in reading about people, so it seemed like a weak way to begin.

I decided to save the Fakahatchee for later in the piece and try starting with Laroche instead. My first attempt was stiff: "John Laroche says he was a weird little kid. This is not hard to believe." Not exactly a thud, but it didn't swing, either. I remember sitting in my office at *The New Yorker* late into the night, listening to the cleaning crew vacuuming the halls, as I wrote one lede after another.

I tried untangling my thoughts. Why was Laroche so fascinating? He was maddening, a perplexing brew of arrogance, candor, and affability, a fibber, a fabulist, but also an earnest striver with enormous, if cockeyed, ambition. He was singular. Even his appearance was discordant. On one hand, he was striking—a pale scarecrow with high cheekbones and a strong jaw. On the other hand, he was scruffy and tattered and missing his front teeth, which had been knocked out in a car accident, and even though that gave him a mad, gapped smile, he seemed in no great hurry to get them fixed. I realized the first thing besides the newspaper article that had convinced me to do the piece was catching a glimpse of him in all his contradictory, clashing glory. I decided to start there, offering the reader the same jarring experience of seeing John Laroche that I'd had when I started reporting the piece.

> John Laroche is a tall guy, skinny as a stick, pale-eyed, slouch-shouldered, and sharply handsome, in spite of the fact that he is missing all his front teeth. He has the posture of al dente spaghetti and the nervous intensity of someone who plays a lot of video games. He is thirty-four years old and works for the Seminole Tribe of Florida, setting up a plant nursery on the tribal reservation near Miami. The Seminole nicknames for Laroche are Crazy White Man and Troublemaker.

It worked. From there, the piece unfolded, a series of concentric circles around the arrest: the story of the Fakahatchee, the story of the Seminoles' immunity to endangered species laws, the story of orchid obsession, the passion that drove people to extremes to collect them. The piece ran in the January 23, 1995, issue of *The New Yorker* with the title "Orchid Fever," accompanied by a striking portrait of Laroche taken by photographer Laura Wilson. I had no special expectations for the piece. I was happy with it, but I wasn't sure if Laroche and his plan to raise rare orchids would resonate with readers. Maybe it was too niche, too odd. The response caught me off guard, in the best way. I heard from countless friends and readers, congratulating me on the piece.

The story felt so abundant that I didn't want to put it aside. Every element of it, from the history of orchid collecting to the backstory of the Fakahatchee, to Laroche's life, to my desire to see the ghost orchid, intrigued me. It seemed like it had more to give, more to tell. I hadn't settled on a book idea to follow *Saturday Night* except for my casual thoughts about *The House in My Head*. I had cooled on that idea, anyway; I was worried that doing another book structured like *Saturday Night*, with stand-alone chapters, wouldn't be wise for me. Anyway, I had been so busy at the magazine trying to win Tina over that pursuing a book seemed impossible. I hadn't formed much of a relationship with my Knopf editor, Elisabeth Sifton, so I never considered calling her to brainstorm a next project.

Shortly after *Saturday Night* was published, I had received a letter from an editor at Random House named Jonathan Karp. He said he admired my work and wanted to do a book with me. He and I met for lunch, and I admitted that I didn't have any ideas, but I would let him know if I did. Karp was as smooth-faced as a teenager, with bright eyes and droopy bangs, but he had been editing for years and had an air of certainty and wisdom. He made me feel like I'd earned his regard and that he expected great things from me even when I sometimes doubted them for myself. He didn't pressure me; he said he was a faithful and patient suitor and that he knew, somehow, we would work together. Maybe that moment had arrived. I wrote a short proposal for Richard, explaining that I wanted to return to "Orchid Fever" and unfold it in every direction, expanding all the facets of the story. It had not been a standard magazine story, and it was not a conventional book idea, but I was passionate about it and stubbornly sure it could work. Karp recalled recently that as soon as he saw the phrase "posture of al dente spaghetti," he was convinced. We quickly came to an agreement on a contract for a book we initially called *Passion*.

The day after the story ran in the magazine, Richard called, saying that director Jonathan Demme wanted to option "Orchid Fever" for a film. I was floored. The story was so quirky and proceeded at such a poky narrative pace that I couldn't imagine it as a movie. In any event, I didn't want a movie to come out before I wrote the book, so I said I'd sell the film rights only if Demme waited until I finished the book. He agreed, so I accepted his offer. To be honest, I didn't envy him the task of figuring out how to make my sprawly, discursive story into a movie. He told us that he had hired Spike Jonze, best known at the time for his music videos, to direct it.

I was working with a film and television agent, Sally Willcox, who coordinated with Richard, and she told me that a promising young screenwriter named Charlie Kaufman had been hired to write the script. I'd never heard of him. "He just finished writing a movie called *Killing John Malkovich*," Willcox said, or at least that's how I heard it. It sounded like a horror film and didn't sound promising to me.

To be honest, I didn't take the film option very seriously. I didn't know much about the film business, but I knew that a lot of material is optioned and then languishes, untouched. I assumed that would be the case with my orchid story. The television series based on *Saturday Night* had yielded a mini-pilot for the studio, but then it ran out of steam and the option expired. *Saturday Night* was optioned again to be developed into a musical. I had encouraging meetings with the producers, and singer Melissa Manchester wrote a few songs for the show, but nothing much happened beyond that. I had disciplined myself to expect little besides a check or two from these relationships. Of anything I'd ever written, I thought my orchid story had the lowest likelihood of turning into a film.

I met with Spike Jonze once or twice, and I thought he was sunny and delightful and seemed genuinely enthusiastic about my story, reveling in its eccentricities, so I was glad of that. But I had a book to write, and that's what was on my mind.

EIGHT

Even though *Saturday Night* was a real book, it was essentially a collection of thematically linked individual stories. This orchid book had to be different. The narrative sprawls and wanders, but I wanted it to be a single story, following a central cast of characters, having a coherent theme. Sustaining a story over the course of three hundred pages would be very different from what I had done with *Saturday Night*. I went into it knowing that, for the first time, I would be writing a conventionally structured book.

I called Laroche to tell him I'd be coming back to Florida. I said that on this trip I'd really like to see a ghost orchid, the focus of his obsession, because I hadn't seen one on my previous trips. He assured me that we would see them, lots of them. Then, almost offhandedly, he informed me that the Seminoles had fired him, and he had gotten rid of all his orchids and was leaving horticulture altogether. He said he was setting up an online porn business.

I was furious. I'd expected to write at length about the Seminole nursery and about Laroche's rapturous love of orchids. Now what? I tried to find comfort in my conviction that a story that doesn't surprise you is probably not worth pursuing, but this was a bigger surprise than I'd counted on. I do believe if you can already imagine the path your reporting will take, it's not interesting enough. You need to be surprised, unsettled, even frustrated by the turns your reporting takes; otherwise, you're too familiar with the material to write it with brilliance. But when a story turns upside down, my first sensation is of vertigo: *Now* what am I going to do? I had counted on Laroche's work at the Seminole nursery as the central storyline of my book. In fact, it *was* the story. But I wasn't in charge. This was non-fiction. The story would take me where it wanted to go.

I decided I had to dig in. I began flying back and forth to Florida, trying to scoop up as much reporting as possible on each trip. My parents had a condo in West Palm Beach, so I stayed there, surrounded by golfers and retirees, driving my father's lumbering sedan to my interviews.

I had a powerful visual image of the book in my mind. The incident, the orchid theft, was a vortex, a small disturbance, that drew together an improbable array of individuals. I pictured that vortex expanding exponentially. I knew I should report in a circle around the theft. I contacted orchid collectors and orchid nursery owners and the American Orchid Society. I dug into the history of orchid collecting. I wanted to learn everything I could about the Seminoles in Florida. I needed to research the court case involving the chief of the Seminoles, James Billie, who had killed an endangered Florida panther but, in a precedent-setting case, had successfully asserted that federal endangered species laws didn't apply to Native Americans. I discovered that the Fakahatchee Strand, the swamp that was one of the few places in North America where ghost orchids could be found, was not the virgin wilderness I had imagined but, rather, the remnants of the largest land fraud in Florida history. The story of that fraud was a rabbit hole I happily went down, since the image of wilderness conquering a planned suburbia was tantalizing and perfectly Floridian in its image of beauty and ruin. The contradiction of the ghost orchid—the jewel of Florida's natural landscape—thriving in the vestiges of a never-built subdivision embodied the tone of the book.

I had a contract at *The New Yorker* to fulfill. In the magazine's early days, writers didn't have formal contracts and rarely committed to doing a specific number of pieces in a year. Tina didn't like the unpredictability of this setup. She wanted to know who was writing, and how often, and whom she could tap when she had a story she wanted to assign. She put most of the regular writers on contracts. There were a variety of arrangements, but many were like mine: I agreed to write six pieces a year adding up to a certain word count. (My first contract had been for four pieces, but I inched up to six the following year.) I would be paid an agreed-upon lump sum delivered in monthly installments over the year. I liked that I got a check every month now, but the arrangement often made me feel indentured, owing stories as soon as the contract was signed. I had to figure out how to write the book while satisfying my magazine contract. I didn't want to find myself in the same situation I'd been in with *Saturday Night*, running out of time and in a jam with my publisher.

I started working as fast as I could. In one instance, I combined a trip to see Laroche with a feature for the magazine about the Super Bowl, held that year in Miami. (I was very proud of the piece until Roger Angell pointed out to me that I'd failed to note which team had won.) Other times I traveled for a *New Yorker* piece—to Pennsylvania, to profile a show dog named Biff Truesdale, say, or to Cuba for a story about a restaurant that had managed to survive the revolution—and as soon as I could, I repacked my suitcase and headed to Florida. I didn't choose easier stories for the magazine to lighten my load. My trip to Cuba, for instance, was a challenge. At the time, most travel to Cuba from the United States was forbidden, so I had to fly to the Bahamas, pay cash for a flight to Havana, and make sure there was no evidence that I had been in Cuba when I returned to the U.S. Before I left, I begged the publisher of *The New Yorker*, Tom Florio, to promise he would rescue me if I ended up in jail, and I wasn't entirely kidding. I had no idea what I'd encounter in Cuba. I knew that phone service was almost nonexistent, so I really felt—and I really *was*—on my own.

As far as I could tell, I was not unhappy, but I was stretched—often overstretched. My method for relaxing was to run five or six times a week, even when I was on the road. I ran past alligators on Florida golf courses, and up and down the side streets of whatever town I was reporting in, and the entire loop of Central Park whenever I was home. When I ran, I did math problems in my head, which was weird, because I am not good at math. I knew I was pushing myself unreasonably. I knew that I had forgotten long ago how to relax. Where was I running? I was running away from a life at home that left me constantly yearning; a husband who left me feeling lonely. I was running for someone to tell me I had done enough, that I was enough. For my dad to acknowledge that I had made it as a writer. I believed it wasn't sufficient for me to be a good writer or even a moderately successful writer. I felt like I needed to be the best writer, the most celebrated, or it wasn't enough.

It also mattered to me—deeply, insistently—to show why I cared about writing, and to promote it. I couldn't rest. I wanted to demonstrate that the world was complex and revelatory and unexpected; that the ordinary was divine and luminous; that familiar things examined closely were magnificent; to show that a scrap of a story in a Miami newspaper about flowers was actually a portal to the timeless tale we all tell, of what we are passionate about, of what moves us and enthralls us, of what choices we make about how we live. I wanted to tell the age-old story of who we are and how we abide in the world.

After a year of this pace—working on the book while writing for the magazine to fulfill my contract—I realized I couldn't continue without collapsing. I mustered the nerve to tell Tina that I had to take a leave so I could finish the book. By that time, I'd forged a good relationship with her. She agreed to almost all of my story ideas, even though they were so contrary to her newsier, buzzier inclinations. She was a tough boss, but she was always encouraging. When I wrote about a Manhattan hair salon, she called it, in a note to me, "brilliant and hilarious—a little classic." She praised my story about life in a trailer park ("a brilliant social topography") and was thrilled when I profiled the one and only reporter at a small-town newspaper. I asked to go to Tennessee to write about children's beauty pageants so I could talk about JonBenét Ramsey without getting into the fray of newspaper stories covering her murder. Tina was game for all of them.

The beauty pageant story was a gamble. Rather than try to unwind the story around JonBenét's murder, I proposed looking at the world in which she was a star. I didn't know child beauty pageants even existed before hearing of JonBenét—who participated in them—or that it was a $250-million-a-year industry. The idea of parading children and judging their looks appalled me, and that was why I wanted to write about it: I knew nothing about this subculture, and yet I had such a powerful, reflexive response to it. I wanted to challenge myself to look beyond my reaction and try to understand why these competitions meant so much to some people. I wanted to try to find the humanity there, even the humor. ("You don't want to go glitzy with the sportswear," one of the pageant coaches told me. "I'll bet you a nickel they won't want glitzy . . . Since she's only eight years old, I think she should wear flat little pumps instead of heels.") I knew the average reader of *The New Yorker* would balk at the topic. That appealed to my mulish love of making people read about, and perhaps find empathy for, a subject they initially resisted.

I didn't write about subjects in order to advocate for them. The objectification of little girls horrifies me, and the sight of four-year-olds lined up to have mascara applied disturbed me deeply. But it is part of the American panorama. Writing about it was a way to ask people to get to know their neighbors, and it was my desire to observe—to view, like an anthropologist, the variety of human experience without judgment. I like to do a gut check anytime I dismiss or deplore something I don't know anything about. That feels like reason enough to learn about it.

Tina was demanding, and she knew how to push to get me to work a little bit harder, a little bit better. But I had to take a break or I would never finish the book. Or I'd go crazy. I wasn't sure I could return to the magazine after I finished the book if it meant working this intensely again, but I decided to worry about that when the time came.

Tina agreed to my leave of absence, and I began spending long weeks in Florida, loving the strange worlds I was discovering. The nights were long. Peter rarely answered the phone when I called, and as usual, he spun excuses that were flimsy, implausible. The one thing we collaborated well on was writing: As bad as our relationship was, I relied on his insight on every piece. It was ironic that he invested so much time and effort in my work because he seemed to resent it so deeply. After thrashing and struggling through those few terrible years following his affair, we'd been therapized and counseled and, for a time, seemed to have emerged victorious, and yet here we were again, enemy combatants, without ever declaring a war.

Sometimes the sheer solitude of reporting is exhilarating, the immersion in an unfamiliar realm remarkable and powerful, but sometimes it makes you feel insane, like you have chosen the saddest, most desolate life imaginable. I slumped into despair after a long day of reporting, calling Peter's phone and getting no answer. I often took myself out to the nicest place near my parents' condo for dinner, which was an Outback Steakhouse, and as I picked at my broiled salmon, I watched elderly couples share their Bloomin' Onions and wondered where I might be in five years. Would Peter and I stay together? Would I ever write this book? Would I ever have a child?

One of the challenges of working on a book like this one, as opposed to the episodic *Saturday Night*, was managing the heap of material I had gathered. I interviewed dozens of people. Gathered volumes of research on the development of South Florida. Read botanical tracts. Took notes of hours of conversation with Laroche. Clipped dozens of newspaper stories about the crime. Collected snippets about wild boars in South Florida and Chief Billie and Miami. I was overwhelmed by the volume of information and puzzled by how to organize it so that I could find specific material when I needed it. I remembered reading that John McPhee used five-by-seven index cards for his reporting material: He broke all the pertinent information into small chunks and wrote them on index cards, and then he arranged the index cards to help him visualize a structure for his books.

I bought a pack of index cards and began digging through my heap. If some information nugget was intact—for instance, a quote I knew I wanted to use—I wrote it in Sharpie on a card. If I had something big that I knew I'd use extensively, such as the bankruptcy filings for the company that had tried to develop the Fakahatchee Strand as a subdivision, I wrote a brief description of it with a reference number that I also put on the legal documents. If I had a peculiar piece of trivia I wanted to include, like the fact that armadillos in South Florida had descended from animals that escaped a leprosy research lab (armadillos are the only creatures besides humans susceptible to leprosy), I gave it its own index card.

Card 123: In 1948, nine riders hired by State of Florida to kill wild cows east of Naples

Card 28: So many orchids in Fakahatchee that early explorers called the smell "nauseating"

Card 320: Huge "Skunk Ape" supposedly lives in swamp. Reported to have the body odor of a skunk; 7 ft tall; 700 pounds

Card 5: Collier County climate v. similar to Australia. First oil in Florida discovered here

I ran out of my pack of one hundred cards very quickly. I ended up using over seven hundred index cards to piece out the material of the book.

To begin creating a structure, I spread the cards on our living room floor (and later, on the biggest table I could find) so I could see them all at once, and then I gathered cards that I knew should appear together in the book. I separated the sets of cards into thematic groupings: Orchid history. Florida history. Fakahatchee history. Laroche's story. The Seminoles. I knew the book wouldn't hew to a simple chronology. It was circles within circles of stories, radiating out from the orchid theft itself. But it needed to make sense to the reader. Even if I detoured into a crazy cul-de-sac of an anecdote, I needed to make sure the reader sensed that I was steering us firmly and I would return to the main road after the detour.

Working this out on a computer would have been impossible. I needed to see all the material and organize it into cohesive sections. A computer was a shuttered view, never allowing me to see the sweep and shape of the story. I had to keep track of the time frames I was writing about. I was convinced that a reader could follow as I moved around in time as long as I was clear within each portion about its purpose, and then I could return to the ongoing chronology of my efforts to see a ghost orchid. Without the index cards, I can't imagine how I would have made sense of all that material or kept it orderly. I've used them on every book I've written since.

My trusty index cards, the finest writing tool

By this point, I had a reliable system for how I worked. I rarely used a tape recorder. It's impractical for the way I work. I liked to spend as much time with my subjects as possible. A lot of that time was spent hanging around, getting used to each other, which gave me a chance to observe them without the rat-a-tat pressure of an interview. Running a tape recorder during that time would have been pointless. I also hated being distracted by worrying whether the recorder was working, whether the sound was clear enough. I didn't pay attention as closely when I knew the conversation was going to be taped. It was as if I could relax a certain amount of my focus, since it wasn't as necessary to listen—but if I wasn't really listening, I wouldn't ask the right questions or follow the nuance of the conversation as well. Also, most people are edgy when a tape recorder is running. Taking notes is more obvious, much sloppier, but it doesn't have the surgical chill of a tape recorder. It's human. It's disarming. With a notebook and pen, I could write down what was pertinent and skip writing what wasn't. Sometimes I did miss a great quote because I hadn't written fast enough or would have to ask subjects to repeat themselves because I couldn't get an entire sentence down. That was the risk. But taking notes felt more natural than taping. I noticed another benefit: Often, when a conversation was winding up and I closed my notebook, my subjects began talking more freely. It was easy to open my notebook again and casually ask if it was okay for me to return to taking notes. I'd never had anyone object when I did that, but I'm sure that clicking on a tape recorder would have made them hesitate.

The act of handwriting is so complex that it demands intense mental engagement. It embeds information in your brain in a profound way. To write well, you need to feel deeply connected to your material; you need to process it multiple times. Listening to my subjects is the first chance I have to connect. Writing down what they are saying fixes it in my head a second time. I review all my notes—the third time I'm engaging with the information—and highlight the good parts. Writing the good parts on my index cards is my fourth engagement with the material. By the time I sit down to write the story, I know it thoroughly and deeply. I sometimes feel like I know it so well that I hardly need my notes. I would be able to tell the story the way I'd tell an interesting story over dinner—from my heart.

I continued the practice of reading my work aloud. At first, sitting alone in my office, I felt unaccountably bashful, embarrassed by the sound of my voice and my sentences. But I came to depend on it. Reading out loud was the best way for me to edit myself. I could hear awkward sentences instantly. I could hear when they dawdled. Sometimes I write sections of pieces with a very intentional meter. For instance, I wanted the lede of my story about Keiko, the whale who starred in the *Free Willy* movies, to have the tone of a nursery rhyme—something about a story on whales seemed to call for that. I wanted my profile of the Jackson Southernaires to have the surging tempo of a gospel song. Would it work? I could tell only by reading out loud. When I began doing the narration of my own audiobooks, starting with *The Bullfighter Checks Her Makeup*, the experience was unexpectedly familiar, because I had already read the material aloud as I worked.

Writing is a mysterious practice, so it feels important to me to apply logic and methods whenever I can, an armature on which to hang the creative part. I know I can't produce a perfect sentence using a system, but I hope to set up an environment in which the likelihood of being able to produce that perfect sentence increases. It is like using the right skillet when you cook: That's the method, the foundation, and then magical things might happen. Throughout my writing life, I have read hungrily, as much as my eyes can take in or my ears can absorb. I read the writers I most admire and take note of what they do that makes my heart flutter. I've always read more fiction than nonfiction, which might be surprising given my profession, but I'm a student of the lovely handiwork that you find in fiction, and I want to make it my own. I also swear by the notion of writing a *lot*. I've never believed creativity is a finite asset that must be portioned out sparingly. To me, it seems more like a muscular action that needs strengthening and practice to perfect.

JOYRIDE

When I first started working on *The Orchid Thief*, the idea of writing three hundred pages in a continuous narrative was daunting. Every day when I sat down to write, it seemed like the only way I would feel accomplished was if I wrote the entire book, then and there. Since I knew I couldn't, I walked away from my desk in defeat. What's the point of writing a page or two, a measly nothing, when I had an entire book to write? The prospect of the entire book yawned, boundless and terrifying. One day I mentioned this predicament to Chip. He advised me to set an achievable daily word quota and stop thinking about the whole book. "Think of yourself as a widget factory," he said, "and sit down every day and make your daily quota of widgets." I decided to try it. I set a daily goal of eight hundred words. I was strict about it to a hilarious degree. If I had written seven hundred and fifty words, I stayed at my desk until I got to eight hundred. If I exceeded eight hundred words, I applauded myself as if I were an Olympic medalist. Having a finite goal was liberating. Before that, I felt terrible all the time, no matter how much work I'd gotten done, since I hadn't finished the book. Now, at last, I could feel like I'd achieved something concrete day-to-day.

After a while I was making it to eight hundred words easily, so I increased my widget production to one thousand words a day, and I reached it most of the time. Knowing how much I could write in a day, I was able to roughly figure out how long it would take me to finish, rather than feeling that writing a book was an unruly, unpredictable, unmeasurable undertaking beyond my control.

And finally, I finished. Along the way, I changed the working title from *Passion* to *The Millionaire's Hothouse*, which was a chapter title in a vintage horticulture book I'd found. I thought it was dreamy and romantic. After Jon Karp read my manuscript, he left me an ecstatic message: "Each sentence bursts! Brilliant, beautiful! You're as good as McPhee and Sandy Frazier and all those guys!" His chief objection: He didn't think *The Millionaire's Hothouse* worked. He had another title in mind: *The Orchid Thief*. I groaned. I thought it was awful. He asked me to think it over, so for the next week or two, I asked my friends which title they preferred without telling them which was mine. Every one of them preferred *The Orchid Thief.* I was beat.

I was busy for the next few months getting ready for the book to be published—helping choose a cover, doing last edits, writing a dedication and acknowledgments. I kept my expectations low; after all, orchid crime was a peculiar and rather singular subject. To my delight, though, the early responses were enthusiastic. Borders, the now-defunct bookstore chain, doubled their initial order, and Random House increased their initial printing from 19,000 to 22,500. Word of the book was spilling out. In one of the more exciting moments of my career, I got a letter from the great writer Oliver Sacks: "I so enjoyed your brilliant piece [about orchids] in the magazine last year and I am agog to see your book when it comes out!"

Would I go back to *The New Yorker* now that I had finished? Tina urged me to sign another contract, but I was wary of returning to that high-pressure arrangement; I didn't know if I could handle it anymore. Moreover, in 1995, Chip, who had been at the magazine for twenty-three years, had one too many tangles with Tina and left the magazine to edit *The New York Times Book Review.* His new office at the *Times* was down the block—you could almost see the Times Building from the *New Yorker* offices—but his departure unmoored me. He had been my editor and stalwart at the magazine from the beginning, and my deepest friend there. I counted on seeing him every day and many nights. I didn't know what our relationship would be like when he left.

During this interval of indecision, Pam McCarthy, the deputy editor, sent me a note: "I wanted to tell you how much Tina and I hope you will, in the end, decide to stay at the magazine . . . everyone here does very much want to see you in the magazine's pages, not to mention the hallways." I was hooked.

* * *

Paradoxically, illogically, counterintuitively, and probably unwisely, I began seeing fertility specialists. Even though our efforts to get pregnant had been lackadaisical, Peter and I were trying, and we were failing. I wasn't as bone-thin as I had been a year or two earlier, but my body was clearly off-balance. I bounced from one doctor to another, each one mystified by why I wasn't getting pregnant. I took Clomid. I did shots of Follistim. I got moody and fat and sweaty and not pregnant. During one ultrasound, my doctor said with disgust, "This is a terrible cycle!" as if my failure to produce enough eggs had somehow insulted him, and as I cried silently on the exam table, I debated whether I could continue with the process. I knew I needed to find a different doctor. But did it make sense to try to have a child within a precarious marriage? Of course not, and if I'd been advising a friend, I would have warned her off. But I was in my late thirties, the age when having a child seems more urgent than having a marriage, so I persisted.

With the cover of *The Orchid Thief* designed and the galleys proofed, I was once again looking for blurbs. I was more successful on this go-round, but I still got several rejections, some of which were so memorable that I kept them in my scrapbook. From John McPhee: "I've been in a maelstrom of teaching and am at this moment in an airplane . . . I don't have a nickel's worth of time and just can't critique a manuscript." From Tracy Kidder: "I got the manuscript, but I am straight out upset, exhausted, and I can't read it right now. Ordinarily I would be delighted to be your blurbist. I just can't until I get through my little period of craziness." From Calvin Trillin: "In 1978 I officially extricated myself from both ends of the comment business, giving and getting. I was acting on what I usually describe as a matter of high principle that I can no longer remember."

The Orchid Thief came out at the end of 1998 into a publishing thicket of big nonfiction books. At the time, Mitch Albom's *Tuesdays with Morrie* had been on the bestseller list for sixty-nine weeks, followed by *The Art of Happiness* by the Dalai Lama and Howard C. Cutler, *The Professor and the Madman* by Simon Winchester, and *Angela's Ashes* by Frank McCourt.

How would my weird little book do against these megahits? I hoped for the best but tried to keep my expectations in check. Upon release, *The Orchid Thief* jumped to number one on the Palm Beach bestseller list, which was wonderful but hardly a surprise, given the local interest. But then the book started popping elsewhere around the country, and in January, it landed on the *New York Times* bestseller list: a dream fulfilled.

Laroche, interviewed by the New Orleans *Times-Picayune*, said he thought the book was "pretty good." He added, "I would tend to disagree with Susan that I'm insane, although I do have my moments." Some orchid professionals were enraged by the book, even though I was convinced many of them hadn't read it yet, since some posted their complaints weeks before it was on sale. "It seems the poor dear spent too much time wandering in the Fakahatchee and not enough time in the library or on the telephone," one of them posted. "It is mostly gossip about orchid growers, with a little history thrown in. The technical terms are full of errors. I would not buy the book." Angry people are always the first to respond to anything published. Within a week of the book's release, I received a letter from a dental hygienist whose letterhead said: IF YOU SEE SOMEONE WITHOUT A SMILE SEND THEM TO YOUR FAVORITE HYGIENIST! She was furious that I had focused on the fact that Laroche was missing his front teeth. She wrote huffily, "Have you written anything else with dentistry in it?" But the rest of the reviews were complimentary, even raves.

I rented a storefront in Manhattan's wholesale flower district for my book party. I invited more than a hundred people. I expected it to be a splendid, jubilant night. I was ecstatic; everything seemed to be going even better than I'd hoped. That afternoon, a few hours before the party, Peter seemed jittery and distracted. He hunched over his laptop, typing frantically. Every time I came near, he slammed his laptop shut. It was comically obvious that he was hiding something, but he rebuffed me when I asked what he was doing. We circled each other for a while, and finally, without a word, he put on his running clothes and left for the park. I immediately opened his laptop and read his emails. Several were from a woman whose name I didn't recognize, saying what a great time she'd had with him over the weekend and asking when they would see each other next.

In the photos from my book party, I look glassy-eyed, startled, pallid. It was a gorgeous night that I drifted through like a specter. Afterward, a few of my best friends came home with me, and I explained what had happened, and they embraced me and told me I would be all right. The final uncoiling of the marriage took a few more brutal months. We went back to a counselor. Peter first claimed he wanted to repair our marriage and that he had ended his relationship with the woman in the emails. She called me and apologized and said their affair had ended. After a few months of this charade, a friend told me that she had run into Peter with the woman, whom he supposedly wasn't seeing, and she was noticeably pregnant. At last, our marriage was truly over—sixteen years of my life tied off like a wound. I could recall how much fun we'd had when we first fell in love in Portland, and how often we had enjoyed each other, and what a life we'd made—how we had, in a sense, grown up together, became adults together. But those memories were now scorched, indecipherable, as foreign as a language I once spoke fluently but no longer understood. After we signed our divorce agreement, I never saw Peter again for the rest of his life.

NINE

Richard sent copies of *The Orchid Thief* to Jonathan Demme, Spike Jonze, and Ed Saxon, the producer working with Demme. I worried they might be disappointed in the book, since the orchid heist had not erupted into something of cinematic proportions—no murders, no car chases—and the narrative wandered off the main track whenever something interesting presented itself to me. I met with Spike, and he asked me a million questions, scribbling notes as I recounted stories that hadn't ended up in the book. The idea that *The Orchid Thief* would turn into a Hollywood product continued to seem absurd to me. But why not enjoy yakking about it? A few months went by with no further word from the film people, so I assumed the *Untitled Orchid Thief Project* would sink like so many other movie ideas.

One afternoon, though, Ed Saxon called and said Charlie Kaufman had completed the script. I was astonished. He suggested that we meet so he could give it to me in person. I liked Ed a lot, but I was busy, so I said it would be easier if he could send it to me. He insisted that we meet. I gave in, and we arranged to have lunch later that week at a restaurant in the Village.

Ed was in a bubbly mood when I arrived. He proposed that we order drinks before lunch. Day drinking isn't my style, but he seemed so eager that I agreed. Did I want an appetizer? Not really, but if you insist, sure. Wine with lunch? I guess if I'm in for a dime, I'm in for a dollar. Wine with lunch. Entrées. Dessert. Coffee. I kept peeking at the floor beside his chair but didn't see any sign of a script so I started to wonder if he was softening me up to break the news that the script wasn't ready or had been rejected or had gone astray. Finally, full of food and drink, I told him I had to get back to work. He reached into his coat and pulled out an envelope.

"Before you read this, I have to tell you something," he said. "It's a little . . . *different* from the book. There are people in the script who are not in your book. But we're very excited about it and hope you love it." He pushed the envelope toward me, saying, "Please call me *immediately* after you read it." I stumbled back to the *New Yorker* office, a little dizzy from the wine, and dropped the script on my desk. I didn't see any rush in reading it, so I glanced at the cover. To my dismay, it didn't say *The Orchid Thief*. It said *Adaptation*. And it credited two scriptwriters—Charlie and Donald Kaufman. Okay, I guess Charlie Kaufman has a brother? I flipped through a few pages. I landed on a scene between me, as a child, with my parents. *What?* I couldn't decide whether to go back to my work or keep reading. I decided to take one more glance at the script. The next scene I read involved a character named Charlie masturbating to an image of Susan Orlean on a porn site.

I slapped the script shut. I was so stunned that I decided to put the script aside for the time being. I couldn't process what I was reading. The next day, when I got to the office, I saw the script on my desk and thought, Okay, I have to read this, but not now.

What I didn't know was that after he was hired to adapt *The Orchid Thief*, Charlie Kaufman was paralyzed by a severe case of writer's block. When he and I spoke recently, he told me that he had loved the book and loved the challenge of writing a movie from material that didn't have an obvious story arc. After *Being John Malkovich* was released, he had been sent scores of projects that were self-consciously weird, but he didn't want to repeat himself, and he was excited to work on a movie about beauty and flowers. He found the book mournful and elliptical, without an obvious Hollywood hook. He couldn't figure out how to write a conventional script or how to make it into a movie without betraying the book. He was stuck. "I thought, I can't do this," he said. "I thought I didn't know *how* to do it." He found it uncomfortable to fictionalize the real people in the book, especially me. After struggling with it for a while, he came up with the device of having the fictional movie live within the story about making the movie. He wanted to focus on the battle between the need to make it a marketable Hollywood movie and his urge to focus on the book's more poetic heart. He saw the sadness I had written into the book that I hadn't realized I had conveyed.

I finally read the *Adaptation* script the next afternoon. It was perplexing. I recognized parts of the book—whole sections taken directly from it, in fact—but it was embedded in a story about my childhood, and then my marriage, and a fictional love affair between me and, of all people, John Laroche—as observed by twin screenwriters, one of whom had been hired to adapt my book. I thought it was a little insane and a little incomprehensible. My biggest concern, though, was that I didn't want to appear as a character in a movie at all. When I'd sold the film option, I'd assumed the script would be about Laroche. I'd never imagined appearing in it in any way.

I called Ed Saxon and said I didn't understand the script, but I didn't want to be a named character under any circumstance. What was more, I was appalled by being portrayed in a romantic relationship with Laroche. "I can't have people thinking I had an affair with Laroche," I said. "This will ruin my career."

He sighed. "Susan, everyone in the movie is a real person, and they're all letting us use their names. And are you sure you'd want your book to appear in the movie with another name as the author?"

He had a point. The book itself is a character in the film, and if I insisted that they use a different name for the Susan Orlean character, *The Orchid Thief* would appear in the film with some pseudonymous person as the author. *The Orchid Thief* by . . . Nancy Jones? Jennifer Stevens? My vanity ached at the thought. I softened. Then I repeated that if I were portrayed as being involved with a subject, it would be embarrassing as well as an ethical violation.

"It's not so bad," Ed said. "Just think about Charlie. He portrays himself as a loser who's constantly masturbating. What we're asking of you is so much less embarrassing." True, but I wasn't persuaded. I said I would think it over. I asked friends for their opinion, and they all urged me not to do it—most stridently Stephen Schiff, who was working as a screenwriter and understood the consequences of movie infamy.

And then I don't know what happened, but I changed my mind. I began to feel like I had been offered a ticket to a very strange amusement park ride and that I might regret it if I didn't try it. That was my constant posture in life, the impulse to say yes even when I wasn't sure of the consequences. I told Ed I would sign on if references to my parents were removed. I didn't know that he had already spoken to them, and they had sunnily agreed to be portrayed in the film, even though in the script, my teetotaling mother was portrayed as a drunk. My parents weren't naive, but I suspect they thought the whole thing was a bit of a lark—as if this were me putting on a show in the garage rather than it being a real Hollywood movie that would be seen by millions of people. They were steadfastly good-humored about it all; in fact, my father told Ed he would be fine "even if you portray me as a drunken astronaut," a notion that seems to have come out of thin air. But I worried they were agreeing to something they might regret. The script was way too long anyway, so Ed promised that Charlie would edit those sections out.

I signed the release, devised specifically for this film:

You have advised me that you may wish to produce a motion picture for theatrical release, tentatively entitled ADAPTATION incorporating parts of my life story as contained in that certain screenplay dated November 21, 2000 written by Charlie Kaufman.

> A. I understand you may desire to portray and/or impersonate me in the Picture and use my name, likeness, and biography in connection therewith . . . and that the Picture may be based on fact, be partially fictitious or completely fictitious.
> B. Material changes to the Screenplay relating to the commission of a felony, illegal drug usage, sexual orientation, and alcohol or prescription drug abuse shall be subject to my approval (not to be unreasonably withheld).

Notwithstanding the foregoing, I pre-approve all changes to the Screenplay which may be made with respect to the murder of Mike Owen, and the usage of the substance "PASH" (which substance is identified in the Screenplay), except with respect to the physical manner in which PASH may be ingested by the character "Susan Orlean."

I hereby waive and agree that I will never make any claim or demand or bring any action against you, your licensees . . . for invasion of privacy, violation of the right of publicity, libel, slander, presentation of me in a false light . . .

I remember sitting at my agent's desk, signing this document and thinking what a funny thing life can be.

I had not met Charlie Kaufman. I knew nothing about him except the bit my agent had told me, but I had a feeling he knew a lot about me. Obviously, he had read my book. But some elements of the script that weren't in the book were uncannily accurate. Some were small things. In the script, the Susan Orlean character drinks only champagne—and at that time, that was almost the only alcohol I drank. There were big things, like the melancholy I felt while writing the book, and the slow-motion dissolve of my marriage. How would Charlie have known that? I hadn't written about it and had concealed it from most of my friends. I suspected that Charlie had come to talk to me at *The New Yorker* and chickened out, as Charlie does in the film. I wasn't sure if it was an implanted memory or it really had happened. Charlie was correct about how incredulous I was when the book was optioned, as he shows in the film, and how I told friends that I'd expected Hollywood to pump up the drama of the story, tossing in murder and romance and spectacle. I was curious to meet him but hesitant, too: I couldn't gauge what percentage of fictional Charlie's obsession with fictional Susan was not fictional at all.

Between the time I wrote "Orchid Fever" and the release of the book, *The New Yorker* had undergone another sea change. In July 1998, Tina jumped, or was pushed, out of her job, and my next-door neighbor at the office, David Remnick, was appointed editor in chief. The transition was far gentler than when Tina had arrived. Remnick had been a staff writer for years and was roundly liked and admired. He seemed more connected to the tradition begun by Harold Ross and William Shawn than an extension of Tina's regime, but like Tina, he believed the magazine needed to stay engaged with the present day. My only beef with Remnick was his penchant for smoking cigars. He and I were next-door neighbors in the office, and his acrid smoke drifted my way, but he found a T-shirt to block the crack under the door and we made our peace. We became pals, although he often shooed me away when he had work to do, and he always seemed to have work to do. He was the most productive writer on staff by a mile. Remnick was tall, dark-haired, with merry dark eyes and a laugh that was surprisingly high-pitched coming from someone of his size. His manner was that of a teasing, tolerant older brother, needling me at every turn but always kindly.

Having him elevated to my boss was disorienting, like a brother taking over a family after the death of a patriarch. But his openheartedness, his devotion to the magazine, and his generosity—he was always ready to compliment a piece and shared Tina's habit of sending notes—made the transition easy.

I was single then, or single-ish. As my divorce mediation was in the works, I went to Bhutan for a *New Yorker* story. The idea came about after I noticed an ad for a Bhutan "fertility trip" in the back of *Outside* magazine. Apparently, this tiny kingdom in the Himalayas is famous for the efficacy of its fertility festivals, so the tour included visits to several fertility festivals and sites. At the time, I wouldn't have been able to find Bhutan on a map, but I was amused by a line in the ad stating that people on the trip were not required to want a baby.

When I first noticed the ad, Peter and I were in counseling, discussing the idea of repairing the wreckage of our relationship, so I suggested that he join me on the trip. I almost always went alone on reporting trips, but I clung to a bit of bruised hope that this trip would have healing properties and we would get back together. Peter loved mountains—for some period of time, he was the youngest person to have climbed Denali, in Alaska. Maybe the setting of mountains and fertility festivals would work. *The New Yorker* liked the idea of the story, so we booked the trip. The day before we were scheduled to leave, Peter told me he didn't want to go with me, so I left for Bhutan by myself, brokenhearted.

Bhutan was the most beautiful place I'd ever been, and the most enchanted. A monk blessed me and told me I would have a baby boy, and I would name him Tenzing Kinley. "Some things are beyond science," he told me. "It will happen if you have the right type of devotion." As he was talking, a heavily pregnant dog wandered past, shuffling and panting; I took it as a sign. I fell in love with the country and developed a crush on one of our Bhutanese tour guides. His name was Tshering Wangchuck, and he was twenty years younger than I was, but we forged a holiday romance that lifted me out of my despair over Peter. I was so sodden with heartsickness that I seized on anything buoyant and hopeful, and in no time, I convinced myself that Tshering and I would get married and divide our time between Bhutan and New York. We would have adorable children who were half Jewish and half Bhutanese. When I got home from the trip, I campaigned to get Tshering a visa in hopes of furthering this mad idea. Visas are hard to come by if you are a single man of color from an underdeveloped country, so it required persistence. I called my congressman and senator and finally made a deal with someone at the American embassy in Delhi, which handled Bhutanese applications. I promised that I would make sure that Tshering left when his visa expired.

Tshering finally arrived in New York and stayed with me for several months. I knew I was out of my mind, but I enjoyed his company and was swept up in the relationship and appreciated that it marked such a bright boundary between my past with Peter and my life as it was now. By the time *Adaptation* was in development, Tshering's tourist visa was about to expire, and he packed to leave. We promised we would stay true to each other from seven thousand miles away, fully aware that we would do no such thing.

The first piece I worked on after Tshering left was one of the few that came to me by way of someone else. People suggest stories to me all the time, but usually the ideas don't click for me, and I politely demur. This time, though, my friend, the writer and editor Kurt Andersen, hit the bull's-eye. He had read a short piece in *The Wall Street Journal* announcing the rerelease of a classic album by a cult band named the Shaggs. Music critics had long debated whether the Shaggs' music was the worst ever recorded or the best. The band was made up of three sisters, Helen, Betty, and Dot Wiggins, from a working-class family in New Hampshire. They had receded into obscurity and quiet lives after enjoying a blast of celebrity in the early 1970s when Frank Zappa declared them "better than the Beatles." Kurt thought that the reissue of their 1969 album, *Philosophy of the World*, was a great hook for a story, and I agreed.

I started my career writing about music, and I returned to the subject many times. I didn't like being a critic, but I loved music, and I loved its capacity to define communities and create them. It wasn't easy to describe music itself, but I was fascinated by fandom and the sociology of music; I loved feeling out the nature of popular success. I had never heard of the Shaggs, and the first time I played *Philosophy of the World*, I would have agreed with the person who posted online that she'd listened to it "in the fetal position, writhing in pain." It was ragged, discordant, nasal, atonal, played by young women who seemed unfamiliar with their out-of-tune instruments. While I worked on tracking down the Wiggins sisters, I listened to the album on endless repeat, and its janky rhythms and artless lyrics started sinking in. I wouldn't say I liked it, exactly, but it had its weird pleasures.

The sisters were wary of the press, which was understandable, considering they'd spent years bouncing between scorn and adulation without ever being fully acknowledged for themselves. I explained my genuine interest in their lives, and was delighted when they agreed to meet with me. I drove to New Hampshire and parked myself in a dreary motel beside a highway; lights from oncoming cars swept my room like the beacon from a lighthouse. The next morning, I arrived early at the Dunkin' Donuts Betty had suggested for our meeting. I waited in my car, listening to the album again. Against the odds, I had grown to love the title song, with its clattering guitar and lumpy, fitful cadence and the cheery but bleak lyrics about how people are never happy with what they have. I had the volume up so high that I didn't hear Betty tapping on my window. When I rolled it down, she heard the music and gasped, "Do you *like* this?" I said yes, and she said, "God, it's *horrible*."

The Wiggins sisters were plainspoken and modest and cordial. They also seemed a bit weary. The weariness was no surprise. Their peculiar flicker of fame led only to exhausting jobs, pricing goods in a Walmart, cleaning houses. Their childhood had hardly happened. Their father, Austin Wiggins Jr., was harsh and unyielding. He was fixated on the Beatles' success and frog-marched his daughters into forming a band, fully expecting them to overtake the Beatles even though they didn't want to play music and had no natural aptitude for it. He homeschooled them, restricting the girls to a regime of calisthenics and band practice, and barred them from having a social life except for the nights when they performed in town. I was wary of treating the Wigginses like a spectacle or with the ironic delight that some of their fans heaped on them. It's true that the sheer discordance of their music was kind of fascinating, but the story of their stolen childhood and their obsessive father and the fleeting effect of renown seemed quite tragic to me.

I spent a lot of time with them, and in the town of Fremont, where they lived. I dug up local newspaper accounts of their performances; I tracked down someone who knew the guy who had worked at the recording studio where Austin paid a few hundred dollars to get the Shaggs' record made. It was a weird, wistful tale about determination and dreams, with an outsider-art angle. The story was published in *The New Yorker* in September 1999, and the reaction was immediate, not only from readers but from a gaggle of Hollywood producers who wanted to option it on the spot.

When I write a piece, I never calculate its viability as a Hollywood property. I'm drawn to stories magnetically, with no calculation of their potential value beyond my story, and I consider it something of a miracle that they see the light of day in print. Their prospects beyond the page are never on my mind. I've never requested a signed release from my subjects. If they agree to speak to me, that's all I need. I have never maneuvered anyone I've interviewed to promise me their life rights—by that, I mean the exclusive right to use their story and name in a project for film or television. Such releases are rarely obtained in the print world. In film and television, though, no project goes forward without the subjects' legal agreement to be portrayed. Papers are signed and money changes hands and the studio is assured that it controls the exclusive rights to tell that individual's story. Studios are meticulous about this. When my story

"The Maui Surfer Girls" was optioned to be the basis of the film *Blue Crush*, the studio secured the life rights of every girl I interviewed in the piece, even though the script didn't use their real names and the story was fictional. Having their rights was insurance against the possibility that one of them might object and claim invasion of privacy and topple an expensive movie project.

There were several different entities vying for the rights to my story, and in the end, the rights to my piece and the sisters' life rights ended up in separate hands, which caused the whole project to collapse. It has remained a snakebit project for twenty years, pieces of it passing from hand to hand among different producers, without much prospect of it getting made. I hope it surprises me someday.

I didn't keep close track of what was going on with *Adaptation* because I was busy with my own work, and frankly, I didn't expect much to come of it besides the usual Hollywood noise. I was amazed when Ed Saxon invited me to brainstorm casting ideas. This made the movie seem more real than I had imagined it was. The producers were most interested in whom I pictured playing me. I drew a blank. "Red hair!" one of them said. "Julianne Moore!" Someone else said Jodie Foster—blond hair, but she could dye it. We kibbitzed for a while. It felt like a party game, naming actors, as if that were all you had to do to conjure them into your film. Someone said, "Meryl Streep." What a loony thought: the most admired female actor in the country in this outlandish movie. I dismissed the idea.

I told everyone at the meeting about my history with Meryl Streep. In my sophomore year of college, when I was in Cleveland for Thanksgiving vacation, a friend asked if I wanted to be an extra in a movie being shot downtown. I had never heard of the film's director, and I thought the title of the movie, *The Deer Hunter*, sounded silly. Also, I hadn't heard of the actors in it except Robert De Niro, who had appeared recently in *Taxi Driver*. I didn't have much else going on, so, along with my friend

Lisa, I agreed to work as an extra. The scene was being shot in a Russian Orthodox church in an old working-class Cleveland neighborhood. For close to six hours, we played the guests at a wedding of the characters Steve (John Savage) and Angela (Rutanya Alda). The wedding party included Christopher Walken, John Cazale, and Meryl Streep. I had never been on a movie set, so the repeated reshooting of the scene baffled me. I thought nothing would come of the movie or anyone in it. When it was released in 1978, *The Deer Hunter* won Oscars for Best Picture, Best Director, and Best Film Editing, and a Best Supporting Actor for Christopher Walken. It was not the first—nor the last—time my predictions were slightly askew.

By the time *Adaptation* was cast, Meryl Streep reigned in Hollywood. The film was different from anything she had done before, and she told me a few years later that her children loved the script and badgered her to take the role. Nicolas Cage was rumored to be interested in playing Charlie and Charlie's twin, Donald. It turned out that a lot of actors wanted their shot at playing the Kaufman twins. While casting was underway, I happened to be at a film screening in New York, seated next to John Turturro. We said hello and introduced ourselves. He recognized my name and began pitching me passionately on why he should get the Charlie/Donald role.

The most fun I had with the film prep was the afternoon I spent with the movie's costume designer, Casey Storm. He wanted to see my clothes so he could outfit the fictional Susan Orlean appropriately. I love fashion; my time at *Vogue* had left me with an abiding taste for designer clothes. At that time, I favored vaguely goth concoctions from Comme des Garçons, snap cardigans from Agnès b., Japanese streetwear T-shirts, and chunky creepers. I met Casey at the door of my apartment in a black wool Comme des Garçons dress with bondage straps, dreaming that he would reproduce it for Meryl Streep to wear in the film. Over the next hour or so, I paraded my favorite outfits, and we had a great time gabbing about design, but at the end of the afternoon, he told me he wouldn't be using any of my clothes. "You don't dress like a journalist," he explained. "In the movie, we need to make the journalist look like a journalist."

At the very least, I assumed I would meet with Streep so she could study my mannerisms and pick up my Ohio accent. I tidied my *New Yorker* office, expecting the call any day announcing that she was heading over to study me. I mentioned it to friends at work, something along the lines of "Oh, Meryl Streep might be dropping by, just in case you see a stranger wandering around," and tried to imagine which gestures of mine she might focus on. Time passed. More time passed. I finally called Ed and asked him when Meryl was coming to see me. He told me she didn't need to because she had already created the character on her own. I was crushed.

Production on *Adaptation* began in 2001, with a blue-chip cast, including Streep, Nicolas Cage, and Brian Cox. Ed invited me to be an extra. Spike wanted me in a scene where a waitress, played by Judy Greer, is serving coffee to Cage, and he drifts into a fantasy about having sex with her. After noticing him leering, Greer whispers about him to another waitress. I was going to play that other waitress, but I was tied up the week they were shooting, so I had to wait for another scene. A few weeks later, they were shooting a scene set in a grocery store in which Charlie/Nicolas Cage notices two women muttering to each other about how odd he seems. I was offered the chance to be one of the mutterers, and I said yes. I got ready to go to Los Angeles and make my appearance in *Adaptation*.

Let me set the scene, with some important new details. In January 2000, I was at the apartment of my friend, the humor writer Patricia Marx, helping her choose paint colors for her living room. Tshering had returned to Bhutan a few months earlier, and I had visited him there after he went back, but it was obvious that our relationship would continue only as long-distance friends. Once again, I was on my own. As we flipped through paint swatches, Patty asked if I knew someone named John

Gillespie. I didn't. She said he was getting divorced and wanted to be fixed up. She asked if I could think of anyone. I suggested myself. Patty wasn't sure if John and I were an obvious match, but she said he was a good guy, so I would have a nice time even if the date didn't amount to much. She gave him my number and left it up to us.

John had gone to Harvard with Patty and, coincidentally, with Peter, so he and I knew a lot of people in common, although we had never met. When he called, we talked for almost an hour about mutual friends, fireplaces, baseball, art. I knew he traveled a lot. He was an investment banker who focused on financing public projects. His specialty was sports facilities, and he had been instrumental in developing Baltimore's Camden Yards and the Staples Center in Los Angeles. I didn't see myself especially suited to a relationship with an investment banker, but I liked talking to him so much that I said yes when he suggested getting together.

Blind dates are never without peril, and this would be one of the first I had ever gone on; I wasn't sure I had the appetite for it. I debated whether to cancel. As the date grew closer, I realized it would be rude to bail out so late, so I decided to go ahead with it to be polite. That day, I was reviewing fact-checking changes for a piece I'd written about Khao San Road in Bangkok, a stretch of cut-rate backpacker hotels and cafés that attracts young people from all over the world. I told the fact-checker, Dan Kaufman, that I was going on a blind date that night and needed an exit strategy if it was dull. I was meeting John at six-thirty, so I asked Dan to call me at eight p.m., and if I wasn't having a good time, I would pretend he was calling me back to the office to finish the piece. That would give me an easy out.

John and I arranged to meet at a fundraiser for the Democratic candidate for Senate from Michigan, whom John knew. It was at the midtown Sheraton in one of those drab event spaces with popcorn ceilings and sand-colored carpeting. I felt keenly out of place. I wished I had asked Dan to call me earlier. After a moment, a sandy-haired man with kind eyes, a soft smile, and a handsome, square-shouldered build approached and introduced himself as John. We mumbled our hellos and then he guided me around the room, introducing me to the Michigan delegation. I liked his face and his manner, his warmth, his ease, but I felt out of my element.

We dawdled at the fundraiser for a while and then, to my relief, left for dinner. When we got to dinner and started talking, time galloped. Before he became a banker, John had been working on a graduate degree in literature, and we discovered that we both adored William Faulkner. John could even quote long passages from *As I Lay Dying* and *The Sound and the Fury*. We began talking about our families, our mutual friends, Faulkner, more Faulkner, travel, dogs. He couldn't believe I hadn't gotten a dog since my much loved Irish setter had died. "We need to get you a dog," he said. I thrilled to the way he phrased it—"we"—and the fact that he was concerned about making sure I had what I needed. I hadn't felt anything like that in so long—honestly, I couldn't remember when. My phone rang, startling me. I fumbled for it in my bag. "Susan, it's Dan," the voice said. For a minute, I was confused. I asked him what was going on. "Umm, you told me to call you? To get you out of your date?" I had totally forgotten. I said something hurriedly and told him I'd see him at work the next day. John and I left the restaurant and went for a nightcap at the King Cole Bar in the St. Regis Hotel and talked for hours beneath its gauzy Maxfield Parrish murals. By the end of the night, I was willing to bet that this was the man I would marry, and I was right.

John and I flew to Los Angeles in the spring for my appearance in *Adaptation*. I thought I would finally meet Meryl Streep, but she had already filmed her scenes and had left town. I was stunned when we got to the soundstage. My book had felt like such a private undertaking—written in the solitary, sometimes leaden quiet at my desk—but it had bloomed into a mini-city, an industrial complex, with dozens of crew members racing around and an expanse of trucks, dressing room trailers, and concession tables. Except for my stint as an extra in *The Deer Hunter*, this was the only time I'd been on a movie set, and it was the first time I'd seen something of mine lifted off the page and into the three-dimensional fictional world.

The day John and I arrived, they were shooting a scene in which Nicolas Cage meets with his impatient, foulmouthed agent. Several people milled around, tidying the set, touching up Cage's makeup. I noticed a slight figure with a froth of curly hair a few yards away from me. Suddenly, Cage bellowed, "Oh, look! It's the real Charlie meeting the real Susan!" Everybody swiveled their heads in my direction. I caught the eye of the curly-haired guy. Evidently, this was Charlie. I stammered and said hello, adding, "This is kind of embarrassing for me."

"It's more embarrassing for *me*," he said, and rushed out the door.

I don't remember seeing Charlie on set the rest of my time in Los Angeles. Anyway, I was preoccupied by my role as an extra (the scene ended up getting cut). Unexpectedly, John was pressed into service as well, playing David Remnick in a long scene in the *New Yorker* offices, faithfully reproduced under the hot Hollywood skies. (That scene got cut, too.)

Scene from the set, with Nicolas Cage

A few months later, I was invited to watch an early version of the film with a handful of people, including Spike Jonze's mother and a French film distributor. The movie was far from finished. It was too long, and none of the music had been added yet, and the color hadn't been corrected. On my way to the screening, I began to panic. Why had I agreed to this? Was it too late to change my mind? I called Richard, who made it clear that it was definitely too late to change my mind. I sat through the screening in a daze. Watching Meryl Streep, projected on a nine-foot screen, say "I'm Susan Orlean" was an out-of-body experience. Did I like the movie? At that point, I was too stunned to really take it in.

I also had other things on my mind. While we were on a trip to Istanbul, John had proposed to me, and we'd decided on a fall wedding. We picked a date—September 15, 2001—and a location (the Explorers Club in New York City) and started planning. We had enjoyed an epic courtship. Shortly after our first date, John had a business meeting in Rio de Janeiro, and he invited me to join him. Even though several of my friends thought I'd said we were going to *Reno*, not Rio, they were happy for me. I packed carefully, wanting to look as cute as possible, and of course our luggage got lost, so we spent several days padding around in cheap clothes from a chain store in Brazil, paid for by the airlines. Not long after, Condé Nast *Traveler* asked me to write about several luxury hotels in Thailand. Off we went to Thailand. On a whim, we decided to try visiting every continent within the first year of our courtship. After Thailand, we made a short trip to London, and then I came up with a story I wanted to write about the Sydney Olympics, which *The New Yorker* was eager to run. Could we really make it to every continent? John had work obligations and couldn't go with me to Australia, so we gave up the game. But it was an exhilarating way to start a relationship.

The highlight of those early days might have been our first Valentine's Day together. I had a pent-up yearning for celebrations, because Peter had pointedly resisted them. I didn't know what to expect from John. On the morning of Valentine's Day, he said he had gotten us tickets for *The Lion*

King as a Valentine's gift; the only hitch was that the tickets were for later in the month. I thought it was a nice idea, but I was disappointed that we wouldn't be going on Valentine's Day. He then mentioned that he had invited his friend Rick Lyon over. I was miffed, since a visit from a friend didn't seem very romantic, especially because John was living in Boston and our time together was constrained. I decided to make the best of it and went to change into something nice. When I came out of the bedroom, John looked me up and down and suggested I put on something more casual. He had never told me what to wear—I wouldn't have tolerated it—so I was peeved. In a pique, I changed into pants and a sweater. He assessed me again and recommended wearing something even more casual. Now I was mad. Without explanation, he began rolling up my hall rug. He said that Rick was bringing his toddler daughter, Sarah, and that she might make a mess. "That Sarah," John said, shaking his head, "she's a real animal."

My dream of a romantic Valentine's Day had buckled. I stomped out of the living room, threw on a dirty sweatshirt and jeans, and stomped back into the living room. At last John approved. Fine, I thought, and screw you.

The doorbell rang. I assumed it would be Rick Lyon, but it was not. It was an African lion—a two-year-old two-hundred-pound tawny-haired lion with golden eyes and soft, round ears and paws the size of baseball mitts. His handler—whom I will call Jason—and two police officers, looking anxious, held the lion on a leash. I squeaked and babbled excitedly. Was this *real*? Was there really a *lion* in my New York City apartment? The lion sniffed the floor, crouched, and coiled. Jason said I could touch him as long as I didn't let him lock eyes with me, because that would entice him to pounce. I laid my hand on the lion's flank; his muscles were taut and radiated a fierce heated energy. "Give him a chicken," Jason said. John went to the refrigerator and took out a whole raw chicken. He placed it in a metal mixing bowl in front of the lion. The lion gulped the chicken in a flash and then settled back on his haunches. "Another," Jason said. Down the hatch with another chicken.

When I could finally focus, John explained how he had orchestrated the lion's visit. He had been seated next to Jason on a recent flight to New York. They'd chatted briefly, and Jason had mentioned that he was licensed to foster exotic animals seized from private owners who owned them illegally. He told John he was currently fostering a young lion. John knew that I loved animals, and he asked if there was any way Jason could bring the lion to surprise me for Valentine's Day. So here we were.

The lion began to get restless. He panted and paced. Jason said it was time to take him home. We joined Jason, the police officers, and the lion in the elevator. I prayed that it would go straight to the lobby, but the elevator jolted and stopped on the fifth floor. The door opened on an older woman with a bird's nest of brown hair. I suggested that she take the next elevator. She looked bothered. "It's just," I explained, "there's a lion in here." She gave an impatient little snort and said, "Yes, but I'm in a hurry." After a moment, she shrugged and waved us on.

The Tuesday before our wedding was a dazzling day. The air was clear, and the sky was a cloudless bowl; an optimistic, brilliant blue. I woke up early to attend to my long list of wedding chores. My main concern was getting my white shoes dyed to match my ivory gown. I was in bride mode; this task felt desperately, urgently important. There was an election in New York that day for some local and statewide offices. As usual, I was half-listening to the news on the radio while making coffee. I remember hearing the announcer say that something—I didn't hear what—was an extraordinary occurrence. I assumed he was referring to the election, and I was surprised because it was a low-stakes, off-year contest. But his tense tone of voice worried me. I flipped the television on. The screen showed a live shot of the North Tower of the World Trade Center. It was spouting a thin, sketched line of smoke, like a silver chimney.

I called John, who was in his car in Boston, and read him the news crawl on the screen, which said that a plane had hit the World Trade Center. John was intimately familiar with the building: He'd worked on the 105th floor of the South Tower for several years. He said it was probably a student pilot who had flown off course. I turned back to the television, where the voices of the newscasters were increasingly strained, anxious. I saw a tiny dot of a plane floating toward the South Tower and then piercing it, like a wasp. At that time, I lived on Riverside Drive, with a view of the Hudson River, and within a minute I heard choppy droning and saw the shadowy form of helicopters tracing the path of the river. John and I had recently gotten a puppy, a Welsh springer spaniel we named Cooper, and just then our dog walker arrived. She and I were both wordless. We sat in my living room for the next hour, watching the news in disbelief.

We hadn't gotten our marriage license yet. John had been planning to come to New York on Wednesday, which seemed like plenty of time before the wedding on Saturday. As soon as the plane hit, City Hall—where the Marriage Bureau was located—closed. The bridges and tunnels in and out of Manhattan closed. The airports closed. The phone lines were jammed. After our initial call, I couldn't get through to John. I couldn't reach my parents.

I knew immediately that we should postpone the wedding. Friends were coming from out of town, including a group from England. My parents and brother were coming from Cleveland. No one could fly into New York. I didn't know if John could join me in New York or if I would be able to leave and meet him in Boston. The weight of horror was suffocating, grievous. I went out for a walk. No one on the street was talking. We shuffled through the rest of the day zombified. That night, people sought each other for some scrap of comfort. My next-door neighbors, knowing I was alone, offered to let me sleep over. When I finally got through to John again, we agreed that I would come to Boston as soon as I could, and we would delay the wedding until—until the world felt normal, which at that moment seemed impossible to imagine.

It was upsetting to postpone the wedding, almost like a bad omen, but I didn't see another option. Among the people we had invited were former president George H. W. Bush and Barbara Bush. Our politics are entirely different, but Barbara was an avid literacy advocate and had convinced me to participate in several fundraisers with her. I had become fond of them, and sent them an invitation mostly as a courtesy because I had told them about the wedding. When we let our guests know we were postponing, Barbara emailed me: "I know that in the middle of a national disaster a celebration seems so petty and small. Both my Georges (#41 and #43) have told me that life must go on and so I am trying to go on. I am sorry you and John had to put off your wedding. You and John were wise!"

We finally got married on November 10. For us, and for many of the people at the wedding, it was the first time since 9/11 that we had celebrated anything. That year I had been spending many Sundays at the New Mount Zion Baptist Church in Harlem, because I was considering writing something about its marvelous choir. Even though the tradition and religion didn't belong to me, I really loved gospel music, and after I had written my Jackson Southernaires story, my affection for it kept growing. Before the wedding, I shyly asked the New Mount Zion choir members if they would consider singing a few songs at our wedding, and they agreed. After the ceremony, they lined the stairway and balcony of the Explorers Club and raised their voices in a transcendent harmony, singing of joy and redemption and renewal, which was what we were all desperate to hear.

A different film based on a story of mine beat *Adaptation* to the screen. My piece for *Women Outside*, "The Maui Surfer Girls," was optioned after it was published in 1998. It was a nice outcome for a story that nearly didn't happen. Susan Casey, the wonderful editor I worked with at *Women Outside*, had approached me to do the piece. At that time, female surfers were few and far between. Susan had heard about a group of girls in Maui who were devoted surfers. I loved the idea of immersing myself in this subculture—I knew nothing about it (always catnip to me), and I liked writing about young people. I was in.

For reasons I can no longer remember, I flew to Maui before contacting the girls on the list that Susan had given me. This is not a wise way to go about reporting, as I soon discovered. I worked my way down the list, calling each girl. One after another, they told me they weren't into surfing anymore. The story was a bust. I delivered the bad news to Susan, who encouraged me to at least enjoy a day or two in Maui before coming home.

There was one name left on the list—a young woman named Gloria who was a bodysurfer. I hadn't called her because I wanted to focus on traditional surfing, but with my idle day, I decided to get in touch with her just because. I was feeling low, so I confessed to her that I'd struck out on the story. "You've got the wrong girls," she said. "The girls you called are down at the mall kickin' it. I'll give you the right ones." She ticked off the names of six girls living on the other side of the island in a small town called Hana. They were avid surfers, and some even dreamed of going pro.

These girls were eager to talk to me, and for the next week or so, I followed them around Maui. I snacked on dried cuttlefish with them; slept over at their coach's house with them; cheered them on in competitions, watching them cut across the waves, as swift as seals. They told me about how they got "landsick" if they were away from the ocean for long. They nagged me to surf with them, but I had never been on a surfboard, and I was terrified. The waves in Hawaii were like brick walls. I stayed glued to my beach towel no matter how much they teased and cajoled me. But the keenness of their dreams—to surf forever, to be independent, to take every wave—animated me, and I wrote the story fast, as soon as I got home.

The film option was icing on a story that had threatened to fall apart, and a reminder to push on when I think I've stalled. I was lucky Susan Casey had been patient. In no time, the studio sent me the finished script, by screenwriter Lizzie Weiss. Released in 2002, *Blue Crush* was moderately successful in its original release but has gone on to be constantly streamed and nearly iconic. It celebrated the toughness of young women and the wild glory of surfing, and launched the careers of Kate Bosworth and Michelle Rodriguez.

I'd had a second encounter with Charlie Kaufman a few weeks before the premiere, when *Adaptation* won several National Society of Film Critics awards. We were seated next to each other at the awards dinner, and after a few bashful moments, we started talking. He was dry and elfish, self-deprecating and sweet. The movie was getting rapturous reviews already, so his big gamble—my big gamble, too, in a different way—seemed to be paying off. I had finally met Meryl Streep a few months before that. In October, Joan Didion, John Gregory Dunne, journalist Marie Brenner, and David Remnick had hosted a screening for tastemakers and journalists, hoping to spread early word about the film. After the movie ended, I headed out to the lobby and felt a hand on my shoulder: Meryl Streep. "Susan!" she exclaimed. "Will you forgive me?" We both started laughing at the absurdity of the moment. For the next few months, we saw each other often. I was asked multiple times to present her with awards for her portrayal of me, and I was invited to sit with the *Adaptation* cast at the Golden Globes, where everyone got tipsy as the film gathered acclaim.

Adaptation had its official premiere in Los Angeles on December 6, 2002, at the Landmark Theatre in Westwood, near UCLA, with limousines, a red carpet, an after-party—all the over-the-top Hollywood trappings. The real John Laroche attended, as well as the fictional one (Chris Cooper); the real screenwriting teacher Robert McKee, who doesn't appear in my book but figures importantly in the film, attended, and so did Brian Cox, who played him in the film. Meryl Streep came and walked the red carpet. I was faced with a question rare for a journalist: What does one wear on a red carpet? I ended up choosing a Jean Paul Gaultier gauze top and skirt in shades of green and blue, decorated with a bedazzled image of what looked like a Renaissance saint.

I sat next to Jodie Foster at the premiere. The film magically had transformed from the messy, illogical version I'd seen at that early screening into a hilarious, shrewd, contemplative work of art. I wanted to freshen up before the lights went on at the end of the film, so I reached into my purse

The Golden Globes red carpet

At the premiere, with Spike Jonze

Handing Meryl Streep one of the many awards she got for her performance

and nervously applied a million layers of lipstick in the dark, thinking I had grabbed a tube of a peachy nude. Without realizing it, I had laminated my lips with a violent, angry purple. I don't remember ever buying such a lipstick. I only noticed it and squeegeed it off an hour later when I saw myself in a mirror. Regardless of my florid lips, Jodie Foster turned to me as the credits rolled and said, "Oh my God, that was amazing!"

The party was across from the theater at the Hammer Museum. The crowd was heavy on Hollywood faces; it was as if the movie industry couldn't resist a movie that made such wicked fun of it. At one point, I was standing at a table with Tilda Swinton, who played a movie executive in the film; Brian Cox; John Laroche; and Chris Cooper's wife, Marianne Leone. It was heady, and fun, and surreal.

The next night, when the film opened to the public, Charlie, Spike, and I arranged to meet, and we bounced from theater to theater in Los Angeles, standing at the back to gauge the audience reaction. When we heard laughter at the right moments, we left and drove to the next theater. A newspaper piece about the movie had asked, "Was there ever a bestseller less likely to make it to the screen?" but the answer, so far, seemed to be that it worked.

As *Adaptation* made its way into the world, I marveled at the difference between publishing a book and releasing a movie. The cultural currency of a film is so potent and wide-reaching that it can almost obliterate the significance of the book it's based on. Some of my readers hated the movie and were angry that I had allowed *The Orchid Thief* to be adapted in this way. My response was to remind them that nothing in the book had changed, no matter what the film had made of it. I drew scores of new readers who had never heard of the book but were intrigued after seeing the film—definitely a net positive. Having work optioned is often treated as if it is evidence of the book's value rather than evidence that a filmmaker sees something in it that could work on the screen. Bad books have been made into great movies, and many great books have been butchered on the screen. They are entities that are linked but distinctive, siblings that share DNA, but each goes its own way.

Being a character in a movie means—what does it mean? Twenty years after the film's release, I continue to be asked what it was like to be played by Meryl Streep. I've never come up with a tidy answer. It was weird, it was disorienting, it was nerve-racking, it was fun, it was great. It was like riding in the sidecar of a fast motorcycle. We see books as beautiful and meaningful and important and profound, but we see movies as dreamlike. In the public's mind, being a character in a movie transports you forever into another, more enchanted realm.

TEN

For some reason, Random House didn't grasp the impact of *Adaptation* and didn't see the point of using it to promote the book. The movie title was different than the book's, it was explained to me, and the movie was so *odd*. I was upset that they didn't take advantage of the moment. Moreover, my editor, Jon Karp, had left Random House by then, so I felt stranded. My contract with Random House was for *The Orchid Thief* and the next two books I wrote, so I owed Random House those books, but we agreed that I could fulfill the contract by assembling collections of my magazine pieces. The first of these, *The Bullfighter Checks Her Makeup*, consisted of profiles. The second, *My Kind of Place*, focused on places.

To choose pieces for the collections, I began reading all my work. In many cases, it was the first time I had read them in their finished form. I resist reading my stories once I've finished. Is it that I don't want to see things I wish I could change, knowing it's too late to do so? I'd been working full-time as a writer for almost twenty-five years. That sounded like a lifetime, and yet sometimes I felt like I was finding my way.

I started by reading the story that ended up as the title of the book—a piece about Cristina Sánchez, a young female matador who was taking the Spanish bullfighting world by storm. I had written the story for *Out-*

side magazine. Before going to Spain, I had spoken with a man who said he was Cristina's agent, and he cheerfully booked many hours for me to spend with her. Can I watch her get dressed for a fight? Of course! Can I travel with her to a few of her engagements? Of course! It all seemed so easy. When I arrived in Spain, I discovered that this accommodating gentleman had no connection to Cristina at all. It was all a pose with no apparent purpose. Mortified, I was ready to leave Spain. There seemed no way I could get time with Cristina on such short notice; she was the trending topic in Spain. My *Outside* editor, the ever patient Susan Casey, urged me to stick around a few more days.

The more I reflected on it, the more fascinating I found it that Cristina was so in demand that someone would pose as her manager, and that made me want to keep stabbing at the story. I hounded everyone I could think of to help me contact her. I had hired an American woman from New Jersey to be my translator. She told me she had come to Spain as a student and then had fallen in love with a matador and stayed. She finally persuaded her husband, who was semi-retired from bullfighting, to help find Cristina's number, and I was at last able to reach her and follow her for several days.

Upon reading my stories, I was struck by how the situation I confronted in Spain wasn't an anomaly. Often my pieces initially teeter on catastrophe. That was certainly the case with my Hawaiian surf girls. When I decided to write about a woman in New Jersey who had twenty-seven pet tigers, I expected her to be eager to tell her story. Instead, she refused to meet with me. Again I despaired. I couldn't figure out how to profile someone who wouldn't speak to me. But David Remnick urged me to stick with it, and slowly, it dawned on me that the woman's secretiveness and taciturnity were exactly how she had come to have twenty-seven pet tigers in the New Jersey suburbs. Rather than undoing the story, this reticence *was* the story, and my job was to circle her, to observe her from a prickly distance, as all her neighbors and state officials had done for years. So many of my stories sprang from what initially felt like defeat, a rough road, resistance. Maybe the friction animated me, helped me abandon my expectations and see what was truly there rather than what I had expected to behold.

I was readying *Bullfighter* in the middle of 2000 and into the early part of 2001. One of the last bits of business was to write the dedication. John and I weren't married yet, but I was in love with him and happier than I had ever been. I was leaning toward dedicating the book to him, but I was nervous. A dedication is a permanent declaration, more durable than a tattoo. It pained me that *Saturday Night* was dedicated to Peter. I could have dedicated *Bullfighter* to my parents, but I was being tugged. I knew it was a risk, but I decided it was a risk worth taking. At last I wrote the dedication: "For John Gillespie, who makes me so happy." I'm glad I did.

Beginning in 2002 or so, I found myself writing a lot of stories for *The New Yorker* about animals. I loved animals, so I was always happy when a story popped up that involved them, and I began seeing these stories as an oblique way to write about human beings. Animals don't exist in a vacuum. Even the wildest of animals are affected by the presence of humankind. How we live with them, and how they live with us, is rich material. After I wrote about the New Jersey tiger lady, I wrote about the woeful saga of Keiko the orca. Then I did a piece about the World Taxidermy Championships (not live animals but animal-centric nonetheless). In 2003, I wrote about the film and television unit of American Humane, the authority that issues the "No Animals Were Harmed" endorsement on movies and television shows. As I followed the American Humane officers on their visits to film sets, I decided to research the history of animals in Hollywood, which was essential to the piece.

One of the first names that came up in the research was Rin Tin Tin. I recognized the name from my early childhood. As I recalled, Rin Tin Tin was a noble, can-do German shepherd who lived with a young boy and a cavalry troop in a Wild West town, in the imaginary world of a television show. I barely remembered the show, but I remembered how much I loved that dog and how I pleaded with my parents to get us a German shepherd. I assumed Rin Tin Tin was a fictional Hollywood character, so I was shocked to learn, after doing some research, that there had been a real Rin Tin Tin. I was even more shocked to learn that the real Rin Tin Tin lived decades before the existence of the television show; his dam and sire were German army dogs used in World War I, and he was born in a kennel in occupied France. A young American soldier found the puppy, cared for him during the war, and then smuggled him back to the United States after Armistice Day and trained him. In the early days of silent film, this dog—this *real* dog—became the most valuable asset of Warner Bros. He starred in dozens of films that were worldwide blockbusters. Then I remembered that when I was a child, my grandfather had kept a plastic figurine of a German shepherd on his desk. It was the one item on his desk we'd been forbidden to touch. As a kid, I assumed the figurine was Rin Tin Tin from the television show, and I was always surprised that my grandfather—a grown man, an immigrant from Hungary—cherished this toy from a 1950s American television show. What I didn't know was that those original Rin Tin Tin silent films had been shown in Hungary when he was a boy, and it was this dog, the silent star who was unimaginably brave and good, that my grandfather had idolized.

I wonder now whether my experience with *Adaptation* primed me to respond to this subject, to the way it toggled between legend and reality and told a story about the mythic power of film. That surely must have been part of it, combined with my affection for animal stories and my astonishment at the truth of what I'd always thought was a made-up tale. Like *The Orchid Thief*, this was a story of devotion verging on obsession, the belief that getting hold of something you deemed precious could give contour to your life.

"As you know, I've often wondered whether I would ever find another story that would be as engaging, unusual, rich, and wonderful as *The Or-*

chid Thief. I'm writing to tell you good news: I have," I wrote to Richard. "The book is the story of an American hero whose life spans this past century and whose influence continues to the present . . . who is a piece of popular culture and an ideal lens through which to view it . . . I love the idea of writing about a figure that everyone recognizes but no one really knows, who inhabits the recess of memory but has never been fully explained." Larry Kirshbaum, the CEO of Time Warner Book Group, loved the idea, and in March 2004 we made a deal to publish the book with Little, Brown, which was part of Time Warner and run by Michael Pietsch. I met with Pietsch and the editor who would handle the book, but Kirshbaum was the book's greatest advocate.

By this time, I had moved to Boston. John and I had lived apart for the first two years of our marriage, burning up the road between Boston and New York to see each other as much as we could. He had left investment banking and was now the chief financial officer of a health care company in Boston and had committed to the job for five years. I wanted to stay in New York, but the travel was exhausting. I woke up alone the morning of our second anniversary and realized I didn't want to continue this way. I didn't want to leave my friends or my hard-won office at *The New Yorker*, but it was more important to be with John. We agreed that when he finished his five-year contract, we would move back to New York, which made leaving New York feel less final for me. I also applied for a Nieman Fellowship at Harvard, a program that offers journalists the opportunity to spend an academic year at the university. If I got accepted, the fellowship would give me some footing in Boston. As much as I looked forward to being with John full-time, I knew I needed something of my own there, something to give me an identity beyond being the wife who showed up, so I was excited to be admitted to the Nieman class of 2004.

Against the odds and the calculus of time, we'd decided to try to have a baby. I loved John's teenage son, Jay, but the desire to have my own kid persisted, even though I was in my forties. John was wholehearted about it, too. If we were going to buckle down and work on having a baby, I didn't want to do it while we lived in different cities. *The New Yorker* let me keep my office even though I would be away most of the time. In 2003, I moved into the loft we'd bought in downtown Boston on the marvelously named Wormwood Street.

I juggled my Harvard schedule with work on *Rin Tin Tin,* stories for *The New Yorker,* adjustment to a new city, and fertility appointments. It was probably too many things to manage—typical for me—but I was happy to finally be living with John and optimistic about the book. On the surface, its subject seemed almost tongue in cheek—a biography of a movie-star dog—but the deeper I got in my reporting, the more poignant and beautiful the story seemed.

Lee Duncan, the American G.I. who found the puppy in 1918, named him after a French good-luck charm. He was a lonely soul who had been surrendered to an orphanage when he was a child until his mother reclaimed him some years later. The experience wounded him. He was intensely, fervently attached to Rinty—his nickname for the dog—and determined to elevate him to an impossible status—a state of immortality. He found a bit of that immortality in having Rin Tin Tin appear in movies, which in the early 1920s were new and seemed nothing short of miraculous. The world was enchanted by on-screen images, with their extraordinary capacity to conjure reality and rewind time. When the original Rin Tin Tin died, Lee trained one of the puppies he sired, Rin Tin Tin Jr., to work in the movies, and continued with many generations of Rinty descendants after that. Lee married and had a child, but he never established a relationship as deep as the one he had with his dogs. When silent films were superseded by talkies and dog films fell out of favor, Duncan's despair was profound. The story would have ended there, a footnote in film history, except that Duncan took Rin Tin Tin on the vaudeville circuit and then to television, making Rin Tin Tin perhaps the only pop culture character who has starred in silent film, vaudeville, feature films, and television. The dog headlined throughout the entire arc of entertainment in modern times.

I thought I would finish the book by 2006, but I felt myself slipping. The amount of reporting was overwhelming. I kept a single-spaced list of research tasks that I titled READ THIS AND WEEP. One list included trips to California (where Duncan had lived); France (where the dog was found); and Texas (where a woman who claimed to be raising the progeny of the original Rin Tin Tin lived). The rest of the list was a frenzy of fragments, including:

Go to Hollywood collectibles show
Go to a German shepherd show
Visit the battlefield in France where Lee found RTT
Rivalry between RTT and Lassie: How do I describe this?
Go to collie show?
Join all Yahoo groups about Rin Tin Tin
More on Duncan's WWI division
Animal use in movies
Do eBay capture of all RTT items
More background on war dogs
Oakland: Visit Duncan's orphanage
Fifties TV—visit Corriganville where they shot RTT show

I loved that the subject had expanded so voluptuously, but I was dismayed. It seemed unmanageable. I had a big advance, so money wasn't the issue. It felt like I was wrestling an octopus of a story that required endless travel, just when I had finally made a new home with John. I stalled. I wrote *New Yorker* pieces, including one about a quixotic search for a lost dog in Atlanta (he ended up being found) and a story titled "Little Wing," about a young girl I'd met while walking my dog; she'd mentioned that she raised racing pigeons. This was a perfect instance of my "Who knew?" story: Here was an ancient sport I hardly knew still existed, being undertaken by an adolescent girl who was decades younger than the usual middle-aged male participant. It was a quirky story, but it had a lot of heart, a tenderness I hadn't anticipated. It turned out that the young girl's family was moving, and she had to give her pigeons away because they'd be unable to adapt to a new home. The day after the story was published, Steven Spielberg called my film agent and told her he wanted to option it. After many years in development, it came to life in 2024 as a feature film called *Little Wing* on Paramount+, starring Brian Cox—our second film project together!—and Brooklynn Prince. I was back in the movie business.

But I was first and foremost in the book business, and I realized I was muddling about, letting time speed by. I knew this melody by heart. I explained my slow pace to my editor at Little, Brown and we revised the contract to give me an additional year. That sounded ample, sort of. In my heart, I suspected I wouldn't make that deadline, either, but I was too embarrassed to ask for more time, even though contract extensions are a regular occurrence in publishing. I was frustrated by how slowly I worked, and I had to admit I was slowing myself even further by taking on other projects. Privately, though, I didn't see why the deadline mattered. The topic of Rin Tin Tin wasn't urgent or timely. I knew I was going slowly, but the book's delivery date seemed like something of an abstract need. My editor assured me that Little, Brown could bide its time.

By this point, Larry Kirshbaum, who had acquired the book with such enthusiasm, had left the company. From experience, I knew that having your book's greatest champion depart is cause for concern, but I didn't hear any complaints from Michael Pietsch, so I assumed all was well.

In the spring of 2004, I enlisted the help of a reknown fertility specialist at Columbia Presbyterian. When he called with the news that my pregnancy test was positive, I slumped against the wall of our apartment; the room teetered, and I thought I might faint. We had been diligent, even exhaustive, in our efforts, and my doctor hadn't been troubled by my "advanced maternal age," as it is so ungraciously named. Science had triumphed. The flood of feelings was disorienting—disbelief, relief, ecstasy, terror.

After all this time, being pregnant had begun to seem notional to me rather than something that might truly take place in this time, this space. I was going to have a baby; I was going to be a mother. I knew I would have to revise the way I lived my life, which had always meant traveling whenever a story called, working late, keeping an irregular schedule. Somehow I convinced myself that I would make the transition breezily. Did I picture strapping the baby to my back and trekking through Florida swamps? To Bhutan? To chase after bullfighters? I didn't allow myself to think about it too much. Over the last decade, getting pregnant had gotten so ensnared in my struggles with Peter that I had lost track of the core concept of what raising a child would entail. I wasn't particularly maternal. I was a youngest child, the youngest cousin, an infrequent and indifferent babysitter. I loved talking to kids and young adults, but I was slightly frightened of infants. One of my closest friends asked why I wanted to have a child when my life seemed so full and not very child-friendly, at least in terms of my work. I was stumped. Should I have a ready answer; did it mean something bad that I didn't have one? I realized having a child felt a lot like my decision to proceed with *Adaptation*: the ride of a lifetime, hard to predict, sure to be life-changing, something I didn't want to miss.

I was asked several times to write about being pregnant, but I didn't want to. I thought having a baby was both the most ordinary and most extraordinary thing in the world, done by billions of people throughout history, but now, privately, mine. I had nothing and everything to say about it. Also, John was a stickler for privacy. I said no time and time again.

I felt good, health-wise, while I was pregnant, except for an excruciating bout of carpal tunnel syndrome. Otherwise, my complaints were few. I went about my life without many changes except giving up alcohol and sushi. I refused to overprepare for birth or parenthood. I approached pregnancy the way I approached my stories: I wanted to dive in and figure it out on the spot rather than do a lot of book learning in advance. I didn't read the usual pregnancy books. I didn't devise a birth plan. I didn't join mommy-to-be groups. I didn't take a Lamaze class, although at the last minute, I worried that giving birth might be more rigorous than I'd anticipated. I hurried to find a short preparatory program and enrolled in a hypnobirthing class led by a ditzy woman who mostly showed us videos of her cat. I kept working throughout the nine months, taking stabs at doing more reporting for *Rin Tin Tin* and a few more *New Yorker* pieces.

As my due date approached, I was swamped by that last-minute anxiety I've felt at every precipice in my life: Is *this* where I want to go? Is it too late to change my mind? The due date came, and it passed. I got a haircut. John and I went out to a nice dinner, knowing we might not do so again for some time. We waited. After I passed my due date, doctors started monitoring me closely, to make sure nothing had gone awry. At first, it seemed like I was simply carrying a stubborn little boy who was in no hurry to be born. Then at one of my endless check-ins, my doctor noted that my blood pressure had spiked, indicating that I had preeclampsia, which she calmly but firmly explained could be cured only by delivering the baby. She said I needed to come to the hospital immediately and be prepared to stay for a while. I didn't know how to interpret "a while." John and I packed a dozen DVDs, my computer, cameras, clothes, phone chargers, and external battery packs, as if we were preparing to go on a long ocean journey. The cruise atmosphere ended abruptly once my contractions began and continued for hours. The stubborn little boy held firm, and after what felt like an eternity, my obstetrician announced that we probably needed to do a cesarean. I was outraged: To have been in labor so many hours and still end up having a cesarean seemed unfair. Rallying whatever strength I had left, furious at the prospect of having wasted so much effort, I summoned the baby out of my body at last. There were five people in the room, and suddenly, there were six. It was a true wonder, a conjuring.

* * *

What made me think having a baby would be easy? When I was pregnant, people told me that I was lucky, since I worked at home and could keep working as usual with a baby. Perhaps they pictured me dandling the baby on my knee while I typed or carting him to interviews like an extra handbag. What nonsense. My baby would tolerate no such thing. He was not fond of naps. If I held him on my lap when I typed, he wanted to do the typing. He started walking at eight and a half months, so that ended the dandling phase, anyway. I adored him. He was the most interesting thing that had ever happened to me, and I was overwhelmed.

On one of our trips to Los Angeles before Austin was born, John and I met a pair of producers. They thought that the story of our courtship would make a great movie and encouraged us to write a screenplay about it. An executive at DreamWorks liked the idea and offered us a contract. Soon after we signed, Austin was born. I sleepwalked into the screenplay. I was so blitzed with baby care, a book to write, and the needling feeling I should be writing *New Yorker* stories that I couldn't think straight. After putting Austin to bed—something he loudly resisted—John and I sat at the dining room table most nights, sketching out scenes. Many times I wasn't sure I

With John and a very young Austin

was awake, even though I was sitting upright. If I laid my head down on the table, I instantly fell asleep. We finally finished the script. It vanished, a little message in a bottle bobbing in the vast ocean of unproduced screenplays, where it remains today.

At last I found some footing. We hired a brisk, officious young woman to help with the baby. At last I felt like I was post-*post*-pregnant, no longer groggy and befuddled, as if encountering the world through a layer of cheesecloth. A few months after Austin was born, John came to the end of the five-year contract with his Boston company, so we were untethered from the city. I was anxious to get back to *Rin Tin Tin*. Almost all the material I needed was in California. Lee Duncan's papers were in Riverside; the Warner Bros. archives were at UCLA. Another important character, Herbert Leonard, had passed away, but his daughter and niece lived in Los Angeles and said they would speak to me. I would need multiple trips to Los Angeles to get everything done. But I couldn't fathom being apart so often, or for so long, from Austin. I had an idea. All of us—the dog,

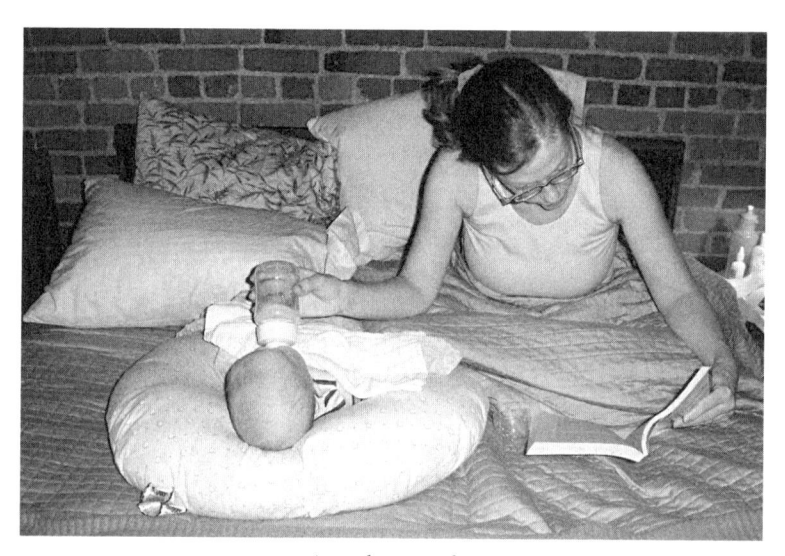

A working mother

the baby, the nanny, John, and I—could go to California. We could rent a house for a month, and I would be able to work during the day and come home at night and not be gnawed by homesickness and guilt and fatigue.

When I first started writing for *The New Yorker*, I was happy to discover that many of the magazine's contributors were women. I'd grown up in a world where almost nobody's mother worked. My mother was an exception. From the time I was five, she worked part-time in a bank. It wasn't a career, exactly: She worked as a teller and then helped people open accounts. She didn't earn a lot, but she was proud of having a job. She reveled in her independence. She kept her salary separate from the main household account she shared with my dad. She called it her "mad money," and starting when I was young, she urged me to always have some money of my own, even if I got married, so I could spend it however I wanted. She couldn't imagine not working. It was part of her sense of worth. She kept

With Lillian Ross

her job until her early eighties, when the bank introduced a new computer system and she didn't want to learn how to navigate it. Otherwise, I suspect she would have kept working until she died on the job.

I was fortunate to have my mother show me the value and pride of being a workingwoman. But that didn't provide answers on how to manage my situation, which was not an ordinary job. I didn't have a set schedule or predictable tasks. I sometimes had to travel for long stretches. I wasn't a prima donna, but when I was writing, I needed solitude and the freedom to work long hours. All those conditions seemed inconsistent with raising a child.

The New Yorker always featured female writers and cartoonists, including, when I first came to the magazine, Pauline Kael, Lillian Ross, Andy Logan, Joan Didion, Veronica Geng, Janet Flanner, Jane Kramer, Roz Chast, Elizabeth Drew, and Liza Donnelly. I took it as proof positive that a woman could work as a journalist and thrive. Foolishly, I never asked any of the women who had children how they managed it, so when I arrived at that point in my life, wobbling with the combined responsibilities of working as a writer and parenting, I didn't have a clue. I knew I was far luckier than most people with children. After John finished his Boston job, he decided to write a book about the inherent faults of corporate boards, so his time was as flexible as mine. We could afford childcare. We had a robust kid. We had space for playpens and strollers and toys. But I felt a filament of guilt and expectation running through me all the time. I believed I was doing too many things and none of them well, especially my job of raising a child. Some ancient voice was always scolding me, saying motherhood was my only true job and I was failing at it.

John liked my idea of decamping to California for a while, so we rented a house in Malibu, packed, and flew west. We planned to stay a month. The Rin Tin Tin material was more abundant that I had thought, and we loved the warm winter, so we extended our stay for a few more weeks. It was nice to see my toddler on the beach, knowing that back in Boston, it was blizzarding.

I never expected to live in California. More accurately, I never thought I quite deserved to live in California. It was too pretty, too cool, too desirable. It was like yearning to date the captain of the football team, a bold, baldly ambitious notion, the belief that you deserved to have the best there was. I never felt I could reach for something so big and shiny. Malibu was ridiculously, seductively beautiful in the simplest physical terms, a sultry mix of mountains and canyons and ocean. I was equally taken with its weird hodgepodge culture of beat-up cowboys, surfers, movie stars, and tramps wandering up and down the narrow artery of the Pacific Coast Highway. The PCH itself was like a string of mismatched trinkets, a bonsai store next to a shitty souvenir shop next to a Michelin-starred restaurant next to a horse-feed store. A city planner would have shot himself on the spot. Me, I found the rattle and jangle of these disparate elements intriguing, a sort of visual jazz composition, dissonant and raw.

When the lease in Malibu expired, we moved down the beach to Venice, which we loved, and then to the Hollywood Hills, an entirely different sort of neighborhood full of nooks and blind corners and late-afternoon shadows, and a view of four different mountain ranges and the long laplike spread of the San Fernando Valley. By then we had talked ourselves into believing that it made perfect sense to buy a house in Los Angeles, even though it made no kind of sense at all. We rationalized it by planning to rent it out except for the occasions when we would use it, which wasn't really such a bad idea. After trying so hard to resist it because it was too easy to love, and feeling not quite entitled to it because it was too exciting and sexy and fast and fun, we grabbed Los Angeles and we got it, a foothold in this mad, maddening, marvelous place.

Before working on *Rin Tin Tin,* I had never realized how exciting and emotional archives could be. I had done some historical reporting for *The Orchid Thief,* about Victorian orchid hunters and on the 1950s-era land scam that peddled swampland to eager GIs. But I had never dug deep into records, diaries, memorabilia. I was biased. I thought only those things you could see and smell firsthand were interesting, not what you might come across in a banker's box in a library.

Lee Duncan was a pack rat. He kept every clip, every flyer, every press photo related to his dogs, which he displayed in his house in Riverside, California, in what he called "The Memory Room." His wife resented his devotion to his animals. When Lee died, his wife sold the house and asked a neighbor if she could store this collected ephemera in his shed. It sat there for a decade, moldering. When the neighbor decided to move, he planned to throw away Lee's boxes, but his assistant, knowing it was material about Rin Tin Tin, couldn't bear the thought of it going to a landfill, so she retrieved it a few minutes before the sanitation department arrived. She sorted through it and eventually donated it to the museum in Riverside. There it sat, a life's work and passion told in clips and flyers and photos. Before I arrived, it had rarely been pulled out of the museum's storage since it landed there in the 1970s.

Dry stuff, or so I assumed it would be. I set up a laptop on a table in the museum's workroom and began making my way through the boxes. The material was filed chronologically, starting with the earliest material. Duncan's birth certificate. The paper his mother signed when she surrendered him to the orphanage. His army identification. The fragments and scraps of one man's existence. The photograph of Rin Tin Tin leaping over an eleven-foot obstacle at a dog show, which was featured on a newsreel and became his ticket to Hollywood. The license for an early marriage of Lee's I hadn't been aware of, attached to a crisp, cursory divorce decree. The letter from Warner Bros. telling Lee that he and Rin Tin Tin were no longer on contract now that talkies had arrived ("Obviously, dogs don't talk"). Entries to Lee's "Name the Puppy" contest. Fan mail. A United Press bulletin announcing the death of the original Rin Tin Tin: "Rin Tin Tin, the greatest of animal motion-picture actors, pursued a ghostly villain in a canine happy-hunting ground today."

I was spellbound. It was the first time I had ever spent so much time learning about someone, falling deeply into their story, more deeply than would have been possible if I'd met them and interviewed them. I had never realized how crackling and alive someone's papers could be. Reading them made me feel as though I had drilled my way inside a still-humming life. It was a kind of intimacy that wouldn't be possible with a living subject: Here were all the details, the ordinariness, the records, the disappointments, the triumphs, the scribbled scraps that wouldn't have been shared otherwise. It was the texture, the woven fibers, of the human experience. Lee came alive for me. As I worked my way through the archives, forward in time, I was filled with dread, knowing where I was heading. Soon there were the records of trips canceled, and doctors' correspondences, and I knew my time with Lee was drawing to an end. I had a bird's-eye view of the road he was traveling and its end point, a perspective he never could have had. The day I reached the cache of funeral announcements for him in the archives, I cried. I was stirred by affection for him, this man I'd never met, and by the realization of how privileged it is to be a writer, to peer into others' stories, travel alongside them, and piece together the way they have lived.

John and I kept extending our stay in Los Angeles. We were having a blast, and my reporting kept going strong. Finally, I had exhausted most of what was available. I had only one more interview lined up, which was with Herbert Leonard's daughter. Leonard had been the producer of the Rin Tin Tin television show, an enormous hit in the late 1950s and early 1960s. Leonard had been just as beguiled by the character of Rin Tin Tin as Lee Duncan had been, but he'd led a more tragic life. At one time, he was producing multiple television hits and had risen to the apex of Hollywood fame. Then he washed out, undone by multiple divorces and bad guesses, and he died in debt and without a home.

His daughter, Gina, warned me that she didn't have much to share about her father, so I kept postponing our meeting. At last I arranged to visit her a few days before we were scheduled to leave Los Angeles and go back east. I went to her house in the Hollywood Hills, and as she had warned me, she didn't have a lot of relevant information, since most of her father's work with Lee Duncan had taken place before she was born. We talked for a while, and as I was leaving, she mentioned that her father had a storage unit that she hadn't emptied yet. She didn't know what was in it. She said if she could find the key, I was welcome to go look. She rustled around in a desk drawer and, with a flourish, held up a key.

The next day, I drove to the storage facility, a sun-battered spot on the flank of a freeway, shaded by a few struggling palm trees. I wandered around until I found Leonard's unit. I teased the key into the lock. It fit, but the rusty shackle was stuck. I thumped it against the sheet-metal door, and it rang like a bell. Another thump and it cracked open.

The storage unit was about the size of a New York City parking space, poorly lit, airless, and so jammed that I could hardly wedge myself in. I took out a flashlight and pointed it at the tallest stack of boxes, which were bulging under their own weight. As I swept the light over the boxes, I could see the labels: "Rin Tin Tin," "More Rin Tin Tin," "More Rin Tin Tin."

We extended our stay another few weeks, and I spent that time hauling squashed boxes out of Leonard's locker and taking stock of their contents, which included thousands of pages of diaries, memos, and notes about his development of the show; his ideas for its revival in the 1980s; prospective film projects starring the dog; ledgers showing how broke he was at the end of his life after he lost his beautiful house in Los Feliz and had alienated most of his powerful friends in town.

Sometimes I shudder to think how much I would have missed if I hadn't done that final interview with Gina, or if she hadn't found the key. Of course, you never know what you've missed, but when an opportunity to speak to another source or look at more material opens, I can't say no, knowing that it might be the missing piece. The material about Herbert Leonard brought the book fully into being. The story now was about three people—Lee Duncan, Herbert Leonard, and a woman in Texas named Daphne Hereford, who continued to breed Rin Tin Tin descendants—and how they had centered their lives and passions around this one dog or, more precisely, the idea of a dog; the indelible idea of a hero, a star, the immortal.

We never expected to live in Los Angeles. At that time, we weren't sure where we would live. We had planned to make our way back to New York City after John finished his job in Boston, but the price of apartments had soared and now seemed hair-raising.

I had been renting a summer cottage in the Hudson Valley since 1990. I loved it, and one of my few demands in my divorce from Peter was that I would keep the lease. The cottage was small, a little shaggy and worn, on a shady road lined with maples and oaks. It wasn't heated, so the season ended with the first frost. I wished I could be there in the winter, and my fingers always itched in vain to freshen up the kitchen, change the floors, give it fresh paint.

One day while John and I were at the cottage, I noticed a for-sale sign on the land across the road. We had never seen anyone there and didn't know the owners. We had sneaked onto the property a few months earlier and discovered it had a lovely swoop and flow, a beautiful view of the Taconic Mountains, and a flock of wild turkeys rustling around in the stand of locust trees. I fantasized about that land, about owning something in the Hudson Valley. We put in an offer, not having any idea if we would ever build on it, but instinctively feeling it was a good idea.

We met the owner at the closing. She had been married to a man named Malcolm McNeil, who had passed away recently. His family had owned the land for generations—in fact, the road was named for his family, and at one time they had owned most of the acreage surrounding it. For many years, it had been a dairy farm, with some fields of corn and soy. McNeil had been a pilot, and he'd dreamed of putting a landing strip in the flattest pasture.

A few days later, a friend of his drove us around the property to get a fuller view. The friend told us that during McNeil's military service, he had flown a plane that was carrying a nuclear device. Unbeknownst to him or the men on board, the device was leaking radiation. Eventually, everyone who had been on that flight developed cancer. McNeil survived the longest, perhaps because he had been at the front of the plane, farthest from the device. He and his wife never built a house on the land, but McNeil visited regularly, sometimes staying overnight in a camper in the pasture, sometimes walking around, listening to the birds, crossing paths with wildlife. The land had meant the world to him. We felt like we were becoming stewards of a cherished place.

We decided to build a house there, and after a few false starts, we found an architect we liked. He designed a long, low house made of glass, wood, and stone, looking out over a meadow and toward the shadowy shoulders of the Taconics. It was stunning. We planned to spend summers there, but then it occurred to us that instead of struggling to find an apartment in New York City, we could live in the house full-time. Neither John nor I needed to be anywhere in particular, so we might as well be there.

Once we got back from Los Angeles, we sold our Boston apartment and headed for the country. Even though I had lived in New York City for seventeen years, and in downtown Boston for four, and had spent a few months in the whirl of Los Angeles, I immediately felt at home in rural New York State. For an animal lover, it was pure gluttony. There were animals everywhere. Wild, domestic, half-wild; with fur, with feathers, with fins; for sale and affordable or, quite often, free. I enrolled Austin in a Montessori preschool next to a goat pasture. Sometimes the goats clambered over the fence and frolicked around the playground equipment like furry preschoolers.

I wanted to get animals now that I lived in the country. I decided I would start with a goat, but my next-door neighbor warned me that goats eat everything, including cars, and that scared me off. My mind roamed from goats to chickens. This directional shift was spurred by a documentary I happened upon called *The Natural History of the Chicken*, which elevated the birds in my mind from quotidian to magnificent.

I decided I would begin with the hardware and then move on to the software. I would find a nice chicken coop, and the rest would sort itself out. Before long, I found a company called Omlet that made sleek plastic coops. The website offered the coop in four colors, and you could purchase a bundle that included a coop and either two or four chickens. The coop would be shipped freight. The chickens would be delivered to the nearest post office. I ordered a chartreuse Omlet and four red hens. A few days later, a clerk called from the post office. "You have a package," she said, "and it's clucking."

ELEVEN

Rural life is ideal for a writer. Rural life is inhospitable and impossible for a writer. Both of these statements are true, and during our four years living in the Hudson Valley, I lurched from one truth to the other. The quality of time in the country was delicious: full, abounding, undulating, in rhythm with the day, with the season, with the weather. We had fifty-five acres—some pasture, some pine forest, some black locust thicket, all cross-hatched with stout stone walls that a farmer in a far-off time had built with admirable precision. A herd of deer arrayed themselves in the pasture in the mornings and then tiptoed off as soon as one of them—ears swiveling like radar dishes—rang the exit bell. Wild turkeys, ugly as boxers but splendid and stern, marched the same route. In the spring, the turkeys were followed by a long line of chicks as black as beetles. The fields greened up in May, blanched in the August heat, browned in October. My friend Jeff Conti designed a garden at our entryway, and among the plantings was a cactus that could tolerate northeastern winters. Each fall, I was sure it had died: It collapsed in a heap, nothing but husk, and by early spring even the husk was gone. But as the days warmed, the flat paddle of cactus would reappear, tender and green, happy to start the cycle all over again.

In time, I collected a menagerie. At my fullest booking, I had eighteen chickens; two fussy ducks; four manic guinea fowl; two irritable Sebastopol geese; and four beautiful white turkeys, all males, who followed me around like puppies and gobbled on command. Every spring, we bought ten young Black Angus cattle, grazed them on our abundant pastures, offered them handfuls of alfalfa cubes and sweet feed a few times a day. They were skittish and silly, but by July, the boldest ones let us stroke their foreheads and touch their wide, wet noses. We didn't have winter shelter for the cattle, so we couldn't keep them year-round; we were operating a summer camp for cows. In the fall, we sold them to a farm down the road. The arrival of the new cattle marked the beginning of summer.

I didn't have a proper office in the house, so I erected a little studio a few hundred yards away, in a tangle of young ash trees and wickedly prickly raspberry canes. It was the first time I had my own dedicated place to work, and I was ecstatic. I had surrendered my office at *The New Yorker* a year earlier and had never figured out how I wanted to work. I had rented a few spaces in Boston, which I ended up never using; then I cordoned off part of our loft and declared it my own; but nothing ever felt right. This tiny cabin studio was it, and I rejoiced in it.

My flock, including my beloved turkeys

Sometimes my turkeys followed me down to the studio. They stood outside patiently, occasionally tapping on the windows with their beaks, as if beckoning me to come play with them. The studio was at the bottom of a slope that fell away from the house, so Austin couldn't see it. When I went to write, I told him I was going to work and would see him at the end of the day. For a while, at least, he thought I was going far away. The ruse worked until it didn't. One day I heard a gentle tapping on the window. I assumed it was the turkeys, but when I glanced up, I saw the shiny face of my little boy, who was overjoyed that he had found me, as if all this time I had been lost.

What was best about living in the country was being immersed in the life of the land, and the fact that almost all the time I spent away from writing, I was doing something physical: weeding my garden, mucking out my chicken coop, visiting the cows, going for a run. It complemented all the hours I spent in front of a computer screen, trying to figure out how to write *Rin Tin Tin*. The worst part of life there was the excess of solitude. We were five miles from a village; twenty-five minutes to the nearest sizable towns of Red Hook and Rhinebeck. Most of our friends lived in Red Hook or beyond. When I hankered for something social, it couldn't be quick; everything and everyone required a thirty-minute drive. When I was trying to write, the prospect of taking at least two hours off to have coffee with a friend was forbidding. Instead, I played with my chickens. Of course, I had John and Austin, but I was often knocked sideways by a wave of loneliness, toppled by it.

In December 2007, a friend told me about a new service starting up that she thought I'd enjoy. It was called Twitter. I didn't understand what it did or why I should sign up, but she opened an account for me to prod me along. Twitter, which described itself then as a "micro-blogging platform," had been around for a year and a half, but its users were mostly in the tech world. In March 2007, though, it was featured at South by Southwest, and from there it quickly grew. Operating as a sort of online neighborhood bulletin board, Twitter was a random collection of 140-character blurts about anything, nothing, and everything in between, posted by people around the world. On the face of it, the whole idea was rather ridiculous, and the initial knock was that it consisted of little more than people posting what they had eaten for lunch. I was intrigued enough to poke around and begin to follow some people who were funny or smart or posting interesting news bits. I didn't write anything of my own until December 22, 2007, when I posted my first tweet, which consisted of one word: "reading."

Nothing happened. No one seemed to have read my tweet; no one commented on it; I had no followers. I didn't return to the site until over a month later, when I dared to post another fragment: "reading email and trying to decide whether to buy an iPhone."

I didn't post again until May, but I began browsing Twitter whenever I took a break from writing *Rin Tin Tin*. I didn't yet understand the cadence of the platform, nor the proportions of what to post, and most vexingly, I couldn't figure out the voice to use when posting. But I was beginning to enjoy the chatter that unfurled on the site. It provided me with the kind of casual interaction that my gorgeous but solitary rural existence made so scarce. I posted once more in May ("reading an incredibly weird book about nonverbal communication with animals") and then retreated until August, when I picked up the pace:

getting over Lyme disease. Ugh!

admiring Austin's new first-ever bike!

Taking Cooper to the vet

just picked my first ears of corn from my very own garden. Amazing.

JOYRIDE

* * *

That August, John and I headed to Denver to work as speech coaches for the Democratic National Convention. John had worked at seven or eight prior conventions and had persuaded the head of the speech coach team, Michael Sheehan, to include me in 2004 and again in 2008. In 2004, at the Democratic convention in Boston, I edited a few speeches, but my main responsibility was to entertain Teresa Heinz Kerry, the wife of presidential candidate John Kerry. By "entertain," I mean that I was assigned the task of keeping her away from the speechwriters so she couldn't meddle, and to make sure she didn't edit her own speech too much. She had a gaggle of friends and hangers-on who regularly suggested additions to her, and the party bosses were uncomfortable with most of them. Heinz Kerry was treated by the press and many DNC insiders like a birdbrain, but I found her smart and warm and solicitous. At the time of that convention, I was pregnant with Austin, and she loved talking to me about motherhood and babies. Occasionally, she took a phone call from a friend and returned to announce something like she had decided to learn a few lines in a different language and do a section of her speech in it. Usually, these epiphanies passed in a few minutes. I loved spending time with her and hated how disrespected she was.

A young Senate candidate, Barack Obama, was giving a keynote speech at the convention. When it was his turn to run through his speech, he came to our workroom in the bowels of the convention center. This was the final step before the speeches were typed into the teleprompter and considered "locked." Obama objected to the small changes that were suggested and bore the process with undisguised impatience. His charisma was chilly, a little forbidding. Consensus among the speech team was that the last few lines of his speech needed tweaking, and I was nominated to tell him. I think I'm good at talking to difficult people, so I waltzed up and suggested the changes with a smile. He fixed his gaze on me for a moment and then turned back to his manuscript. "I won't be changing it," he said coolly, and he didn't. The rest of the speech team—all men, for the record—found this awkward interaction entertaining and they were proud of having set me up.

The convention in 2008 was a different matter. Obama, now the presidential candidate, brought a battalion of his own speechwriters, and there were snippy, snarly turf squabbles between the Obama people and the DNC team that John and I were part of. But his speech, obviously, was magnificent. Being in the stadium in Denver to see him accept the nomination was one of the most moving experiences I've ever had.

Being at the convention gave me an on-ramp to Twitter that made sense, and I started posting several times a day. After the convention, I went to France to do some additional reporting for *Rin Tin Tin,* and that was another easy opportunity for tweeting. I didn't know whom I was talking to on Twitter, but it began feeling natural, the sort of casual observational chatter you might do with your office mates—an exchange that isn't necessarily consequential but seems contextually valuable, cumulative in its meaning and its capacity for making you feel known. A few friends started following me, and then a few strangers, and then a few more. Twitter became my regular break during the long days working alone.

If I hadn't been working in such isolation, I might not have embraced Twitter so enthusiastically, but in my studio on that bosky hillside, with my turkeys tapping at my window, it provided the bite-size socializing I missed most about city life. I sometimes tweeted about working on my book, and people on Twitter cheered me on whenever I posted my word count. Was it the equivalent of posting that I had a ham sandwich for lunch? Did it matter that almost all the people who applauded my growing word count were strangers? Were they strangers once they responded to me and I replied? Were they any less known to me than people in the office I hardly knew but with whom I might chat when I bumped into them? I never confused my Twitter relationships with real-life friendship, although over the years I did meet some of my Twitter conversation partners in the flesh, and we've stayed in touch: They qualify as real friends. Twitter wasn't a facsimile of society. It was a new kind of culture, boundaryless and outside of time and space. It kept me company, and amused me, and forced me to figure out how to write well, to be engaging or funny or smart, in a very brief bite. I liked the challenge of making those few words sing.

I happened to know a few people who worked for Twitter, and I suspect they wiggled a few dials to build my audience, which eventually reached more than three hundred thousand followers. I'm sure some of those followers were bots or fake accounts, but a lot of them were living, breathing humans who seemed to enjoy reading my snippets. I welcomed their company.

That is, I welcomed it most of the time. In September 2018, I was glued to the televised coverage of the Senate Judiciary Committee questioning Brett Kavanaugh, who had just been nominated to the Supreme Court. Many of us were also following the public statements of Christine Blasey Ford, who had accused Kavanaugh of assaulting her during high school. It was an emotional, troubled time, lining up people against each other. While watching the hearings, I was struck by how many aging Caucasian men were on the judiciary committee. I have strong feelings about such matters, but I didn't want to post them on Twitter, where my postings were rarely political; I never wanted to incite growling and fighting and name-calling. But the sight of that monolithic committee irritated me, and I tweeted, "I'm so tired of old white men." I thought it was both clever and true. I went back to watch the hearings and stayed off Twitter for a while.

When I came back to my computer, I saw that my tweet had attracted thousands of comments—literally tens of thousands. I read the first few and then slammed my laptop shut. The tone of the responses was acid, accusatory, bellicose. One of them smirkily informed me that I had been "ratioed"—that is, I had attracted more responses than likes. This person explained that I had been singled out by Q, the pseudonymous head of QAnon, the extreme right movement behind such events as Pizzagate, the incident that claimed Hillary Clinton and other leading Democrats were engaged in a satanist child molestation cult.

Why would QAnon single me out? By Twitter standards, my remark seemed fairly ordinary, at most a bit sassy, and I would have wagered that most of my followers didn't look to me for political direction and might well have agreed with the sentiment of this one. All I can guess is that because I had a lot of followers, I had attracted the group's attention, and they were monitoring my account. The ferocity of the response terrified me. I refused to read the comments after I saw those first few; I knew they were vicious and threatening. I was days away from leaving on a book tour. My public appearance schedule was posted everywhere. I didn't know what to do. Within a few minutes, my publicist called and told me to look at my Wikipedia page. In the hour since I had posted the tweet, someone had gone into my Wikipedia page and edited it, inserting wherever possible the fact that I'm Jewish. (*Susan Orlean is a Jewish American writer . . . from a Jewish family . . . both of her parents are Jewish.*) In the section mentioning my marriage, they had added something to the effect that I was "married to an old white man" and it wasn't known whether we were still married. My publicist edited the page back to its original form.

What remained, though, was my genuine fear about going on my book tour, appearing at events open to the public. I'm never afraid appearing at open events, although I know there is a certain vulnerability in doing so. Except for a few unwelcome flirtations and a few encounters that were uncomfortable, I've never had a bad experience. But now I was scared. I weighed canceling the tour but knew that would be a death knell for the book. A friend who had some familiarity with right-wing groups advised me to do nothing, say nothing. Don't give them the satisfaction of seeing you upset, he said, and they'll get bored and move on.

I left for my tour a few days later and held my breath until the first few events went by without incident. Apparently, QAnon had indeed gotten bored with me, and I never heard from anyone affiliated with the group again. In my life, I've never been happier to have attention withdrawn.

None of my books has been easy, but each time I've come up with a book idea, I've convinced myself that this was the one that would be a breeze. The best analogy is the old maxim about childbirth—that the minute you give birth, you instantly forget how hard it was, because otherwise you'd never do it again. This is the experience of writing a book. In the beginning—the day you get your positive pregnancy test/ sign your contract—you are tipsy with excitement and convinced you'll whiz through, that writing it will be a cinch. Midway, misery settles in; you lose all hope that you'll even make it to the end or that it's worth the trouble. The final rush is blinding, ecstatic, peculiar, galvanic. It's a short, fast plunge, and it obliterates any memory of how grueling the process was. Immediately after delivering my baby, I told John that I wanted to get pregnant again as soon as possible, and I know I'm not the only person who has had this experience. Nor am I the only writer who has suffered through writing a book and then been boosted into such ecstasy upon cradling the finished copy in my arms that I instantly thought, What's my next book going to be, and when can I start? It's a rapturous form of insanity, a spellbound delusion.

I did think *Rin Tin Tin* would be easy. At least one thread of the book was chronological, which seemed more manageable than the radiating chapters of *The Orchid Thief*. I also assumed I'd toggle between the story of the original Rin Tin Tin and the story of Daphne Hereford, who continued to breed Rin Tin Tin puppies and train them as service dogs for children with special needs. Now I had to weave in the story of Herbert Leonard. Initially, I pictured his story as a sidetrack, but the more I learned about him, especially after discovering the material squirreled away in his storage unit, the more I realized he was essential. What I had imagined as a singular, linear story had grown far more complex. This made it a better, fuller book, so I didn't mind.

But getting the voice right was challenging, especially with the historical material. Telling the story of events I had observed firsthand gave me an authority that made it easy to write, much the way I might have told a story out loud to a gathering. But history was different. I wasn't able to draw on my sensory experience of learning the material, living the experience. Most worryingly, I didn't feel confident. I am not a scholar. I'm not a historian. Who am I to tell you what it was like for Lee Duncan to be on the front lines of World War I?

The single essential element in good writing is confidence. You need swagger to be a writer at all, to be convinced that readers should listen to you. You must believe passionately that you have something to say. Someone else might have the same observations, but in choosing to be a writer, you choose to broadcast your observations and reckon that they are of value. It's a state of mind, a matter of willing yourself to trust yourself. I often picture this as walking along a narrow ledge and willing yourself to not look down: If you do, you'll lose your nerve, and you'll fall. If I'm writing about someone I've interviewed or an event I've observed, conjuring that sureness is relatively easy. I've done something that my readers haven't done, and I'm going to tell them about it because it will interest them. I'm the authority: I'm the one who experienced it.

But much of what I'd learned for the book had happened long ago, and I'd learned about it second- or thirdhand, through published material or archives. I didn't have the certainty to write it. It nagged at me that anyone could access this same material. What was I bringing to it? What made it mine?

At some point, I confessed this insecurity to my editor. "Anyone could read those archives," I said. My editor nodded and said, "But they won't."

But they won't. I wondered what this meant at first, and then it dawned on me. This was my story. Everything I'd learned in service to it was part of the story, whether it was a person I interviewed or a cemetery I visited or an account of Lee's days as a pilot in the war. The reader relied on me. The reader wanted the whole story, all the threads from different sources spun into one magical veil. I wasn't delivering new information about World War I, but I was delivering it as part of a story that wasn't well-known, with context that was fresh, and that was what I owed the reader.

Grappling with this hesitation, and feeling that I could overcome it, changed everything about how I write. For the first time, I understood that I had anointed myself as a storyteller, and the way I gathered the fragments of the story was secondary to the end product and the embrace of the reader. Anyone could look up Lee Duncan's military record, but they wouldn't. They would, however, love to hear about it from someone who had done so. I finally sat down to write those chapters with more pluck than I had ever felt.

In August 2007, my father died. He was ninety-two, and while he had heart issues and other maladies, he had been as engaged and present as ever. He was still working, although he gave himself more afternoons off to play golf, and he remained curious about anything new, anything extraordinary: Shortly before he died, he had gotten an iPod. He visited us in the Hudson Valley and assessed the construction of our house the way he might have considered one of his own construction projects. Then, while recovering from a minor fall, his heart stopped, and he was gone. I felt completely betrayed: He had given every impression that he would live forever. His youthfulness made his age seem like a math error. Many of my friends had lost one or both of their parents by then, and my parents were old enough that I should have been prepared. But they kept us fooled. At eighty, my mother won a seniors tennis tournament. At ninety-two, my father was planning new real estate ventures. His death left me flabbergasted. I knew I owed him everything: my comfortable childhood, my safeguarded adolescence, my ongoing reliance on him for steady wisdom and companionship. But so much more. His example to stay wide-eyed in the world, to notice, to listen, to learn, had been imprinted on me. He had been grudging with his praise, but as I got older, I came to understand that he wanted to spur me to work harder, do better. I continued to ache for a little indulgent approval from him, but I know he never intended to hurt me. I knew he was proud of me. Toward the end of his life, we'd talked more freely than we ever had. I finally asked him about so much that I'd wondered about—his thorny relationship with my mother, his own feelings about an afterlife, about the minutiae of our family dynamics. I sure wasn't ready for him to go, but I felt lucky we had that intimate time.

In September 2008, the subprime mortgage business disintegrated and the financial firm Lehman Brothers fell apart, leading to the largest American bankruptcy in history. The world economy went off a cliff. Around us, local stores shuttered and houses sprouted for-sale signs. There was an eerie, vertiginous sense that there was no bottom, nothing to stop the fall.

Every business was in alarm, including publishing. I heard rumors about contracts being canceled and proposals going begging. I fretted about my Rin Tin Tin project, but I convinced myself that Little, Brown had invested so much in the book already that they would continue to nurture it, with an eye on the investment paying off in the end.

I knew I needed another deadline extension. I had puzzled out the structure of the book, but I was a long way from a finished draft. I turned to my editor for reassurance. We chatted on Facebook, and my nerves eased. To be honest, as was the case with *Saturday Night*, I didn't think timeliness mattered. There was nothing pressing about the topic. No other writer was going to beat me to market with their book about Rin Tin Tin. I wouldn't get any more of my advance until I handed in my manuscript, so it didn't cost Little, Brown anything to wait for me. Publishers legitimately worry that a book is late because it has problems, and thus the writer will never finish it, and the advance will be lost. But I had published three books successfully; it seemed a safe bet that I'd finish this one, too. I told my editor how difficult it had been for me to structure *Rin Tin Tin*, but I had finally figured it out, so I felt optimistic. I never said I couldn't, or wouldn't, get it done. He said that another extension wouldn't be a problem, and it was just a matter of processing the paperwork.

One slate-gray day in late fall, with filmy snow floating sideways with the wind, I got a call from Richard Pine. His tone was tense, odd. He said that Little, Brown would not give me an extension. They said that I had to turn in the book by the end of the year—a few weeks away—or they would cancel the contract. "Cancel" meant I would have to return the portion of the advance I'd already received. The wind picked up, and the snow clotted into wet, white shapes that stuck to the patio furniture in little piles, like flocking on fabric. I held my phone to my ear, speechless. Richard, too, was speechless. I felt tricked, betrayed, furious, embarrassed. My stomach curdled. I was so fucking slow. Why couldn't I write faster? Where had the time gone? But I was also dumbfounded. Who cared when a book about this subject was published? It made no sense.

I knew it's never good to have the person who first championed your book leave the company, as was the case at Little, Brown, but I had felt fully embraced by the company, especially by my editor, even after Larry Kirshbaum left. I opened my Facebook account to look back at the messages my editor and I had exchanged about the extension. I took a screenshot of them, because I noticed that he had apparently unfriended me; suddenly I could no longer see his account. His messages to me were as plain as day: Don't worry about your deadline, the extension is nothing but a bit of paperwork, keep going, I'm excited to read it.

I'm sure one reason I was so angry was that I was ashamed: ashamed of how slow I am, ashamed that I'd let other projects distract me from the book, ashamed that I wasn't perfect and hadn't done everything perfectly. The shame was as hot as a branding. No one except John knew what was happening that day, but I couldn't leave the house or see friends: I believed everyone would know instantly that I was a loser, a failure. I was nauseated for days. I felt the jig was up: I had been unmasked as a fraud. I wasn't a real writer, ever. I never had been. It had been a performance, and a shoddy one at that.

The only thing that rallied me from this wretched state was to reignite my fury about how illogical Little, Brown's position really was. John, who understood the business world, believed it was a purely financial move. In the feeble economy of 2009, Little, Brown wanted to prop up its bottom line, and reeling in my large advance instantly gave them a significant amount of cash. I assumed that Michael Pietsch, the publisher, was skeptical about the book and thought it would ultimately lose money. Perhaps he didn't think much of me as a writer. As for my editor, I'll never know. I never spoke to him again, and his Facebook account remained invisible to me.

Whatever the reasons, the situation was irreversible. I couldn't finish the book in a few weeks. It would not be easy to fish the advance out of the bank and return it. When I'd received it, I had deposited it in our family bank account, and over the years it had been portioned out for food and flights and childcare and mortgage payments—the stuff of daily life, the way anyone would spend a salary. That's the way people use book advances, sustaining themselves while working on a book. I doubt many writers put their advances in a hidey-hole, separated from the rest of their income, retrievable at a finger's snap.

Once I gathered my wits, I called John Pelosi, a friend who practiced entertainment law. I explained my situation, especially the fact that my editor had told me to not worry about the deadline. Pelosi was irate on my behalf. I would have to pay something back to Little, Brown—the contract was undeniable on this matter—but he was certain they would settle for a smaller amount to acknowledge that I had been misled about extending the deadline.

Richard wanted to circulate what I'd already written of the book to other publishers as soon as possible. I was so bruised and upset that I hardly wanted to look at what I'd written or talk to other publishers in that chipper, optimistic, retailing tone you use when trying to convince someone to buy your book. I tried to remind myself that I was good at making sentences. I had a knack for language, an ear for melody, a good eye for detail. I was able to talk to people. I could be witty on the page.

I could have made a living as a writer doing something routine. I could have spent my entire career writing celebrity profiles or travel stories or writing about issues that were crisp and obvious. I understood writers who had done that. Why hadn't I? From the beginning, I couldn't help but approach topics obliquely and get curious about unlikely things. I was intrigued by the ordinary, the odd, the unexpected, the disruptive. I liked the stories adjacent to the more obvious stories, the unexamined worlds butting up against the well-known ones. This wasn't calculated. I simply couldn't think any differently. Somewhere along the way, I had developed an insistent appetite for surprising readers, the urge to show them something new, or at least show them something in a new light. I was so used to people telling me bemusedly that they hadn't planned to read my story on X, or my book on Y, and yet they'd found themselves beguiled by it. Was it the beguiling that I loved? Knowing that I had captivated someone, even somewhat against their will, and yet sensing that I had ended up pleasing them? I had a lot of ego riding on that; I derived a lot of joy out of doing that.

But wasn't it also true that I believed, stubbornly and avidly, that these oddball topics were genuinely meaningful? At my most crestfallen during this interlude, I thought I was a failure, but it never, ever occurred to me that a book about Rin Tin Tin was a bad idea. I absolutely believed in it. In the simplest terms, I knew it was a fascinating story about a cultural icon who was little known and usually misunderstood. Most people who remembered the Rin Tin Tin television show had no idea that its genesis was with a real dog born in France during World War I. People who didn't know the television show would read the book and discover a media sensation that reflected the beginnings of Hollywood. And the engine of it all was something deeply emotional—namely, the persistent, determined loyalty of the three main characters to this mythical beast, within whom they saw the outlines of eternity, an everlastingness that was beyond human. To delve into that devotion was to examine the workings of human nature. To see what they saw would be to touch the fabric of dreams.

I didn't believe in myself at that moment, but I fervently believed in the value of these stories, these tales about dogs and Saturday nights and gospel and basketball, about bullfighters and ten-year-olds and even shower curtains. I wanted to tell them all.

After hearing from my lawyer, Little, Brown admitted that there had been a "misunderstanding" about the deadline extension and agreed to accept a smaller amount of money to settle the contract. I didn't feel great, but at least I felt validated: I had been working under the impression that I could take the time I needed, and then the rug was pulled. The experience felt like a penetrating stab; the nerves that were cut never knitted back together. Many years later, after the book was published, I was in New York City to attend the National Book Awards. I had stopped to talk to a friend, and over my right shoulder, I sensed someone hovering. I finally turned and saw Michael Pietsch, whom I hadn't seen or spoken to since our meeting about *Rin Tin Tin* when Little, Brown first acquired it. He had never called me during or after the contract debacle. My throat seized and my heart started thundering. I decided to look at him as blankly as I could. He introduced himself and then said that he had recently been "running the numbers" on *Rin Tin Tin*—I assumed he meant he was looking at the sales figures—and he realized that Little, Brown would have made money on the book. He said canceling it had been a bad business decision. He didn't say "I'm sorry" or "I'm glad you were able to place the book elsewhere" or "Congratulations, it was a good book." He said that it had been a miscalculation, which seemed to vex him slightly. My first instinct—always my instinct—was to say something assuaging, mild, even consoling, something like, "Well, it all worked out okay!" or "Ah, so it goes!" or "No problem!" but for once in my life, I simply couldn't. I fixed my gaze on him and said, "I want you to know that was the worst experience of my professional life. It truly wounded me." I was shocked to hear myself say this—shocked that I wasn't backing away from my discomfort and his but rather leaning into it and laying at his feet the truth of how brutal the experience had been. I realized that I was shaking. He must have been shaken, too, because by the time I got home and called Richard to tell him about the encounter, Pietsch had already called him to report it.

Back in that cold late autumn, Richard began circulating my chapters of the book, and the publisher of Simon & Schuster, David Rosenthal, told Richard he was interested. Rosenthal, whom I knew slightly from his days as an editor at *Rolling Stone*, is impish and irreverent, and clearly, sticking a finger in Little, Brown's eye tickled him. He boosted my confidence when I was most dejected, raving to me about how much he loved the book and how we would "make trouble" with it; I assumed "making trouble" meant getting attention and perhaps making money and most of all upending expectations. He sent the advance immediately. It covered what I owed Little, Brown and left me enough to fund the remainder of the work on the book. I started savoring the revenge fantasy that the book would be such a success that Little, Brown would rue their decision. Most of all, I felt renewed, ready to get back to the story and sew it up.

I pounded away in my studio, the winter easing into spring, the soft curve of the hill greening, the chittering of summer insects rising at dusk. My studio was an eccentric assemblage of my life at the moment. With Gina's permission, I had shipped some of Herbert Leonard's archives to my house. There were several VHS tapes that I wanted to watch, including old episodes of the Rin Tin Tin television show, so I bought a VHS player on Craigslist, since we didn't have one anymore. It was a rackety old thing built into the bottom of a small television set, and I balanced the unit on a handmade chair I'd found at a yard sale. On a shelf behind it was my collection of bird nests, some as tiny as thimbles, that I'd found around our property. Leonard's journals and notebooks and memos were in a yellow heap on the floor, like a pile of fallen leaves. My bookcase creaked under the weight of my books about animals in Hollywood, about World War I, about silent film, and the official handbook of the German Shepherd Dog Club, alongside my collection of toy typewriters, a flyswatter, and a few handfuls of dried corn in case the turkeys stopped by. On Etsy, I had stumbled upon Rachel Denny, an artist who took Styrofoam deer forms, manufactured for use in taxidermy, and knitted decorative "skins" for them. My prize office possession was the head of a ten-point buck with Denny's turquoise cable-knit covering, casting a cool blue eyeless gaze over my desk.

And there I labored, writing and rewriting. I bought a fresh pack of index cards and began.

Card 40: Army dogs fed carefully—meat but never corned beef. In Army brochure about military dogs: "Ice cream and sweets are taboo."

Card 43: Hero dogs in WWI: Tubby, Buster, Daisy, Chips, Queenie, Skippy, Chub. Queenie was killed in combat.

Card 140: From a 1930s vaudeville program: "Rin Tin Tin is known as the Wonder Dog of Stage and Screen. He gives his performance with the precision of a human being and behaves less like a trained canine than any animal ever before the public."

Card 252: "The Courage of Lassie"—1946 film starred Elizabeth

Taylor. Promotional line: "Lassie has been turned into a killer by military training."

Card 324: In WW2, Army had goal of recruiting 300,000 dogs for use in the combat. Used dummies of Hitler and Hirohito to train the dogs.

Card 698: "Adventures of Rin Tin Tin" television series ran in 70 countries.

Card 710: Just met a guy with a tattoo of RTT on his chest! Said, "I think in my previous life I was a German shepherd."

I filled almost eight hundred index cards. Then I spread them out, organized them, reviewed them. I wrote questions for myself: "Animal use in movies: What were the themes and were they reflecting anything going on in the culture at the time? Does my idea of orphans/grasping for memory/loneliness of heroism apply or not? Rivalry between Rin Tin Tin and Lassie: How do I describe and use in the book?"

Of course, nothing ever stays still in publishing; it is a tossing, roiling sea, flinging bodies here and there. In 2010, less than a year after Rosenthal had bought my book for Simon & Schuster, he was pushed out of the company, which was shuddering in the bad economy. Before I could panic, it was announced that he would be replaced by Jon Karp, the editor who'd held my hand all those years on *The Orchid Thief*. This was as close to a win as I could get. As publisher, Karp wouldn't have the time to edit individual books, but he promised he'd keep a close eye on me. My new editor, Jofie Ferrari-Adler, drove up to the Hudson Valley to meet me one afternoon, and he made me feel like he couldn't wait to work on the book. Now it was up to me to finish it.

I spent months at my desk. When I found myself too distracted at home, I went to two artists' residencies—Yaddo and MacDowell—where I worked without being interrupted by children and turkeys and husbands and gardens, and I wrote thousands of words. Finally—triumphantly, and somewhat astonishingly—I finished. The book had taken me almost ten years, start to finish. To congratulate me, Austin made me a card featuring a plastic figure of a German shepherd and a cardboard doghouse. I realized that I had been working on *Rin Tin Tin* since before he was conceived. As far as he knew, a mother's job was to write a book about a dog.

On one of our trips to Los Angeles, John ran into a former colleague who asked if he might be interested in helping with a start-up for a year or two. We were content in the Hudson Valley, but the previous winter had been cruel, with thirteen raging snowstorms. I liked the idea of taking a break. It also meant a chance to use our house in Los Angeles more than for occasional visits; we had been renting it out for all but a few weeks a year. The local elementary school had a great reputation, so it would be easy to enroll Austin there.

Around that same time, Simon & Schuster was planning the publicity tour for *Rin Tin Tin*. I had suggested pairing my readings with a screening of my favorite Rin Tin Tin silent film, *The Clash of the Wolves*, which had been restored as part of the Library of Congress's film classics program. The response from theaters and bookstores was keen, so I anticipated a long book tour. It would be easier to fly in and out of Los Angeles for these trips than to manage it from the Hudson Valley, where every flight meant driving two hours to an airport in New York.

Friends agreed to house-sit for us if we left for L.A., which meant chicken-sitting and turkey-sitting and duck-sitting as well. It seemed like a nice short-term adventure. We hardly said goodbye because we pictured returning in the spring. This was a West Coast idyll, a respite from winter, nothing more.

I have always loved L.A. I love its arch glamour, and its grubbiness, and the jarring, jangling mix you encounter everywhere you go. I love the posh parts of the city, and I love the mishmash of small businesses in dingy strip malls. I love how the houses seem like stage sets, every house someone's fevered fantasy: an English Tudor with palm trees, a miniature Spanish castle, a mid-century clerestoried jewel box. Los Angeles has a randomness, a quality of haphazardness, that delights me. I couldn't wait to wander through all the neighborhoods: Thai Town, Little Ethiopia, Little Tokyo, Boyle Heights. There was so much to explore.

I knew the time would go fast. For the first part of our Los Angeles stay, I was on the road promoting *Rin Tin Tin*. Its publication had started on the highest of high notes: a front-cover review in *The New York Times Book Review* calling it "fascinating" and "sweeping." The good reviews stunned me in the best sort of way. Perhaps the one that moved me the most was written by Michael Schaub of NPR, who said, "Brilliant . . . if there were any book [Orlean] was born to write, it's this one. The product of years of dogged research, it's her magnum opus, a work filled with fascinating stories . . . [and] stunning prose that is both compassionate and perceptive."

Some readers complained that the book contained too much meandering, too many sidetracks and too much self-reflection, but I expected that, and the acclaim far outweighed the complaints. When *Rin Tin Tin* landed on the bestseller list, I was overjoyed. Despite the difficult journey, it felt worthwhile.

I bounced from coast to coast, doing readings from the book following a screening of *The Clash of the Wolves*, which was a little over an hour long. In some venues, a pianist or organist accompanied the film, just as they would have when it was released in 1925. It's a fantastic movie. In it, Rinty—then in the prime of his life and at the height of his silent-film fame—plays a half-wolf, half-dog leader of a wolf pack. He is gravely injured in a fight. Rather than put his pack at risk, Rinty decides to head off on his own, leaving his mate and their new litter of pups. He intends to die of his injuries alone or to commit suicide. It sounds crazy to say, but Rin Tin Tin's performance is truly moving. You feel his despair as he slinks away from his mate and gazes over the edge of a cliff, considering his fate. It was a treat watching audiences be surprised by how good it is. Many people had never seen a silent film before, and certainly not a silent film starring dogs. I wanted them to read my book, but I was just as excited to introduce them to another experience they might not have had otherwise.

In the spring of 2012, I had a peculiar experience while I was trying to put on mascara: My right arm wouldn't raise up to eye level. It happened again the next day and the next. Always happy to diagnose myself, I assumed I had done something to my shoulder and was annoyed at the thought that I might have to do physical therapy or get an injection. The problem persisted, so I finally decided to see my doctor and sort it out. He watched me struggle with lifting my arm and said he wanted me to have an MRI of my neck, even though my problem was with my shoulder, because he suspected it originated elsewhere.

The next day, my doctor called and said I needed to see a spine surgeon immediately. He said my upper spine—from right below my skull to midway down my upper back, known in spine language as C3 through C7—had essentially collapsed. Apparently, my spine looked like whiplash after ten years of wear and tear. I had never been in a car accident. Then I recalled one of my first times snowboarding. I took up the sport because my stepson Jay loved it, and John thought it would be a nice way for us to bond. I was never much of a skier, but I liked snowboarding immediately, except for an early lesson when I fell so hard that I saw stars. That must be it, the surgeon said, typing into his computer. And how does one fix this sort of thing? He explained that it would be two days of surgery: One day to replace my discs; one day to put in a rod to stabilize the new discs. It sounded grisly. I told him I would think about it. He explained that it wasn't the sort of thing you "think about"; that if I had a minor accident like stumbling or falling off a bike with my spine in this condition, I might end up paralyzed.

I was mad at myself for caring about putting on mascara, as if I had caused this to happen by noticing the weakness in my arm. I was in such disbelief that I got a second opinion, and then a third, and a fourth. They were consistent: Get this surgery as soon as possible or *else*. That June, I headed to Cedars-Sinai for a weeklong stay that I can only describe as excruciating. I fantasized that I would spend the summer reading as I recuperated, but holding a book proved uncomfortable, so I hardly read. I don't really remember how I spent the time, but it passed. It was months before I didn't feel like I was made out of balsa wood, ready to snap at the slightest jostle. The surgery left me with thirty-seven titanium screws in my neck and enough scaffolding to hold up a small building. It was a tough process, but I ended up as good as new.

In June, as soon as I could travel after my surgery, we returned to the Hudson Valley, relaxing again into the gentle cadence of the countryside—the unhurried unfolding of days, measured in chores and the cycle of the gardens and fields. Our new summer cattle arrived, shy and stumbling, with high hips and long eyelashes and big, damp noses. The hay fields sprouted. My chicken coop, though, was empty. My turkeys were now living with the friends who had given them to me when they were babies. The ducks and geese, which actually belonged to my neighbors, had been sent back home. My guinea fowl, Prince Charles and Camilla, had decamped for points unknown during the winter and apparently weren't coming back.

The chickens had been waiting for me. But in April, before we returned, a raccoon fiddled with the lock on the door of the coop until it opened and killed all fourteen chickens. I knew I was no kind of real farmer, because when I got the grim news from our house sitters, I cried until my eyes were sore. I didn't think I could have chickens again. It was too upsetting; they were too vulnerable. Having chickens was guaranteed heartache unless you viewed them as a commodity that would come and go. I couldn't. When I got my first chickens years earlier, my neighbor's lazy, floppy-haired old mutts loped onto our property and, with unaccountable energy, clawed open the coop and killed two of my birds. Soon after, I lost my prettiest chicken to a hawk: She was lifted from the ground without a trace. My favorite chicken, Beauty—my friendliest, calmest bird, who laid big brown eggs and loved being held and stroked like a kitten—developed a fatal neurological disorder called Marek's disease. My vet gave her antibiotics (the label on the bottle listed the patient as "Chicken Orlean"). The drugs didn't help, and she was suffering, so I had her euthanized. After the vet administered the phenobarbital, I went out into the waiting room and bawled. A husky woman with an overweight pug crossed the room and put an arm around me, saying, "Oh, honey, I'm sorry. Was it your dog?"

"No," I sobbed, my face in my hands, "it was my chicken."

Before we'd left Los Angeles for the summer, John's colleagues asked if he was willing to come back in the autumn for another year with the company. I was happy to do it. I loved living in the Hudson Valley, but in certain ways, living in Los Angeles was easier. It might seem counterintuitive to find the tumult of living in an enormous, clattering city easier than the tranquility of the Hudson Valley. But I spent much less time in a car in Los Angeles than I had living on the farm. In L.A., Austin could walk to school; in the country, his school was a half-hour drive from our house. In L.A., almost everything we needed, day-to-day, was in our neighborhood. In the Hudson Valley, the closest big grocery store was sixteen miles away. My friends in Los Angeles lived closer to me than my Hudson Valley cohort, which meant I could incorporate socializing into my workaday life without it feeling so disruptive.

We loved our house in the Hudson Valley, and we loved our house in L.A.; we were unbelievably fortunate. The house in L.A. was a mid-century bungalow designed in 1946 by architect Rudolph Schindler. It was on a drowsy dead-end street and had a view of the San Fernando Valley and a lawn on the roof of the garage. Its tidiness and its clever nooks and crannies made it feel more like a sailboat than a house. We converted the garage into an airy office for me, so I had an ideal arrangement for work—a space separate from the house but close to it. I sorely missed my New York friends, and I got a pang every time I thought about the sweep of our land there, the waving hayfields, the animals. Maybe we would be able to toggle back and forth between these two worlds indefinitely, savoring each one in its time.

With *Rin Tin Tin* finished, I was a little at loose ends. I turned my energies to working on *New Yorker* pieces. Someone sent me a clip about a tiger on the loose in a New Jersey suburb. I dove in. I profiled artist Brendan O'Connell, who set out to do a series of plein air paintings inside a range of Walmarts across the country, winning unlikely support from Walmart itself. At that time, I used a treadmill desk, and I walked while I worked. An editor at *The New Yorker* persuaded me to write about it, and I discovered a whole subculture of treadmill-desk aficionados who verged on fanaticism. The piece was published decades ago, and I am asked regularly whether I still use my treadmill desk. (I gave it up when we moved to a different house in L.A., where my office was too small to accommodate it.)

But what about another book? Richard nudged me about it now and then, and Jon Karp said he was ready for another whenever I was. But I wasn't ready. *Rin Tin Tin* had been such a battle. When I mentioned the idea of writing another book, a friend discouraged me. "You've already done it," she said. "Do you need to go through that again?" It did feel like something I'd *gone* through, an expedition that was emotional, professional, artistic. It made me grapple with the idea of immortality, which naturally beckoned the uncomfortable idea of mortality, more real to me than ever before. After all, I had given birth and lost my father in the course of completing *Rin Tin Tin*.

But creating a book is miraculous. You have no guarantees—there is no promise that your book will be printed forever—but books do have a quality of permanence, of foreverness, that you can't deny. That quality enthralled me. Writing a book made me feel I was scratching a mark on the smooth face of existence that would endure. I pinned my sense of mattering on creating books. I was lured by the same unattainable but irresistible figment that had enchanted so many of the people I had written about—Lee Duncan, Herbert Leonard, and John Laroche—all of whom had been determined to lick the ultimate foe, the acid wash of time, the inevitability of erasure, the hard fact that we come and go and may be little remembered.

Rin Tin Tin attracted readers who knew nothing about the character, who were discovering his story for the first time, as well as devotees, mostly early baby boomers, who had fallen in love with the 1950s television show. One of those happened to be the exceptional writer Nick Hornby, who reviewed it for *The Believer* so glowingly that I almost cried. Later, in a wonderful circular piece of happenstance, he was hired to adapt the book for a screenplay, after it was optioned by Amazon Studios.

Another fan was George R. R. Martin, the legendary author of *Game of Thrones*. Martin is a small, stout, elfish man whom you could mistake for a clerk at a head shop. I was struck a little dumb when we met, at a literary gathering—like most of the universe, I was addicted to *Game of Thrones*—but he immediately began telling me how much he loved my book and loved the character of Rin Tin Tin. Then, with a lift of his shaggy eyebrows, he said he had a great idea: He owned a bookstore and movie theater in Santa Fe. What if we screened a Rin Tin Tin film and held a weekend of Rin Tin Tin–related events at the theater? A month or two later, following a screening of *Clash of the Wolves*, he and I judged the one and only Santa Fe Rin Tin Tin Lookalike Contest. The contestants included several German shepherds; a few dogs that were, at best, shepherd-adjacent; and a lot of ringers—pugs, mutts, cockapoos, spaniels, and dogs that looked less like Rin Tin Tin than I did. Martin devised a cocktail for the occasion—he called it a Rin-Tin-Tini—which we downed while we awarded the trophy to a shepherd mix with a charming expression and one ear that flopped and rose at regular intervals, like one of those inflatable air dancers flailing in front of a used-car lot.

TWELVE

I didn't have a new book idea and felt like I never would. Maybe I was truly done writing books. I would write magazine stories that were manageable in size and ambition, and that would be that. To be honest, it would be easier. I would try to learn to push myself less, even be a little lazy. It didn't feel like a resignation. It felt like the lightening of a load, almost a relief.

When John and I returned to Los Angeles in September, I got a call from Ken Brecher, the head of the Los Angeles Library Foundation, which raises money for the library system. He asked me to speak at one of the foundation's sponsor lunches. As it happened, libraries had been on my mind. One of my events for *Rin Tin Tin* was in a public library. While walking through the building, I was struck by a contrary thought: Libraries were incredibly familiar, and yet I really didn't know anything about how they worked. My heart jumped. Here was a "hiding in plain sight" story, that perfect brew of deep recognition and unexpected mystery. How *did* libraries work? What did they feel like, day-to-day? And why did they have such a hold on our hearts—I mean, who doesn't love libraries? I was so excited by the idea of a book exploring libraries that I mentioned it to my publicist, who was at the event with me. Libraries are beloved, she agreed, but wouldn't a book documenting the workings of one be a little dry?

It did sound dry, and furthermore, I was set on the idea that I was done with books. Maybe libraries were a good topic, but not for me. I filed it away mentally along with a bunch of stories I'd considered but never done, stories about sourdough devotees, about a chef in Peru who was thinking of running for president, and a dozen others that had flitted through my mind but never come to be.

Not long after that, I returned to Los Angeles. Austin, now a leggy, saucy red-haired kid, was in kindergarten at the elementary school down the street. He came home one day and said he had a homework assignment to interview a public service worker. We talked about whom he should choose. I tried to imagine what municipal employee might interest a five-year-old boy.

"Why don't you interview a sanitation worker?" I said.

He thought for a moment and answered, "Why don't I interview a librarian?" And I thought: Wow, I'm such a good mother.

We looked up the location of the closest branch library. It was a few miles away, a white building with turquoise trim, a swooping roof, and a cramped parking lot you almost needed to fold your car in half to use. From the outside, the Studio City building looked nothing like the branch library I'd grown up visiting several times a week with my mother: The Bertram Woods branch of the Shaker Heights library system was a russet-colored brick building with a butterfly roof built in 1960. The moment Austin and I walked in, though, I was overcome with the chiming, almost physical sense of recognition. Some of it was the timeless ritual of a mother bringing a child to the library, which I had experienced so often with my mother, and now I was a mother bringing my son. But it was more, a sense of being swept back in time but also being out of time, being in library time, where everything lingered; where the sounds were as they always had been, the flicking of book pages and the hushed rumble of the book carts and the half-whispers of patrons at the reference desk. There were the same sturdy worktables that I remembered from my childhood library, and the same wide front counter, like a mother ship in this quiet sea. I was transported to an enchanted place in my memory, of being with my mother, of quickening at the sight of all these books, all these stories that could be mine. As poet Louise Glück wrote in her poem "Nostos," "We look at the world once, in childhood. / The rest is memory." Being in the library was a fusion of those two views, one original and intimate, the other memory.

But why was this memory so potent? I had many happy childhood experiences and many shared moments with my mother. This felt different, exquisite. It was as if my feelings about my mother and being young were distilled in the library itself. What about libraries was so special? My son did his interview, and we headed home, my mind whirring. What a great idea for a book, to examine why libraries evoke such emotion—perhaps the only public buildings that make us feel that we belong, that we are rich, that we can travel anywhere in our minds.

I resisted. I didn't see a narrative arc for the story. It was evocative and socially meaningful and deeply personal. But I didn't want to write another book, especially one that was so amorphous. A book about libraries would have to be someone else's to do.

I had begun noticing my mother slipping. She was in her late eighties, living in the house I'd grown up in, and until recently, she'd seemed younger than her years. She gardened ferociously, drove herself to do errands, and was chipper when I called her. She refused to move to a smaller house but finally agreed to have someone come in a few days a week to help. However, on one visit home, I noticed that her refrigerator was empty except for some mayonnaise and mustard. She was peevish when I asked her about it. She'd always had an overflowing refrigerator, a stuffed pantry, things she'd baked lined up on the counter. She said she hadn't had time to go to the store. I took her shopping, encouraging her to stock up on as much as possible, and made her promise she would go to the store when she needed more. On my next trip to Cleveland, I again found the refrigerator empty. This time she didn't try to excuse it; she simply didn't answer when I asked why she had nothing to eat. She had been a fastidious housekeeper, but now the house was dirty. I found stains on some of her clothes and took an armload to the dry cleaner. It was sudden and all at once, the realization that she was flagging, withdrawing from life because it had begun to puzzle her. Our phone conversations had seemed routine. But I began ticking through our last few conversations and realized with a sick thud that all she had really done on those calls was ask general questions and tell me about her garden, which she could see while she was on the phone. It was her prompt; it gave her something to talk about when she couldn't think of what to say. I had been too preoccupied to notice that the outlines of her world had drawn closer; I was too pained to admit to myself that she wasn't the same. I don't even need to tell you what a five-minute cognitive test revealed: the awkward handwriting that had taken the place of her immaculate script; the clock that the doctor asked her to draw a wobbling circle with no hands.

As my brother and sister and I fretted about what to do, the police found her wandering, directionless and confused, one day, and we knew she couldn't live alone anymore. We signed a lease on an assisted living facility run by a Jewish community group, where a few friends of hers lived. She certainly wouldn't go willingly, so we had to devise a scheme to get her into the facility. My brother and sister left it to me, my mother's favorite, to perform the script: I told her that we were going for lunch at a nice place out in the country, a place where some of her friends lived, just to look around. Over the previous week, her home care worker had surreptitiously packed up some of her clothes and personal items and took them to the blank little apartment so it might feel a bit cozier.

Our lunch was pleasant, but as had become her habit, my mother quickly grew impatient and said she was ready to go home. I wouldn't meet her eye. I saw panic flicker across her face, and she crumpled in on herself. I felt sick. I was panicking, too, undone by this wrenching dynamic, of holding my mother against her will. My mother. My champion.

My mother, who always cheered me on, who brightened to my voice, who told me regularly how proud she was of me. With whom I had also tangled furiously at times, resisting her possessiveness and insistence that I could never—should never—disagree with her or do things my own way. I was anguished. I fumbled for a moment and then asked her to wait a bit and let me finish my food. But she knew that I was fibbing and she bubbled up with tears. "We aren't staying here!" she whimpered. "I want to go home now. Take me home."

I stayed with her that night, resting fitfully on an inflatable mattress in the second bedroom of her apartment. Before she went to sleep, she perched on the edge of her bed for a long time, hovering there like a small prey animal that had been captured. My heart hurt more than at almost any moment in my life.

I returned to Los Angeles, shaken and sad. That fall, I spoke at the Los Angeles Library Foundation luncheon as planned. After the lunch, Ken Brecher asked if I'd ever visited the main branch of the library, Central Library, downtown. I hadn't, so he offered to give me a tour. The day of my visit was hot and dry. As I headed downtown, the spiky skyscrapers at the center of the city shimmered in the heat and haze. Even after a year, I felt new to L.A., fumbling as I drove from one end to the other, my eye constantly catching on an intriguing house, a shop, a shrub, an overlook. I felt so Midwestern, an Ohio girl gone wandering, shocked by the hulking mountains, the ripping waves at the beach, the knurled canyons and flattened valleys that fanned out to the edge of my vision. It seemed like infinity, the city barely secured to the landscape, merely tacked down here and there—a temporary assemblage that could wash away or be shaken apart or burn up or be lifted into that endless sky.

I was expecting the library to be a grand marble edifice, the typical central library of a big city. Instead, it was a curious, quirky structure built of tan stone, punctuated by dozens of small windows and a modest entrance. Everywhere I looked, there was a Juliet balcony or a terrace or a ledge or some other ornamentation, the whole thing rising to a pyramid tower clad in colored tiles and topped with an enormous bronze sculpture of a torch held in a huge, meaty bronze hand. The surface of the building had bas-relief stone figures on every wall: Virgil and Plato and da Vinci, woolly buffaloes and galloping horses, sunbursts and nautiluses, scrolls and wreaths and waves. Quotes about knowledge and learning, in English and Latin, were carved around the building like the crawl on the evening news. It was fantastic. Brecher led me through the library, pointing out each feature excitedly, as if seeing it for the first time. The library had been built in 1926, and it showed its layers of history; I could almost sense the decades of people who had passed through.

When we arrived at the fiction department, Brecher stopped in front of a bookcase and ran his fingers across the spines of the books, settling at last on one volume. He pulled it off the shelf, flipped a few pages, and then held it close to his face and took a deep whiff. He stood for a moment, then held the book out to me. Maybe this was the way people in Los Angeles appreciated books. Should I take it from him and whiff it, too?

He looked at me and said, "You know, you can still smell the smoke in some of them."

I asked if the library used to let people smoke near the books.

"No!" Brecher exclaimed, shaking his head. "From the fire. You can still smell smoke from the fire."

"The *fire*?" I asked. I had no clue what he meant.

"Yes, the *fire*," he repeated, clapping the book shut. "The big fire!"

"*What* fire?"

"The fire," he said. "The one that shut the library down."

As I soon learned, the arson fire, which occurred in 1986, was the largest library fire in American history. It destroyed 400,000 books and damaged 700,000 more. What was almost more astonishing was that I had never heard of it. It was both a story hiding in plain sight and a "Who knew?" It was an incredible story. Someone needed to write a book about it, and I knew—and was glad—it would be me.

As soon as I signed my contract for *The Library Book*, I called my mom to tell her the good news. She remained unhappy in her new quarters, but her determination to leave had lessened, or at least she seemed resigned. I knew she'd be excited that I was writing about libraries. "I'm the one who got you interested in libraries," she said proudly. I agreed. Even as her sense of direction and awareness of the world around her narrowed, the library was one of the last places she continued to visit. She used to tell me often, wistfully, that if she could have been anything in the world, she would have been a librarian. "You can still do it, Mom!" I always replied. "It's not too late!" She usually answered with a sigh, and that was all. The unattainable. She looked at the librarians at the Bertram Woods Branch Library as secular priestesses, wise and benevolent and all-knowing, able to summon up a thick book that would carry you wonderfully away.

How did I leap from my decision to stop writing books to embracing another one? Maybe my decision to stop writing them hadn't been staunch. Maybe I had just been tired after *Rin Tin Tin* and now I'd gotten a second wind. Maybe I was like a hit man returning for one last job, one that I convinced myself would be nice and simple, the settling of accounts. I did think the library and the fire was a manageable topic. Almost all the research was in L.A., and unlike most of what I wrote, this story had a narrative with a fiery climax; it had *plot*. Unlike "The American Man, Age Ten" or *The Orchid Thief* or *Rin Tin Tin*, it wouldn't be "that meandering *New Yorker* shit," as the character Charlie Kaufman complains in *Adaptation* when he can't figure out how to write a screenplay for *The Orchid Thief*.

When I first talked to Jon Karp about the book, I also made a completely foolish boast. I knew that someone had been arrested on suspicion of setting the fire, but he had been acquitted, so the crime was, at least in theory, unsolved. Maybe, I said to Karp, I'll solve it.

What I did solve, at least, was the question of where we would live. I figured it would take me a year to report the library story and perhaps a year to write it. It was our second year in Los Angeles, and we loved it. If we extended our stay one more year, I could polish off the reporting and then—well, who knew? We spent all summer in the Hudson Valley and felt attached there, but I wasn't sure I wanted to return for good.

When I began working on *The Library Book*, I assumed that the arson suspect, Harry Peak, was alive. He would have been only fifty-two years old. I found a phone number for a Harry Peak near Los Angeles, but it belonged to his father. From him I learned that Harry—his son, the Harry I was looking for—had died of HIV/AIDS in 1993.

I always remind myself that, in nonfiction, the story is in charge. Whatever you may expect it will be, wherever you thought it would take you, doesn't matter at all. The story goes where it goes. It's hard not to fight back when you find yourself immediately undone, your assumptions upended. But isn't that the mechanism of really seeing? The reorienting from what you expected to find, to what you are encountering? I believed that—I *preached* that—but learning that Harry had died was a rough shake, and I began the book knowing that the person I'd imagined would be the central character—from whom I'd hoped I would extract a fresh version of his involvement in the fire—was gone.

Very quickly, what I pictured as the singular thread of the story split into several strands. I wanted to tell the tale of the fire in detail, especially since it had been overshadowed in the news because, as I learned, it occured the same day as the meltdown at the Chernobyl nuclear plant, which dominated world news. But how could I explain the significance of the fire without exploring the value of libraries? And I couldn't tell the story of this fire without recounting the long, sad history of book burning and library fires, beginning with the Library of Alexandria. And what about arson itself? There was a lot to say about that. Also, I wanted to document life in the library today, to portray its daily tempo—the way books course through the system, the way its many employees do their jobs, the experience people have when they visit. That demanded a full-throated accounting, too, of the history of this one particular library, and how it came to be built, and the people who had been in charge of it over the years, and how it figured in the history of the city itself.

The story kept teasing me, beckoning me further into each segment. At first, I hadn't considered writing about the previous heads of the Los Angeles library system, who are given the official title of "City Librarian." I'd thought it was nothing more than an administrative job, without much color. But as I researched the history of the library, I realized I needed to include them, at least a short bit of biography.

I began with Charles Lummis, who ran the library from 1905 to 1910. Then I fell down a fabulous reporting wormhole. Born in Massachusetts, Lummis was a poet and a bohemian. He was working as a newspaper reporter in Ohio when he was hired by the *Los Angeles Times*. He decided to walk from Ohio to California. Along the way, he became infatuated with indigenous culture. He abandoned the conventional menswear of the day in favor of corduroy cowboy suits, suede boleros, and bell-bottom pants, topped by a Stetson sombrero. He was a passionate reader and writer: In addition to books and poetry, he wrote a magazine column for several years in the voice of a mountain lion. As head of the library, he commissioned a branding iron with a skull and crossbones and branded books he considered quack science with it. To make sure no one in the library ever felt lost, he created a position called the Human Encyclopedia, an individual who would roam the library and pounce on any patron who looked like they needed help. He hired his friend Dr. C.J.K. Jones, a collector of books about citrus farming, for the job.

How could I describe Charles Lummis in a paragraph? At one point, I even considered writing a biography of Lummis instead of a book about the library fire. He wasn't the only amazing City Librarian, either. There were pioneering pre-suffrage feminists, whiny hypochondriacs, and jazz-playing magicians, and they all begged for fuller treatment. Each one drew me in, and each one embodied its moment in time and the library's triumphs and traumas.

So now I had a story with a protagonist who had passed away and a lot of unexpected tributaries I wanted to travel. There are no easy books to write, but I had tricked myself into thinking this would be one. I would need to work my way around Harry Peak's absence, and I would let myself plunge into all these unexpected new veins. It would unfold the way it was meant to unfold; it would show me the way.

Bit by bit, I was losing my mother. Each time I visited, she was a little quieter, a little paler, a little less sure who I was. As she declined, she was moved from assisted living to a memory care unit, the section of the facility for those whose memories were beyond care. For the first time, I realized that one day she wouldn't remember me at all, but I didn't realize I was hurtling toward that day sooner than I knew.

As I was working on *The Library Book*, I threw my net as wide as I could, sometimes googling the word "library" to see what I would snag. One day I happened on a mention of a Senegalese expression used to express that someone had died: You say his or her library has burned. I didn't understand it at first, but I wrote it on an index card and hung it over my desk.

Finally, it happened. I flew to Cleveland for a visit, and as I drove to my mom's facility, I had a tightening in my gut, a premonition that this visit would be different. My mother, who until the last few years had had a sparky, even furious energy, refused to walk and was now a tiny, hunched figure in a wheelchair. Her hand worried the armrest in a repeated, distracted motion, and she gazed at me passively; I knew that the memory of who I was and what we had been to each other had slipped, like a hardcover book off a shelf into a smoldering pile, crumbling into a puff of ash, a wisp of smoke, a vanishing fragment. Her library was burning.

There is no pain like losing a parent, however it goes: fast, without a chance to say goodbye, or slow, in bits, where the farewell feels like a lingering ache. Losing my dad fast was a cold shock. Losing my mom in these tiny subtractions felt unbearably hard.

The book took on new meaning for me. I now understood why the loss of a library is such a collective sorrow: A library is our shared memory, the shared stories and wisdom of a community. A library isn't merely a municipal building, although it is that, too, and it isn't merely a valuable resource for books, although it is certainly that as well. Libraries are something more than that, something essential and emotional, the public soul. Maybe we recognize ourselves in them. The way our mind and memory function is library-like, a storehouse of individual volumes, each containing a thought or a dream or a sliver of knowledge, and we search through it when we seek to recall something or to savor a thought. I feel this keenly as I've gotten older, how sometimes I pull out a favorite recollection, a tidy booklet of a moment in time, and leaf through it, and then, satisfied, place it back on my mind's shelf, and how, even more vividly, I sometimes have to run my fingers along those shelves to remember something—a lost thought, a wayward word or fact. That Senegalese expression, once so puzzling to me, now seemed vivid and precise. It captured the way a person's death or memory loss takes with it a vast internal library, and how the disappearance of a library feels like a death to the people it serves.

The year I thought it would take to research the book stretched into two, and then three, and then four. I finally reached what I thought was almost the end. Then one day a librarian who had worked at the Los Angeles

Public Library for decades asked if I had looked at the boxes in the storeroom. I hadn't known these boxes existed. I had visions of Herbert Leonard's storage locker: the eleventh-hour cache that ends up transforming the book. And it did. There were volumes of material, including minutes from meetings of the library board in 1926, and flyers from the 1960s introducing "controversial" topics to library patrons (books about sex and drugs), and lists with recommended books spanning most of the library's existence, a timeline of social history. I broke out a new pack of index cards and continued. It was hard to complain when the material was so interesting. There was so much to read that I pressed John into service to help me go through it. We sat side by side at a worktable in the library for weeks, scribbling notes feverishly.

Each time I write, I search for the story or book's theme. The theme is different from the subject of the book, although it's obviously coupled to it. The theme is the bass line, the warm, low note that underscores the topic, which is the melody. I need to find the theme before I can write, although sometimes it evolves once I begin writing.

In *Saturday Night*, the theme was "specialness"—how we want to feel that one night of the week is special, to give shape and tempo to the rest of our lives. I touched on the idea throughout the book, and a reader might have deduced that I used it as the organizing principle. But mostly the theme was a tool for me, the foundation upon which I could rest all these individual stories and digressions and explorations. I was convinced readers liked surprises and sidetracks if they sensed that there was a unifying whole.

Rin Tin Tin was about immortality and the yearning for something to last forever, to beat back time and tide, to endure. The research had presented so many obstacles—disintegrating film, forgotten characters, dead subjects—that my search to overcome them and create something lasting with the book fell into step with all the characters I was writing about, who looked to Rin Tin Tin to hold time in place for them.

Now I felt like I knew what *The Library Book* was about at its core:

It was about the quintessence of memory. It was about Harry Peak, who desperately wanted to be remembered for something, even if it was something as terrible as burning a library. It was about how, throughout history, libraries have contained our shared intelligence, which was why we embraced them so dearly and why they'd been targets for tyranny, because destroying them was a statement of dominance, a whip hand on society to exert control. It was about recovering the story of the Los Angeles library fire itself: Because of Chernobyl, it had been a bit overlooked, so it bore retelling.

For me, of course, the book was also a chance to grapple with the agony of watching my mother lose her memory and feel myself erased from her consciousness; it was a chance to pin down, on paper, who she was and how she had taken me, all those times, to wander the library, looking for a portal into a new and wondrous world. It was about celebrating books as our most durable companions, our memories and stories and understanding written down forever, to outlast us and be the permanent reminder that we once inhabited this world.

When you are frail, the most banal infections become rapacious, greedy. My brother called and said our mother was in the hospital with a urinary tract infection that had taken root and wasn't yielding to antibiotics. I flew to Cleveland to see her. She looked so small in the cottony whiteness of the hospital bed, like a child. She didn't say anything, but she held my hand and patted my arm, her skin dry but so soft that it felt almost weightless, like a touch of a dream. I believed, irrationally, that if I remained there, by her side, I could will her to stay alive. I also knew without knowing that I might not see her again. I flew home at the end of the weekend, and my brother called me the next day and said she was flagging. I flew back to Cleveland, urging the plane to go faster, as if I were urging on a plodding horse, as if I could beat a clock that had been set by an unknown hand. I burst out of the jetway as soon as we landed and called my brother to say I was on my way to the hospital. He didn't say anything for a moment, and I knew I was too late.

The Library Book was released on October 16, 2018. I wish my mother could have been alive to see it. It would have meant so much to me to put it on her lap and tell her it was for her. She passed away February 6, 2016, a bleary, cold day. I finished the book without her.

John had urged me to hide myself away somewhere while making my final push to complete it, so in the middle of that winter, I packed my notes and a heavy wool jacket and headed to our place in New York. It had always been a family place, full of visitors and friends and animals. Empty, it had a slumbery, soothing atmosphere. We had a huge mahogany dining room table that seated sixteen. It was like a writer's fantasy desk. I could spread out my notes on the table rather than having them on the floor, where they invariably attracted the dog and cat. (I have pawprints on a few as evidence.) I went to the grocery store and stocked up so that I didn't have to leave the house for meals except the occasional dinner with friends. This might sound dreary, but it wasn't at all. It was a chance to fall deeply into the book, undistracted.

I knew I had great material, and I was confident about my structure, moving from my "snapshots" of the current life of the library, to the tale of the fire and the investigation and Harry Peak, to the history of the library and libraries in general, and then back. I had one unrequited desire, which was to convey somehow what it *feels* like to be in a library, how you let your eye roam over the shelves and are surprised by what you find. How could I express that in the book? My other ambition was to have some kind of repeated motif that stitched the sections together. I wasn't sure what that would be.

One night I was writing a short description of the Peak family. They had migrated from Missouri to California in the westward rush of the 1940s. I happened to have the Los Angeles Public Library's online catalog search page open on my computer. I made a wager with myself: I bet there weren't any books about migration from Missouri to California in the 1940s in the L.A. library collection. After typing the query in the search box, I was presented with a score of books on the subject. I had lost my bet, but I felt like I'd won. I loved realizing that other writers through the course of time had pursued the subject. Even more deliciously, I loved realizing that the L.A. Public Library had such a deep bench. I put another random search term in the catalog—knitting with pet hair, because why not? Again there was a score of results. I was obsessed. I kept throwing terms in the search bar and didn't strike out once.

It dawned on me that playing around in the catalog this way was a lot like the physical experience of being in a library. Even if you have your Dewey Decimal call numbers and know exactly where your desired book sits in the library, many other books will be revealed to you. There are the books you pass on your way to the book you want, and there are the books tucked around it, those kindred volumes that iterate on the subject, each a little different, or newer, or older; endless variations on a theme, handed off from one book to the next, following the mysterious, marvelous path a thought traverses in our minds.

I had an idea: What if I walked the reader through the library at the start of each chapter? What if I dug out four or five books from the catalog that touched on themes within the upcoming chapter, listing them as they appeared in the catalog, and then, after a line break on the page, began the chapter, replicating the way you might come upon the chapter if it were a book in the library that you had sought? I love the device of a preamble, a brief overture before the main event. Sometimes it helps me write, giving me a ramp into whatever I'm writing. I don't always keep these preambles in the finished piece. For instance, when I was writing "Where's Willy?" my *New Yorker* piece about Keiko, I kept turning to *Moby-Dick* in my mind. I decided to introduce each section of the story with a sliver from that novel. In the end, David Remnick thought I didn't need the quotes from Melville, so we excised them. I missed them—who doesn't like a bit of *Moby-Dick*?—but I saw his point. But having them in the working document had helped me write the piece, almost as if they were cue cards.

I loved this card-catalog idea. I decided to put it on the page to see if it made sense. Since I was working on the chapter about the Peak family, I looked for titles that would hint at what the chapter was about. I looked for a few older titles, to demonstrate the incredible breadth of the library's holdings. I found *All About California, and the Inducements to Settle There*, a book by the California Immigrant Union published in 1870; and then *Migration and the Southern California Economy*, from 1964. I liked the way the listings of these books, with their call numbers, looked at the beginning of the chapter, like found art, documentary footage. My editor and I had already settled on calling the book *The Library Book*, and planned to have the cover resemble a quintessential library book; it was winkingly meta but also entirely the point. The catalog listings fit that design scheme perfectly.

I began searching the catalog for books to introduce other chapters. My options seemed endless. For the chapter on burning books during war, I found a book by Joseph Goebbels, the architect of the Nazi regime's book burnings, and a more recent collection called *The Holocaust and the Book: Destruction and Preservation*. For the chapter that included the story of a city librarian, Tessa Kelso, who was fired after she purchased a controversial book for the library, I discovered that the book in question remained in the library's collection, so I was able to include it at the start of that chapter: *Les Caresses* . . . which was written by Jean Richepin in 1921.

I was sure it worked. I'd managed to do the two things I hadn't really thought were possible: to give the reader the sensation of being in the library while reading the book, and linking the pieces of the story into a harmonious whole.

There were perils in writing a book about libraries. As much as we love them, we also picture them as hushed, sober places. Would anyone be willing to take a chance on reading such a book? Would they put aside their assumption that the book would be boring, and take a look?

Unlike fiction, in which the author is the sole expert on the world he or she has created, nonfiction pits the writer against the authorities in the field. When you write about a factual subject, you have constituents who may or may not welcome you to town. When I wrote *The Orchid Thief*, I knew I would be challenged by orchid devotees who would feel I'd trespassed on their turf and that I was less knowledgeable than they were. It was true. I'd ventured as an outsider into a subculture and didn't have the expertise they did. But I was confident in who I was: an explorer, visiting a subculture to glean as much understanding as I could, with the great advantage of having only curiosity and no stake or agenda that might cloud my view.

There are 146,000 librarians in the United States, and thousands more worldwide, plus thousands of retired librarians. There was Wyman Jones, who had been the City Librarian at the time of the fire. He was blustery and arrogant, the authority on libraries and on the Los Angeles library system in particular, even though by the time I interviewed him he had been retired for many years. He told me that he wouldn't talk to me because he was planning his own book about the fire, but then he proceeded to keep me on the phone for an hour to share his opinions and reiterate that he had no intention of letting me interview him. Librarians are a mighty cohort, and I was attempting to define and describe a world they knew well. Would they feel I'd gotten it right? What about the other players in this saga, each of whom was an authority on their portion of it? There were the firefighters who fought the library fire and the arson investigators who studied it. There were scholars specializing in the history of Los Angeles. There was Harry Peak's family.

They all knew their story better than I did. What distinguished me if it was not authority? What I had, which they didn't, was omniscience. I had the birds'-eye view. I had identified a focal point—the fire—and tracked it three-dimensionally, examining it like a gem from every angle and then seeing it as a whole. I didn't need to compete with those other perspectives. I could stake my claim on what I did have: the voyager's openness, the viewpoint from above, the alchemist's desire to bring it all together into something surprising and new.

I wanted librarians to embrace it, and even though the book received reviews I could only have dreamed of, the approval that made me happiest was hearing from so many librarians telling me I had gotten it right. They told me they felt honored, which they clearly deserve, but as municipal employees working in a quiet profession, that honor is something they don't often feel. Everything about publishing *The Library Book* was happy-making. And there was no eleventh-hour marital turmoil, no dropped shoe, no heartbreak. John cheered me on through the whole long process, even when I was distracted or anxious or neglectful or tired or cranky. The book was a beautiful object; it seemed important to have a book about books be a celebration of the literal thing itself. I did most of my book tour events at libraries, starting with an appearance at Central Library in a room that had been gnawed by flames three decades earlier. I felt grief at my mother's absence, but she would have been happy to know that I also did an event at Bertram Woods Branch Library, which I will always, forever, think of as our branch.

THIRTEEN

The Library Book kept me busy for months. I spoke at libraries in Tulsa, Calgary, Boston, Chicago, Denver, San Diego, and so on, crisscrossing the country several times. But amid the excitement was the fact that the downslope of publishing a book can be flattening. It's exactly like being postpartum: All the energy you had mustered for years to arrive at this point suddenly dissipates. The book exists. It's a marvel, but it also has earthly proportions. It is no longer the unfathomable achievement that, in its previous disembodiment, could seem perfect in your imagination.

I have a puritanical belief in the curative properties of work. I knew the solution to feeling postpartum with *The Library Book* would be to get busy again. I started researching a *New Yorker* feature about the "consignment managers" who gather designer clothes for the Real Real, a resale website. I also cooked up an idea for another book. From the beginning of my career, I have written about animals. I love them, so I'm attuned to stories that include them, and I'm inclined toward writing about them. And animals make great subjects. I'm interested in how we coexist with them, how we've incorporated them into our lives, dominated them, fallen in love with them, depend on them, are frightened by them and awed by them. I'm equally interested in how they put up with us. Coexisting with animals is the equivalent of having Martians land on Earth—complicated, sophisticated, mysterious Martians we can't entirely understand but to which we are ineluctably drawn.

I've written about cats, whales, chickens, cattle, oxen, tigers, and lions, among other creatures. Obviously, I wrote an entire book about a dog. Some years ago, *Smithsonian* magazine offered to send me anywhere in the world to write a piece. I opted to write about a veterinary hospital in Fez, Morocco, that treats the town's large population of working donkeys. One of my favorite *New Yorker* projects was writing about mules in the U.S. military, and in particular, about a harebrained scheme in 1987 to ship twelve hundred mules on a Boeing 747 from Sumner County, Tennessee, to Islamabad, Pakistan, to aid in the war in Afghanistan. The U.S. military still uses mules, particularly as pack animals in harsh terrain, so in addition to writing about the Tennessee fiasco, I went to the Marine Corps Mountain Warfare Training Center in the Sierras, where the mule corps is located, and spent time with soldiers there.

My two previous collections were organized around themes. *The Bullfighter Checks Her Makeup* included "The American Man, Age Ten" and profiles I'd written of Bill Blass, Tonya Harding, and Cristina Sánchez, among others. *My Kind of Place* highlighted the idea of "place." Some pieces that I included were traditional travel stories, such as my piece about Bhutan and an account of my ascent of Mount Fuji. Others were more anthropological and cultural, like a story I did about an African music store in Paris, or "Rough Diamonds," about a Little League team in Havana.

I began to tally my animal pieces. It looked like I had more than enough to make a book. My editor was eager for it, so I compiled them and began fine-tuning. We kicked around titles for ages and finally settled on the simplest and most natural: *On Animals*.

In the meantime, I kept up a steady schedule of speaking engagements. In January 2020, I was booked to give a lecture in Denver. Buried in the news were stories about a flu outbreak in Wuhan, China. The reports were then revised: It wasn't the usual flu. Revised again: A first case was recorded in the United States. And again: A few more people infected with this virus that nobody recognized. Unease drifted in and settled, like a light snow. My sponsors in Denver warned that more than a hundred people had canceled for the lecture. When I arrived, gallon bottles of hand sanitizer were stationed around the room, which was the only thing anyone could think to do.

The night before lockdown, we went to a little sushi restaurant with our friend, the food critic Ruth Reichl, who was in Los Angeles for a visit. The tables were inches apart; the dining room was nearly communal. Ruth fretted about how she could get back to New York and whether it was better to fly or to drive. I wondered if the whole virus thing might blow over in two or three weeks. Really, what could I know? How could I have known this was the last time we'd be in a restaurant for months?

Then it was a runaway train. Except for a scattering of events, my book tour for *On Animals*, which was to be a hopscotch of twenty cities, was canceled. Schools closed. Austin, now in middle school, sat in his bedroom and stared disconsolately at a blank computer screen. His teacher appeared as a cube talking into the ether, like a first-generation video game. We bought masks. I looked for cute patterned silky ones, not yet aware that they did practically nothing.

In 2021, in the gloomy throes of Covid, I got a call from my film agent, telling me she'd gotten a note from the staff of an HBO television show complimenting my work. Evidently, they had read *Saturday Night* and used it as a sort of model for their first season. That night, I planned on watching one episode of *How To with John Wilson*, because I'd never seen the show, but I liked it so much that I binged most of the season.

The next day, my agent asked if I was open to having a Zoom call with John Wilson, the show's creator, and Michael Koman, who executive-produced (along with Nathan Fielder and Clark Reinking). It was a lively call. John showed me his dog-eared copy of *Saturday Night*, and we talked about how all of us loved nonfiction—the adventure of it, the serendipity that makes you sometimes feel you're just along for the ride. Wilson asked if I had any interest in consulting on the show, and I said yes. A few days later, my agent called to say they'd proposed instead that I join the writing staff for season two.

There aren't many television shows with which I have felt immediate fraternity. When I was a kid, I watched Charles Kuralt on CBS News and was jealous of his wanderings, his apparent freedom to choose a place and turn his lens on it. But most nonfiction television felt prosaic—a crime documentary, a toothless travel piece, a history study. On the other hand, *How To with John Wilson* was wild. It was found art, a series of oblique inquiries that were never about the nominal topic but, rather, about odd adjacencies in life. When we worked on an episode called "How to Appreciate Wine," John began by telling the writing staff that he didn't want any wine information in the episode. Occasionally, people described the show as goofy because it wandered into so many irregular situations, documenting so many unorthodox conversations and people, but I saw it as affectionate and heartfelt, a tribute to individuality and eccentricity and the possibility of staying surprised even in your own backyard. John Wilson and Michael Koman were in New York. Perhaps in ordinary times, they would have assembled the writing staff there, which would have made it impossible for me to work on the show. Because of Covid, the writing room was on Zoom, and we could all work from wherever we were.

So this was my pandemic: Three days a week, I logged on to the *How To with John Wilson* Zoom at eight a.m. and spent the day online with the show's writing staff. There were usually two or three other writers, plus John and Michael and me, pounding out ideas. It was not an easy task. While the show was nonfiction, it was paced and plotted. Each episode combined footage that John and his camera crew had already captured with ideas the writers proposed, organized very loosely around a lesson about how to do something. Each episode was revised in the editing room once again, so the result often bore little resemblance to the outline we created.

The show documented John's own curiosities, so the writers somehow had to channel him and his interior world. We began by brainstorming "how to" topics: how to appreciate wine, how to wash your clothes, how to train your dog, how to park your car. Sometimes we were stumped and sat for long minutes staring at the checkerboard of Zoom faces. Everyone on the show was smart and funny. The usual staff included Conner O'Malley and Alice Gregory. Once or twice, Nathan Fielder joined the Zoom and said hello.

This was my first time in a writers' room, and I enjoyed the contrast to my usual solitary work life. Sometimes I wondered why I hadn't chosen a career in Hollywood, since I loved collaborating, but I knew my truer nature was to venture out on my own. Zoom was hardly the typical experience of a writers' room. There were no cheese platters and boxes of doughnuts and no drink dates after work. Because of the strange, stultifying nature of being online, especially for so many hours straight, it could feel draining and effortful rather than fun. But didn't everything feel that way during Covid? I capped my nights off by watching Trump's daily news conference with John and Austin, wondering where the world was heading as the weeks ticked on.

Midway through that awful year, Austin was in such despair over doing school online that we looked for alternatives, and he landed on Bard Academy, a program affiliated with Bard College, on its own campus in Great Barrington, Massachusetts. I didn't want him to leave, but this would allow him to do classes in person, so as much as I knew I would miss him, we got him ready to go.

A few years ahead of schedule John and I became empty nesters. I had not given this phase of my life much thought, because I assumed I had three more years of hands-on parenting. My views on empty nesting were formed primarily by a television commercial I remember from some years back, in which parents send their kid off to college with weeping and wailing and wringing of hands, but the minute the kid leaves, they race into his bedroom, pitch out his furniture, rip down his heavy-metal posters, and turn the room into a plush home theater.

I never pictured myself celebrating at all. If anything, I was bereft. Parenting had wiped out my sense of time: One minute I was buying maternity pants, and the next minute my son was demonstrating how easily he could pick me up and hold me five feet off the ground. It made no sense. I never fully adjusted to the notion of me as a parent, and now it felt like a job I'd held without noticing, and already I was being retired. Because of Covid, we couldn't visit campus, and after he arrived in January, Austin had to stay on campus until school concluded in May. For the first few weeks after he left, I wandered around the house in a daze, not sure what to do. My life had shifted momentously. I needed to remake it anew.

Ever since we'd moved to Los Angeles, we left town in June and relocated to our farm in the Hudson Valley until the end of summer. This Covid year, we didn't know what to do. Should we fly? Flying seemed like something to be done only in emergencies. But driving seemed perilous, too. We finally decided that we would drive with our dog and cat and try to interact as little as possible with other people. We spent our first night in Las Vegas, in a hotel that was peculiarly empty, bearing what would become familiar hallmarks of the pandemic: Lucite dividers at the reception desk, yellow plastic "safe distancing" footprints on the floor.

We crossed the country hurriedly, dashing into fast-food outlets to grab a sandwich and run, registering in vacant hotel lobbies as fast as we could. We drove like maniacs, as if we were outracing a tornado, arriving at our farm winded and relieved to be home. Was it home? We had been in Los Angeles since 2011 and had hardly noticed how much time had gone by. Without knowing when the pandemic would ease, the effort to manage these two places seemed herculean, especially because it required travel that suddenly seemed menacing. I had been in the Hudson Valley since 1990; it was as close to a home as I had. In L.A., I continued to picture myself as a newcomer, forgetting to call highways "the One-Oh-One" and "the Five" the way locals do. I didn't have the deep well of memories that felt foundational, although, like layers of lacquer, they were accumulating slowly, taking on the gloss of time.

We pushed the question aside. Covid made everything seem in the moment, since it so little resembled the past and raised so many questions about the future. I weeded the garden and swam in the pond and wrote and dallied on Twitter and drank cocktails to while away the last half of each day.

Our place abutted a beautiful farm belonging to Eliot Spitzer, the former governor of New York. He was a great neighbor, and we had dinner together now and again. He called one day to say that one of his horses had foaled and invited us to come see the baby.

I did not set out to become the patron saint of pandemic drinking, but it seems to have turned out that way. It began with the horse. The barn smelled warm and milky. The mare obliged us by stepping to the back of her stall so we could see the foal, who was dark and damp. I squealed when I saw him because he was so perfect. He nuzzled each of us in turn, skittering back to his mother when he finished. He returned for another sniff, and when he got to me, he nosed at my hand and then tried to suckle my thumb. Damn, I thought, he's not even a day old, and he has already learned the meaning of disappointment.

Eliot invited us to have a glass of wine. It was a day shimmering with heat, and I had been working all morning and hadn't eaten anything. His wife, Roxana, brought a platter of sushi and placed it in the middle of the table, where it was punished harshly by the sun. Several bottle-green flies, sensing an opportunity, dive-bombed the platter. Everyone was giddy about the foal, so we were in cheery moods. Anything life-affirming in this bleak time warranted celebrating.

The rosé flowed. I knew I should line my stomach before drinking, but I didn't like the looks of the sushi sweating in the sun. We talked and talked and drank and drank; the sun slid around in the sky; the horses nickered in the distance. We sat there for close to two hours, enjoying the day. When we got up to leave, I discovered how drunk I was. Up until then, my all-time record of drunkenness had occurred when I was in college. On that occasion, I was wearing a clown costume I had borrowed from a friend, and much of it disappeared to parts unknown that evening. This felt like a close second.

I mumbled goodbye and took John's arm in a death grip to be sure I made it to the car. I felt like I was wearing a sandwich board sign saying I AM DRUNK, although no one blinked an eye. When we got home, I said I was going to bed. It was perhaps seven-thirty p.m., well before my usual bedtime, but I figured I should end the evening early. I heaved myself into bed and let the room rotate a bit. After a moment, I started worrying that the Spitzers would think I was an idiot. I lay in the dark fretting. From the rumbling in the hall, I knew that John and Austin and my stepson and his wife were watching a movie, which inexplicably filled me with indignation, as if their movie-watching were a personal insult. Then I decided I didn't want to be with them: I just wanted my cat. Though Leo was affectionate, he rarely submitted to anyone's bidding. I knew calling him would be fruitless, and I gave up.

My phone was on my nightstand. Lying sideways in the dark, I decided to console myself by posting on Twitter. I typed out "Drunk" and posted it. The tweet racked up over ten thousand likes, although I noticed this only the next day. I'm a good typist and fussy about typos, and even on social media, I am always fastidious about spelling and grammar, but tonight was an exception. I sloppily tapped on the keyboard whatever came to mind. I was furious at the cat for abandoning me and annoyed at my family for enjoying a movie without me, and I couldn't stop thinking about that exquisite foal and what was surely his disillusionment with my milkless thumb, and how somehow all the innocence in the world seemed lost. I thought I could say something meaningful about it, so I tweeted:

> Ok a newborn colt rocks it totally and he thought my hand was his mom. It was not. He has tasted life's infinite tragedy. As I mentioned Earlier I am inebriated.

And then:

> BTW where exactly is my fucking cat whe
> I need him

I was hungry. I staggered to the kitchen and opened the refrigerator. During Covid, I had adopted the national pastimes of baking bread and making yogurt. There was a pot of fresh yogurt in the refrigerator, but I couldn't remember making it.

> i@had no idea I made yogurt today. Wow.

I tiptoed through the living room. Engrossed in the movie, no one looked up.

> No one on my house is talking to me right
> Now ok!! YeH whatever I hzte you too

I flopped back into bed. After a moment, John appeared in the doorway and asked if I was okay. "Of course I'm okay!" I snapped, turning over in bed. "Go away!" He explained gently that a few people had texted him, asking if my Twitter account had been hacked. I was outraged, the way only a drunk person can be outraged—idiotically, inconsolably, irrationally. I could not have been less hacked!

> Maybe I am drinking too much during THE FUCKING PANDEMIC

Followed by:

> I have SO NOT BEEN HACKED

John went back to the movie. I remembered again that I was hungry, but I didn't want dinner. I just wanted some chocolate candy. Puzzlingly, I first tweeted something angry about recycling, and then I announced that I was going to look for candy, "which I bet doesn't exists l. This house godd@@ Min it." I sneaked out of the bedroom and poked around in the kitchen, where the evening's second—or third, if you count the foal's—disappointment occurred. We had no chocolate in the house. We had nothing that would be considered candy except some sugar-coated fennel seeds I'd bought at an Indian grocery.

> Having l f the stupid fennel seed candy because
> I ha e no options

No candy, no cat, intoxicated, and the source of a newborn colt's baptism into life's pain and sadness: I'd had it.

> WHO IS SICK AND TIRED OF EVERYTHING

I tweeted a little bit more over the next hour or two, and then, exhausted and dizzy, I fell asleep. I hadn't watched the likes or comments piling up; I was letting off steam and feeling like I was writing notes to myself.

The next morning dawned fresh and bright and full of promise. My eyes were glued together with the grit and glue of sleep, but I eventually stirred. I had a nagging feeling that I had been a little uncensored the night before, but I was pretty sure that the only thing I had slandered had been fennel seeds.

I was perhaps a little sheepish, and very hungover, and I guessed that I had surprised a lot of people who knew me, or at least who followed me on Twitter, by tweeting as wildly as I had. I was surprised to get calls from the press about the episode. When I checked Twitter, I realized how viral it had gone, and I was astounded. I knew how social media could have a multiplying effect once it was jump-started. A few years earlier, I'd profiled the young men behind the Twitter account @Horse_ebooks, who posted fragments of text from promotional ebooks that, out of context, had the disjointed, portentous quality of Zen koans. The account became an Internet phenomenon and inspired incredible passion. ("Everything happens so much" was one of @Horse_ebooks' most popular tweets.)

Evidently, that woozy night, I accidentally captured some widespread feeling of outrage, exhaustion, annoyance, discontent, hysteria, mania, worry, and the desire for candy. Maybe the drumbeat of bad news that year made everyone want to guzzle rosé and rant about life's small and large indignities. Maybe the performative nature of public life, the artificiality of what we usually encounter, made this moment of off-script ranting by someone with a somewhat public profile seem refreshing. Covid taxed us mightily. Perhaps anything that lifted that load, even for a brief time, seemed refreshing, a crisp breeze in a suffocating time. I was glad to have lifted it that night. The Spitzers saw the tweets and let me know that, despite my drunkenness, I had comported myself politely, and that I could come over for a glass of wine anytime.

By the end of the summer, John and I knew the inevitable. We simply couldn't keep managing two houses so far apart as the uncertainty about Covid persisted. We listed our Hudson Valley house and sold it to the first people who saw it. Our long chapter there was done.

We went back one more time to clear it out for the new owners. It was a hard goodbye. I'd always dreamed that someday I would have animals around me—in the house, in the yard, watching me in the garden, dotting the landscape, crowing in the morning, lowing in the moonlight, barking at the wind—and I had experienced that there. I had reveled in the animals' friendship and their mystery; the way they were so obvious and so unknowable; their colors and textures, their fur and feathers; the sounds and smells of their presence. I loved the way their needs set the rhythm of every day, and how caring for them felt so elemental. I had been so happy there. If working on my last few books had taught me anything, though, it was that memory persists, that memory is real, so my happiness there, while it might not have been continuing, was a permanent part of who I was. I made my way through the trees and across the fields, around the pond and over the hill. I passed the bare patch of ground where my chicken coop had been. On my last walk, I collected a few things that would remind me of the farm forever and perhaps betoken some place in my future that would feel the way it had: a chunk of quartz, a pine cone, a chicken feather, a knob of moss.

When Covid roared in, *The New Yorker*, like most media outlets, focused on covering it as thoroughly as possible. I felt all thumbs: I didn't have any science or public health knowledge, and the magazine didn't want us traveling more than was absolutely necessary, so I'd have to figure out a story I could manage from Los Angeles if I wanted to contribute to the effort. I had no ideas, nothing that came at the subject in a way that wasn't already being done to death. One day my stepson, Jay, mentioned that he hadn't been able to take his pet rabbit to the veterinarian because the clinic, which specialized in rabbits and small mammals, was temporarily closed. He said he had heard that some virus had killed several rabbits boarding at the clinic, and the facility was closed so it could be sterilized.

The word "virus" stuck in my head—after all, we were living in a virus-dominated world. I did some quick research and learned that the disease, rabbit hemorrhagic disease, was highly contagious, usually lethal, and spreading around the world. It had originated in China and traveled globally through the trade in rabbit meat and fur, as well as live rabbits. Its eerie parallels to Covid made it seem a perfect story for the moment. I had never given much thought to rabbits, but the research fascinated me. They are the only animal we keep both as pets and as food. They occupy a peculiar liminal place, culturally and socially and zoologically. That this virus was spreading around the world made it a perfect story for the time.

It was also the first story I'd ever done entirely from my desk. I have always counted on getting my hands right on a story; meeting my subjects face-to-face and attending events or gatherings to get a sense of the story, the way it feels, the way it looks. When I started "The Rabbit Outbreak," I looked for rabbit shows I could attend and rabbit owners I could meet, then remembered the world was locked down. Could I write a story vividly while sitting at my desk? My experience writing books that contained a lot of history was good training. I had to find material and conduct telephone interviews that gave texture and immediacy, since I wasn't going to get it in person. Given the choice, I would always rather experience something firsthand, hear it and smell it and see it for myself, but writing that piece confirmed that if I scrape together the best details however I can find them, I can put together a story that sings.

It was a season of dark thoughts, nightly death tolls, risk assessment, masks, somber moods. That summer, David Remnick asked if there was a column I wanted to write for the magazine, and I blurted out, "Obituaries." It was an idea of the moment, this grim moment, but it was also one that wasn't out of the blue for me. I'd read obituaries since I was a kid, marveling how each one was a little capsule, a story contained wholly. Even if the person hadn't done anything momentous or celebrated, an obituary honored them. Everyone was someone's son, someone's daughter. Often they were someone's parent, someone's boss, someone's employee.

They were good at something, proud of something; they discovered a groundbreaking drug or had a great pie recipe or "enjoyed crossword puzzles" or were the founder of something. Death was the great leveler and the great magnifier. It came for everyone, and when it did, it picked out each bit of your life that was distinct and lifted it up: Here was your true measure at last, here was your mark on the world. What was more, I had reached a critical marker of my own age. I used to read obituaries and marvel at how old the people were. Now I read them and marveled at how young they were. What had changed was me.

I planned to find the recently deceased subjects who were distinguished in some way but also weren't the kinds of luminaries to merit an obituary in *The New York Times*. I laughed at myself as I began, realizing how consistent I have been in my interests after all these years. Here, once again, I was exploring the idea of commonality, like I had in *Saturday Night*; the drive to fight the dim gloom of obscurity, as I'd explored in *Rin Tin Tin*; the yearning to master something, to have intense focus, as I had explored in *The Orchid Thief*. As usual, I was intrigued by how a small life, when sympathetically examined, could burst, effloresce: its simplicity opening into a complex and astonishing tale. I believe this; I believe it completely. I inhabit the world believing this, and I'm rewarded by it, because every encounter feels freighted with enormous, exhilarating possibility, the promise that I might learn something amazing, that I might meet someone who will tell me something I didn't know.

I started preparing to do the column late that summer, scrolling through the listings on Legacy.com and poring over the obituaries in local papers around the country. I read of the passing of bank presidents and truck drivers and homemakers and restaurant owners. It was a somber undertaking, broody but moving: These were only names to me, but they were a world to the people who knew them, and I thought back on that lesson from the Talmud about each person containing the universe and how, when that person is gone, their individual universe stops spinning. It was the one argument with existence that you could never win.

One morning John and I were having coffee and watching the fog thin as the air warmed. My phone rang, startling me. It was my former sister-in-law, Brenda Sistrom, who is married to Peter's brother Chris. She and I had been dear friends during my marriage to Peter, and we had remained friends even as my marriage ended. It was a great friendship on its own merits, and it also offered a thread connecting me, however tentatively, to Peter. I had not seen him, not been in the same room with him, not heard his voice, since our last session with the lawyer finalizing our divorce agreement in 2000.

I had stayed friends with all my old boyfriends, even though the original relationship had withered away. We had faced the world together for a while, and even if that had ended, I liked knowing we would always hold each other dear. But Peter would have none of it. He was an absolutist: When it was over, it was over. There was no friendship to be fished out of the rubble, no Christmas or birthday greetings to be exchanged, no phone calls or cups of coffee every few years. The only news I ever got about him came from Brenda or from the one friend who had remained in touch with both of us. I sent Peter an email when Austin was born, and when my father died. For some reason, I felt that I needed him to know about these watershed events; it was almost a reflex. His responses were polite but final, clearly not encouraging further conversation. He never sought me out. Even though we both lived in New York after our divorce, I never bumped into him, never ran into him at a party, never saw him on the street. I assumed it would happen eventually, so I rehearsed how I would act when I saw him, with all this bad road between us. But it was a one-act play that never had an opening night. Now that I lived in Los Angeles, the chance of it happening was slim to none. And yet I never stopped feeling that someday, at least once, I would see him again.

"Susan," Brenda said, the phone crackling lightly, "Peter died."

I lost my breath. My entire body started to pound, as if my heart had consumed my limbs. I was dazed. I felt like someone had recited a math problem to me and I couldn't make sense of it and didn't even understand if I was to add or subtract or multiply. She kept talking, and I caught bits of what she said: out for a run, had just dropped his son at college, didn't have his cell phone, not sure yet but probably a heart attack, wanted you to know right away.

"I don't know what to say," I stammered. "I don't know what to say." It was the first time I could remember struggling to find a word for how I felt; I could not. I didn't know the word. Shock, certainly, but acute pain, and then something eerie, a feeling like I wasn't entitled to any feeling; who was I, now, to claim any feeling about this? I felt angry, too: robbed. I always pictured a moment in which we would see each other and, with the buffer of all these years apart and lives that had gone on with new spouses, children, new jobs, new social lives, that we would at last be friends, or friendly, or at least acknowledge that there were memories we shared that belonged only to us and to no one else. I didn't want an apology from him about the things he'd done that hurt me, nor did I picture offering him an apology for ways I'd contributed to our ruin. All I yearned for was some confirmation that those memories existed and mattered, because otherwise they were a broken circuit within me, as if I had the lock but not the key. Closure wasn't really what I wanted: I knew there would never be a tallying of accounts or an attempt to find the sum of our life together. It was more like there had been a sound—a keen, high tone coming from my younger life—and I wanted to know that he'd heard it, too. That we had heard it together even though it had ceased. Now there would be no such reckoning, ever. There would never be a recognition of how we had been the main characters in each other's lives for some time, until the story ended, and we went on our ways.

I have no wisdom about death and loss. I find the calculation itself baffling: The world contained a person and then suddenly it doesn't. Subtract one, solve for zero. How does that happen? Where do they go? Have they received a secret sign letting them know they will be leaving, and they're not allowed to tell anyone? I looked at some old notes from

Peter; maybe I could find the message there. But no. There was nothing profound, nothing coded; everything was predicated on the assumption that life goes on and on. How else could we live?

Maybe death is a dumb, blunt instrument that delivers no subtle message, and there is no secret whispered to you informing you it's time to go. I don't know if that's worse or better than thinking death has some intelligence and cunning. Either way, it punches a hole in your soul.

I started my obituary column, Afterword, in November 2021. I wrote about the death of the woman in charge of Table Talk Pies; the first wolf to make it to Southern California in decades, only to meet his fate on a highway overpass; the man who drew the original Keebler Elves; the first female magician to perform on the Vegas Strip. They were portraits in miniature, and I loved writing them, teasing out everything that made these subjects singular, even if their worlds were small and specific. I decided to include animals when their stories were interesting, and then I expanded to trees (I wrote an obituary for the tallest known tree in New York State, which fell that winter) and objects (the bankruptcy of the Instant Pot, once Amazon's bestselling item).

I had been unrealistic about how many obits I could write. Remnick wanted them often—ideally one a week—but even finding the right subject took time. Because I wanted to write about people who were not well-known, tracking down family members or friends who could speak about them was challenging. As soon as I finished one column, I had to begin work on the next without a beat in between. It was intense.

I got Covid in the spring of 2022 with its usual aches and pains, but after a week or so of dragging myself around, I recovered. That is, I mostly recovered. My rib-cracking cough would not go away. It persisted for weeks, getting more ragged all the time. I felt fine, except the cough left me shaken. It was more an annoyance than anything else, but I was exasperated and wanted it to stop.

In July, I had a pleasant distraction when I found out that an episode I'd worked on for *How To with John Wilson* ("How to Appreciate Wine") was nominated for an Emmy. An Emmy! We didn't win, but this was one of those times when the cliché that being nominated is as good as winning actually felt true.

My cough continued to dog me, so I finally went to my internist, who passed me along to a pulmonologist, who sent me for X-rays and thumped on my chest and told me he wanted a biopsy of my right lung. My annoying cough was morphing into an annoying set of doctor's appointments, but I dutifully booked the biopsy. I was more scared by the thought of a needle piercing my lung than I was of the possible results. In fact, I don't think I worried what the biopsy might reveal, because I was too distracted by the ickiness of the procedure.

I asked for lots and lots of anesthesia—redheads have a proven resistance to anesthesia and need more than most people—so I was numb as a rock and surprised by how fast the procedure was. I'm also surprised by how placid I was for the few days between the biopsy and when the doctor said he would have the results. What exactly was I thinking? I suppose I should be grateful that I had no preapprehension, no dread, of what I might learn.

My doctor called me. "It's cancer," he said.

Oh, I said, what does that mean, exactly? He spoke calmly, steadily: We will schedule surgery, we will take care of it, we will take care of you. Did I cry? Maybe a little, but my bewilderment blunted most of my ability to respond. Was it my occasional cigarettes at Cafe Un Deux Trois back in New York? Could it have been? I didn't remember if I'd ever bought a pack of cigarettes in my life; I'd bummed the few I'd smoked. No one in my family had contracted lung cancer. My grandmother had smoked unfiltered Camels until she died at ninety-two of causes having nothing to do with her smoking.

Of course, it doesn't matter how it happens; when illness comes for you, it comes unbidden and on its own terms, and you accommodate or else. Within a few weeks, I was in the hospital for surgery—brutal surgery with days of equally brutal recovery—and then months of a teeth-rattling ache in my ribs where the drainage tube had been. I met with an oncologist who was perhaps the most tender, pleasant person I've ever met. He seemed as pleased when my post-operative scans came back clean as if he'd been scanned himself.

For someone who is always looking for the telling detail, for the morsel of personal history that reveals a greater narrative, I suppose I should draw great meaning from having had cancer, some grand conclusion from the experience, but even now I don't. It was neither metaphor, nor simile, not a signifier or something signified. It was an unwelcome visitation, hustled out the door almost as quickly as it came, hopefully forever.

By this time, John and I had come to see ourselves as people who actually lived in Los Angeles, rather than people who were here for a year that had accidentally expanded into a decade. Selling the house in the Hudson Valley furthered that point. I loved being in Los Angeles, but I did appreciate the disadvantages: the knotty traffic, the dirty sprawl, the tragedy of thousands of unhoused people, the costs, the vagaries of an economy based on the fickle entertainment industry. Even the beauty of Los Angeles had its darkness. The sliding plates of earth had created dazzling mountains and also mighty earthquakes; the marvelous ribbed canyons funneled winds that could become treacherous; the clear, dry weather was fire's dearest friend.

The horrible fires of January 2025 came close to our house. The first outbreaks were far away, but any fire in California feels like a wicked Whac-A-Mole, ready to pop up somewhere new wherever you've smacked it down. Embers really do fly miles from their origin, and they do light new fires far from where they were first set ablaze; fire is canny in its capacity to find new fuel to consume. Despite the perception that Los Angeles is a disconnected jumble of small cities, the city is a cohesive entity, and a fire in Altadena registered with me at home in the Hollywood Hills as something to worry about, a terror in town.

By midafternoon of January 7, we knew of several friends whose houses in the Palisades had been vaporized; all that remained was the chimneys, poking out of the rubble like blackened goosenecks. We started walking around our house, figuring out what we needed to do in case we had to leave. We didn't really *do* anything; it was more to keep ourselves busy as we kept refreshing the fire department app and staring at the local television news channel, dry-eyed and panicked. We worried about our dogs, especially Ivy, our elderly spaniel, and we worried about our house, which is built entirely of wood and would light up like a lantern and be gone in an instant. Our house, built in 1946, is landmarked and is often regarded as R.M. Schindler's best work. Besides being our home, it's a piece of Los Angeles history that could never be replaced.

When the fires were in the Palisades, far west of us, and in Altadena, far east, they seemed remote. Then a fire started up the street. Our phones blared with an emergency alert from the city telling us to prepare to evacuate. The fire near us had grown and was given a name: the Sunset Fire. We packed dog food and our prescription medications and a few changes of underwear as a precaution. A few minutes later, our phones rang again, and an automated voice told us that we were now in a mandatory evacuation zone. We started to scramble.

I'd often wondered what I would grab if I had only a few minutes to leave my house, and I'd always been stumped. I imagined I would start with the jewelry I inherited from my mom, and then I'd stall: I couldn't think of what I'd take next. Everything seems important, and nothing seems essential. My books? My photographs? I thought if the moment really arose, I'd snap to it and immediately know what I'd take, but in the moment, under evacuation orders, I blanked out. I packed a warm sweater that I didn't particularly like and a shirt that I did. Then I couldn't make my brain work. In the last minute, I grabbed my iPad, and John got our passports and birth certificates. Austin, who was home on holiday break, packed respirators and emergency equipment and a six-pack of hard cider. We loaded the dogs in the car and drove to the home of friends who lived outside the evacuation zone.

We huddled around their computer, watching the news while John checked our security camera to see if our house was safe. Then the wind heaved and shifted, pushing the Sunset Fire in the other direction, away from our house. A pilot flew over and released gallons of water on the flames and snuffed them out. We breathed. Then another fire broke out down the street from where we'd taken shelter, and we faced the prospect of having to evacuate with our friends somewhere else. They started packing. None of us had raised the question of where, exactly, we were going. On the news, we saw that this new fire had been contained, and we could stay put. We ordered Thai food and spent the next few hours watching the news unspool, like a horror movie.

When the fires were finally dowsed many days later, an uneasy quiet settled over the city, like the invisible glassy simmer of a pot just taken off a burner. As I drove to the grocery store a few days later, jittery from what had transpired, I saw flames in the middle of Ventura Boulevard. A small pile of trash was burning in the left-turn lane—not merely smoldering but truly burning, with licking flames and dark gray smoke. I pulled over and dialed 911, my fingers trembling. In a minute, a fire truck seemed to materialize out of thin air, and the firefighters blasted the flames. As the truck drove away, traffic returned to its usual roar on Ventura, and the hot little pile, now a wet black splotch on the road, was flattened by the oncoming stream of cars. It had flared, it was extinguished: a blazing moment in time, a small drama, and then life rolled on.

I resisted the idea of even saying the word "memoir." I said I was writing "a book" that was "kind of a memoir," and I always said it sheepishly, my voice soggy with apology. Why was I so embarrassed? I blame it on the glut of memoirs in the last few decades, some written by people who seemed much too young to have experienced a full book's worth of memories, others so fraught with gut-spilling trauma that I worried I couldn't compete. I didn't want to heave mine onto that already teetering heap.

The other reason was heartfelt. I've spent my working life writing about other people. My desire was to illuminate their stories, and I simply didn't know how to turn that attention on myself; what's more, I wasn't convinced I deserved that attention. I've often been present in my writing, the tour guide leading the reader by the elbow, pointing out this and that. I was especially present in my books, even without my noticing or intending it. Each book answered a personal question or evoked a private memory I wanted to explore. I wasn't squeamish about using first person, but I always positioned myself as the narrator, a few steps offstage, rather than being the subject. Now I proposed myself as the subject, and I didn't know how to start.

I called my friend, the writer Manjula Martin, who interviewed me some years ago for her magazine, *Scratch*. She was precise and probing with her questions in a way no other interviewer had been. I asked if she would interview me for the sake of this project, this forgive-me-for-saying-it's-a-memoir, so that I truly would be the subject and would be able to hear myself explain myself out loud, the way I would have wanted from someone I was profiling. She and I began meeting regularly, talking for hours. Hearing myself speak, I began to notice the through lines and patterns of my life. In the end, I hardly consulted the transcripts of our conversations while I was writing, but they were the entry point for feeling I could tell my own story in my own voice.

My instinct to report and research is fundamental to how I write. What material can I read? Whom can I talk to? What should I explore to understand what I'm writing about? *The art of fact* is how I always viewed the work I was doing: even writing about myself, I needed facts. I thumbed through my books, looking for clues about how I crafted the stories and where they arose in the larger timeline of my life. My mother had maintained scrapbooks of my clips, beginning with my scant college newspaper output, and kept them current until she died. I leafed through them, surprised by stories I didn't even remember writing.

A few years ago, I arranged for my papers to go to Columbia University. Around that time, John and I were in the middle of moving out of our house in the Hudson Valley, and I was too busy to look through the stuff I had socked away over the years. When the Columbia library staff came to collect it, I instructed them to take everything out of my office, sight unseen. Now, trying to understand myself, I needed to know what it consisted of. I booked a week's worth of appointments at Butler Library and requested access to the Susan Orlean Papers. ("This collection documents Orlean's career as a writer and a journalist, and also includes some personal materials and school papers . . . address books, appointment books, audio recordings, clippings, computer files, contracts, correspondence, drafts, interviews, notes, notebooks, photographs, proofs, publications, research materials, school records, and video recording. 30.75 linear feet.") I went to New York twice to read through the papers. They surprised me, riveted me, amused me. Most of all, they made me savor the sheer, crazy good fortune I've had to have been able to do what I've done—to wonder about something or someone and then make it my task to learn about it, and then, just as miraculously, to have the job of telling other people what I've learned. Indexed and filed, these papers also felt somehow detached from me: "Box 24, Folder 3"; "Box 29, Folder 5." I saw them now as foreign documents, expired tickets to my travels in other worlds—these scraps of paper, jotted notes, messages from editors, tattered notebooks, tokens of my history, my autobiography.

As I noted earlier, I've always prided myself on writing good ledes. I'm a good tease, able to dangle enough in those first few sentences to tempt you to keep reading. I work hard at it because I know I often ask you to read things you didn't think you cared about. I'm comfortable playing to skeptics. I might even enjoy it a little too much: I take enormous, head-swelling pride in knowing I've lured you into a story you at first might have dodged. Writing about an obvious subject is fine, but writing about something unexpected, or even off-putting, and managing to charm a reader is intoxicating. It's what I've most enjoyed. My favorite compliment is probably a variation on "I never thought I'd read a book about orchids!" My task, always, is to override your misgiving, to keep you pinned to the page long enough that you fall in fully, and then you become as captivated as I am in this unlikely story, and when you emerge, you're pleasantly surprised and find yourself thinking about things you never thought you would think about. I want you to see that so much lying beyond what's comfortable or familiar is amazing—or at least worth appreciating. Our default, as humans, is to want to reinforce what we already know, so I realize what hard work my ledes have to do.

Conclusions, though, bedevil me. What are they supposed to accomplish? You've already followed me to the end of the story, so the act of seduction has succeeded; what do I do with you now? How do we say goodbye? It's confounding. Stories *do* have beginnings, but do they ever truly have endings? The real finale of the story, the terminus, is the end of my relationship with the reader. I've led you all this way, and now I'm setting you on your way; our journey together is done. The story doesn't finish—but our time together, yours and mine, does. That's the conclusion, that separation of storyteller and listener, the small sorrow of the journey's end.

My first significant editing experience at *The New Yorker* had to do with the ending of a piece. When Chip chopped off that wagging tail of a conclusion I had written at the end of my story about Benetton, I was dismayed. I thought it was like someone had stopped the action midmoment, the reading equivalent of inhaling sharply and holding it, holding it—and not letting it out.

After my initial shock at this excision, I read the piece again, and this time the abruptness felt right. Had I gotten used to the lingering note of the unfinished end? The way it left the reader falling forward, to complete the piece in his or her own head? I began to unlearn my habit of writing those summary upsurging conclusions, rehashing what I'd already written and then, effortlessly, trying to round out the story, complete it, give it ballast, make it *matter*. But does a story end because the journalist's eye has drifted from it? Can any of us set the seal on a story, ever? Should I tell you what a story meant, or is the point that you read it and then it's up to you to determine what it means? I've come to understand that no story is ever over, and it's the reader's duty and privilege, not mine, to take stock of the story and give it weight.

What began to appeal to me was to leave you with an incomplete melody that lingers in your head, in the air, in a way that feels beckoning, like an invitation to keep playing the story over in your mind. This propels the story forward, invisibly, internally, eternally, bouncing off the page into the boundless realm of imagination. It abandons the pretense that stories are mathematical constructs that have a final sum, because, of course, they don't. They can't.

This story here, the one I've just told you—it doesn't have a tidy resolution, either. It is a river journey we've taken together, and I've done my best to point out highlights along the way. See that rock outcropping? See that broken branch? See that whirlpool, that eddy, that cresting wave? See my failures, my triumphs, my heartbreaks, my joys? See my story? It will continue, off the page, into time, into a future I can't wait to meet.

Stories don't conclude, but they do have consequence. They are documents of our humanity, shimmering trails of time spent alive. Who we are, why we live the way we do, what we've loved, how we've managed, what we looked like, how we sounded, how we've faltered, what we've achieved: This is what these stories and books attempt to chronicle, what I've attempted to chronicle. The story of my life is the story of my stories, some private and many public; the glimpse, the glimmer of the world around me, captured for a moment only, but put down on paper to last, I hope, beyond me.

ACKNOWLEDGMENTS

Without the encouragement of Jofie Ferrari-Adler, I would never have written this book. My heartiest thanks to him for unwavering support and the sharpest insights, always. I couldn't ask for a better, more inspiring editor.

Many more thanks are in order:

To the wonderful team at Avid Reader Press, and in particular Meredith Vilarello; Alison Forner (for the beautiful cover design); Carly Loman; Beth Thomas; Annalea Manalili; Eva Kerins; Carolyn Kelly; and Alexandra Silvas. What a pleasure to work with you!

To Jon Karp, the greatest ally. Add one more book to our partnership!! How fortunate I am to know you.

To Richard Pine, for decades of wisdom and friendship and business sense.

To Alexandra Primiani, Ilana Gold, and Lena Little, for great help in getting this book out in the world.

To the Ragdale Residency, in Chicago, and the Mudhouse Residency, in Agios Ioannis, Crete, for providing me with space (beautiful), time (ample), and quiet (but not *too* quiet) to work. What a gift.

To Ruth Lloyds and Bil Ehrlich, for generously letting me create my own little residency in their stunning guesthouse, where I managed to write pages and pages.

ACKNOWLEDGMENTS

To Ellen Hexter and Steve Petrie, for hosting me as I dug through my papers at Columbia.

To David Remnick, Virginia Cannon, and the glorious institution of *The New Yorker*, for giving me the best writing home imaginable.

To Manjula Martin, for her thoughtful questions, which helped me form the first ideas I had for this book.

To Steven Beauregard, the most helpful hand.

To my brother, David, and sister, Debra, as always.

To Jay and Gabbie and Izzy and Vivi, with love.

To my amazing friends, who are (*knock on wood*) too many to list here without looking braggy. You know who you are, and you are my favorite people and greatest champions.

To Austin, apple of my eye; pride, joy, beloved.

And most of all, to John Gillespie, my first and best reader, greatest cheerleader, and finest sounding board, as well as the heart of my heart, forever and ever.

Los Angeles, California, 2025

APPENDIX

I began this book imagining that I would choose a few of my pieces and take them apart, unmaking the sausage, so to speak, to illustrate how and why I write. I began with "The American Man, Age Ten," because it was so important to me as a project, and because I thought it was the best example of the kind of stories I most love to do. But I realized I needed to give it context, and that context grew and expanded, and suddenly I found myself telling the entire story of my career, and my life, besides detailing this handful of pieces. But before I let you go, I want to provide you with a few of those significant stories; I suppose they are either very long footnotes for the book, or the book is a very long footnote to these pieces. And then, for fun, I'm including two pieces from my younger years, examples of the work that paved the way to where I've landed.

THE AMERICAN MAN, AGE TEN

Esquire
December 1, 1992

IF COLIN DUFFY AND I WERE TO GET MARRIED, we would have matching superhero notebooks. We would wear shorts, big sneakers, and long, baggy T-shirts depicting famous athletes every single day, even in the winter. We would sleep in our clothes. We would both be good at Nintendo *Street Fighter II*, but Colin would be better than me. We would have some homework, but it would never be too hard, and we would always have just finished it. We would eat pizza and candy for all of our meals. We wouldn't have sex, but we would have crushes on each other and, magically, babies would appear in our home. We would win the lottery and then buy land in Wyoming, where we would have one of every kind of cute animal. All the while, Colin would be working in law enforcement—probably the FBI. Our favorite movie star, Morgan Freeman, would visit us occasionally. We would listen to the same Eurythmics song ("Here Comes the Rain Again") over and over again and watch two hours of television every Friday night. We would both be good at football, have best friends, and know how to drive; we would cure AIDS and the garbage problem and everything that hurts animals. We would hang out a lot with Colin's dad. For fun, we would load a slingshot with dog food and shoot it at my butt. We would have a very good life.

HERE ARE THE PARTICULARS about Colin Duffy: He is ten years old, on the nose. He is four feet eight inches high, weighs seventy-five pounds, and appears to be mostly leg and shoulder blade. He is a handsome kid. He has a broad forehead, dark eyes with dense lashes, and a sharp, dimply smile. I have rarely ever seen him without a baseball cap. He owns several, but favors a University of Michigan Wolverines model, on account of its pleasing colors. The hat styles his hair into wild disarray. If you ever managed to get the hat off his head, you would see a boy with a nimbus of golden-brown hair, dented in the back, where the hat hits him.

Colin lives with his mother, Elaine; his father, Jim; his older sister, Megan; and his little brother, Chris, in a pretty pale-blue Victorian house on a bosky street in Glen Ridge, New Jersey. Glen Ridge is a serene and civilized old town twenty miles west of New York City. It does not have much of a commercial district, but it is a town of amazing lawns. Most of the houses were built around the turn of the century and are set back a gracious, green distance from the street. The rest of the town seems to consist of parks and playing fields and sidewalks and backyards—in other words, it is a far cry from South-Central Los Angeles and from Bedford-Stuyvesant and other, grimmer parts of the country where a very different ten-year-old American man is growing up today.

There is a fine school system in Glen Ridge, but Elaine and Jim, who are both schoolteachers, choose to send their children to a parents' cooperative elementary school in Montclair, a neighboring suburb. Currently, Colin is in fifth grade. He is a good student. He plans to go to college, to a place he says is called Oklahoma City State College University. OCSCU satisfies his desire to live out west, to attend a small college, and to study law enforcement, which OCSCU apparently offers as a major. After four years at Oklahoma City State College University, he plans to work for the FBI. He says that getting to be a police officer involves tons of hard work, but working for the FBI will be a cinch, because all you have to do is fill out one form, which he has already gotten from the head FBI office.

Colin is quiet in class but loud on the playground. He has a great throwing arm, significant foot speed, and a lot of physical confidence. He is also brave. Huge wild cats with rabies and gross stuff dripping from their teeth, which he says run rampant throughout his neighborhood, do not scare him. Otherwise, he is slightly bashful. This combination of athletic grace and valor and personal reserve accounts for considerable popularity. He has a fluid relationship to many social groups, including the superbright nerds, the ultrajocks, the flashy kids who will someday become socially successful juvenile delinquents, and the kids who will be elected president of the student body.

In his opinion, the most popular boy in his class is Christian, who happens to be black, and Colin's favorite television character is Steve Urkel on *Family Matters*, who is black, too, but otherwise he seems uninterested in or oblivious to race. Until this year, he was a Boy Scout. Now he is planning to begin karate lessons. His favorite schoolyard game is football, followed closely by prison dodge ball, blob tag, and bombardo. He's crazy about athletes, although sometimes it isn't clear if he is absolutely sure of the difference between human athletes and Marvel Comics action figures. His current athletic hero is Dave Meggett. His current best friend is named Japeth. He used to have another best friend named Ozzie. According to Colin, Ozzie was found on a doorstep, then changed his name to Michael and moved to Massachusetts, and then Colin never saw him or heard from him again.

He has had other losses in his life. He is old enough to know people who have died and to know things about the world that are worrisome. When he dreams, he dreams about moving to Wyoming, which he has visited with his family. His plan is to buy land there and have some sort of ranch that would definitely include horses. Sometimes when he talks about this, it sounds as ordinary and hard-boiled as a real estate appraisal;

other times it can sound fantastical and wifty and achingly naive, informed by the last inklings of childhood—the musings of a balmy real estate appraiser assaying a wonderful and magical landscape that erodes from memory a little bit every day. The collision in his mind of what he understands, what he hears, what he figures out, what popular culture pours into him, what he knows, what he pretends to know, and what he imagines, makes an interesting mess. The mess often has the form of what he will probably think like when he is a grown man, but the content of what he is like as a little boy.

He is old enough to begin imagining that he will someday get married, but at ten he is still convinced that the best thing about being married will be that he will be allowed to sleep in his clothes. His father once observed that living with Colin was like living with a Martian who had done some reading on American culture. As it happens, Colin is not especially sad or worried about the prospect of growing up, although he sometimes frets over whether he should be called a kid or a grown-up; he has settled on the word *kid-up*. Once, I asked him what the biggest advantage to adulthood will be, and he said, "The best thing is that grown-ups can go wherever they want." I asked him what he meant, exactly, and he said, "Well, if you're grown-up, you'd have a car, and whenever you felt like it, you could get into your car and drive somewhere and get candy."

COLIN LOVES RECYCLING. He loves it even more than, say, playing with little birds. That ten-year-olds feel the weight of the world and consider it their mission to shoulder it came as a surprise to me. I had accompanied Colin one Monday to his classroom at Montclair Cooperative School. The Coop is in a steep, old, sharp-angled brick building that had served for many years as a public school until a group of parents in the area took it over and made it into a private, progressive elementary school. The fifth-grade classroom is on the top floor, under the dormers, which gives the room the eccentric shape and close-

APPENDIX

ness of an attic. It is a rather informal environment. There are computers lined up in an adjoining room and instructions spelled out on the chalkboard—BRING IN: 1) A CUBBY WITH YOUR NAME ON IT, 2) A TRAPPER WITH A 5-POCKET ENVELOPE LABELED SCIENCE, SOCIAL STUDIES, READING/LANGUAGE ARTS, MATH, MATH LAB/COMPUTER; WHITE LINED PAPER; A PLASTIC PENCIL BAG; A SMALL HOMEWORK PAD, 3) LARGE BROWN GROCERY BAGS. But there is also a couch in the center of the classroom, which the kids take turns occupying, a rocking chair, and three canaries in cages near the door.

It happened to be Colin's first day in fifth grade. Before class began, there was a lot of horsing around, but there were also a lot of conversations about whether Magic Johnson had AIDS or just HIV and whether someone falling in a pool of his blood would get the disease. These jolts of sobriety in the midst of goofiness are a ten-year-old's specialty. Each one comes as a fresh, hard surprise, like finding a razor blade in a candy apple. One day, Colin and I had been discussing horses or dogs or something, and out of the blue he said, "What do you think is better, to dump garbage in the ocean, to dump it on land, or to burn it?" Another time, he asked me if I planned to have children. I had just spent an evening with him and his friend Japeth, during which they put every small, movable object in the house into Japeth's slingshot and fired it at me, so I told him that I wanted children but that I hoped they would all be girls, and he said, "Will you have an abortion if you find out you have a boy?"

At school, after discussing summer vacation, the kids began choosing the jobs they would do to help out around the classroom. Most of the jobs are humdrum—putting the chairs up on the tables, washing the chalkboard, turning the computers off or on. Five of the most humdrum tasks are recycling chores—for example, taking bottles or paper down to the basement, where they would be sorted and prepared for pickup. Two children would be assigned to feed the birds and cover their cages at the end of the day.

APPENDIX

I expected the bird jobs to be the first to go. Everyone loved the birds; they'd spent an hour that morning voting on names for them (Tweetie, Montgomery, and Rose narrowly beating out Axl Rose, Bugs, Ol' Yeller, Fido, Slim, Lucy, and Chirpie). Instead, they all wanted to recycle. The recycling jobs were claimed by the first five kids called by Suzanne Nakamura, the fifth-grade teacher; each kid called after that responded by groaning, "Suzanne, aren't there any more recycling jobs?" Colin ended up with the job of taking down the chairs each morning. He accepted the task with a sort of resignation—this was just going to be a job rather than a mission.

On the way home that day, I quizzed Colin about his world views.
"Who's the coolest person in the world?"
"Morgan Freeman."
"What's the best sport?"
"Football."
"Who's the coolest woman?"
"None. I don't know."
"What's the most important thing in the world?"
"Game Boy." Pause. "No, the world. The world is the most important thing in the world."

DANNY'S PIZZERIA is a dark little shop next door to the Montclair Cooperative School. It is not much to look at. Outside, the brick front is painted muddy brown. Inside, there are some saggy counters, a splintered bench, and enough room for either six teenagers or a dozen ten-year-olds who are getting along well. The light is low. The air is oily. At Danny's, you will find pizza, candy, Nintendo, and very few girls. To a ten-year-old boy, it is the most beautiful place in the world.

One afternoon, after class was dismissed, we went to Danny's with Colin's friend Japeth to play Nintendo. Danny's has only one game, *Street Fighter II Champion Edition*. Some teenage boys from a nearby middle school had gotten there first and were standing in a tall, impenetrable thicket around the machine.

"Next game," Colin said. The teenagers ignored him.

"Hey, we get next game," Japeth said. He is smaller than Colin, scrappy, and, as he explained to me once, famous for wearing his hat backward all the time and having a huge wristwatch and a huge bedroom. He stamped his foot and announced again, "Hey, we get next game."

One of the teenagers turned around and said, "Fuck you, *next game*," and then turned back to the machine.

"Whoa," Japeth said.

He and Colin went outside, where they felt bigger.

"Which street fighter are you going to be?" Colin asked Japeth.

"Blanka," Japeth said. "I know how to do his head-butt."

"I hate that! I hate the head-butt," Colin said. He dropped his voice a little and growled, "I'm going to be Ken, and I will kill you with my dragon punch."

"Yeah, right, and monkeys will fly out of my butt," Japeth said.

Street Fighter II is a video game in which two characters have an explosive brawl in a scenic international setting. It is currently the most popular video-arcade game in America. This is not an insignificant amount of popularity. Most arcade versions of video games, which end up in pizza parlors, malls, and arcades, sell about two thousand units. So far, some fifty thousand *Street Fighter II* and *Street Fighter II Championship Edition* arcade games have been sold. Not since *Pac-Man*, which was released the year before Colin was born, has there been a video game as popular as *Street Fighter*. The home version of *Street Fighter* is the most popular home video game in the country, and that, too, is not an insignificant thing.

Thirty-two million Nintendo home systems have been sold since 1986, when it was introduced in this country. There is a Nintendo system in seven of every ten homes in America in which a child between the ages of eight and twelve resides. By the time a boy in America turns ten, he will

APPENDIX

almost certainly have been exposed to Nintendo home games, Nintendo arcade games, and Game Boy, the hand-held version. He will probably own a system and dozens of games. By age ten, according to Nintendo studies, teachers, and psychologists, game prowess becomes a fundamental, essential male social marker and a schoolyard boast.

The *Street Fighter* characters are Dhalsim, Ken, Guile, Blanka, E. Honda, Ryu, Zangief, and Chun Li. Each represents a different country, and they each have their own special weapon. Chun Li, for instance, is from China and possesses a devastating whirlwind kick that is triggered if you push the control pad down for two seconds and then up for two seconds, and then you hit the kick button. Chun Li's kick is money in the bank, because most of the other fighters do not have a good defense against it. By the way, Chun Li happens to be a girl—the only female *Street Fighter* character.

I asked Colin if he was interested in being Chun Li. There was a long pause. "I would rather be Ken," he said.

The girls in Colin's class at school are named Cortnerd, Terror, Spacey, Lizard, Maggot, and Diarrhea. "They do have other names, but that's what we call them," Colin told me. "The girls aren't very popular."

"They are about as popular as a piece of dirt," Japeth said. "Or, you know that couch in the classroom? That couch is more popular than any girl. A thousand times more." They talked for a minute about one of the girls in their class, a tall blonde with cheerleader genetic material, who they confessed was not quite as gross as some of the other girls.

Japeth said that a chubby, awkward boy in their class was boasting that this girl liked him.

"No way," Colin said. "She would never like him. I mean, not that he's so . . . I don't know. I don't hate him because he's fat, anyway. I hate him because he's nasty."

"Well, she doesn't like him," Japeth said. "She's been really mean to me lately, so I'm pretty sure she likes me."

"Girls are different," Colin said. He hopped up and down on the balls of his feet, wrinkling his nose. "Girls are stupid and weird."

"I have a lot of girlfriends, about six or so," Japeth said, turning contemplative. "I don't exactly remember their names, though."

The teenagers came crashing out of Danny's and jostled past us, so we went inside. The man who runs Danny's, whose name is Tom, leaned across the counter on his elbows, looking exhausted. Two little boys, holding Slush Puppies, shuffled toward the Nintendo, but Colin and Japeth elbowed them aside and slammed their quarters down on the machine. The little boys shuffled back toward the counter and stood gawking at them, sucking on their drinks.

"You want to know how to tell if a girl likes you?" Japeth said. "She'll act really mean to you. That's a sure sign. I don't know why they do it, but it's always a sure sign. It gets your attention. You know how I show a girl I like her? I steal something from her and then run away. I do it to get their attention, and it works."

They played four quarters' worth of games. During the last one, a teenager with a quilted leather jacket and a fade haircut came in, pushed his arm between them, and put a quarter down on the deck of the machine.

Japeth said, "Hey, what's that?"

The teenager said, "I get next game. I've marked it now. Everyone knows this secret sign for next game. It's a universal thing."

"So now we know," Japeth said. "Colin, let's get out of here and go bother Maggie. I mean Maggot. Okay?" They picked up their backpacks and headed out the door.

PSYCHOLOGISTS IDENTIFY ten as roughly the age at which many boys experience the gender-linked normative developmental trauma that leaves them, as adult men, at risk for specific psychological sequelae often manifest as deficits in the arenas of intimacy, empathy, and struggles with commitment in relationships. In other words, this is around the age when guys get screwed up about girls. Elaine and Jim Duffy, and probably most parents who send their kids to Montclair Cooperative School, have done a lot of stuff to try to avoid this. They gave Colin dolls as well as guns. (He preferred guns.) Japeth's father has three motorcycles and two dirt bikes but does most of the cooking and cleaning in their home. Suzanne, Colin's teacher, is careful to avoid sexist references in her presentations. After school, the yard at Montclair Cooperative is filled with as many fathers as mothers—fathers who hug their kids when they come prancing out of the building and are dismayed when their sons clamor for Super Soaker water guns and war toys or take pleasure in beating up girls.

In a study of adolescents conducted by the Gesell Institute of Human Development, nearly half the ten-year-old boys questioned said they thought they had adequate information about sex. Nevertheless, most ten-year-old boys across the country are subjected to a few months of sex education in school. Colin and his class will get their dose next spring. It is yet another installment in a plan to make them into new, improved men with reconstructed notions of sex and male-female relationships. One afternoon I asked Philip, a schoolmate of Colin's, whether he was looking forward to sex education, and he said, "No, because I think it'll probably make me really, really hyper. I have a feeling it's going to be just like what it was like when some television reporters came to school last year and filmed us in class and I got really hyper. They stood around with all these cameras and asked us questions. I think that's what sex education is probably like."

At a class meeting earlier in the day:

Suzanne: "Today was our first day of swimming class, and I have one observation to make. The girls went into their locker room, got dressed without a lot of fuss, and came into the pool area. The boys, on the other hand, the boys had some sort of problem doing that rather simple task. Can someone tell me what exactly went on in the locker room?"

Keith: "There was a lot of shouting."

APPENDIX

Suzanne: "Okay, I hear you saying that people were being noisy and shouting. Anything else?"

Christian: "Some people were screaming so much that my ears were killing me. It gave me, like, a huge headache. Also, some of the boys were taking their towels, I mean, after they had taken their clothes off, they had their towels around their waists and then they would drop them really fast and then pull them back up, really fast."

Suzanne: "Okay, you're saying some people were being silly about their bodies."

Christian: "Well, yeah, but it was more like they were being silly about their pants."

COLIN'S BEDROOM is decorated simply. He has a cage with his pet parakeet, Dude, on his dresser, a lot of recently worn clothing piled haphazardly on the floor, and a husky brown teddy bear sitting upright in a chair near the foot of his bed. The walls are mostly bare, except for a Spider-Man poster and a few ads torn out of magazines he has thumbtacked up. One of the ads is for a cologne, illustrated with several small photographs of cowboy hats; another, a feverish portrait of a woman on a horse, is an ad for blue jeans. These inspire him sometimes when he lies in bed and makes plans for his imagined move to Wyoming. Also, he happens to like ads. He also likes television commercials. Generally speaking, he likes consumer products and popular culture. He partakes avidly but not indiscriminately. In fact, during the time we spent together, he provided a running commentary on merchandise, media, and entertainment:

"The only shoes anyone will wear are Reebok Pumps. Big T-shirts are cool, not the kind that are sticky and close to you, but big and baggy and long, not the kind that stop at your stomach."

"The best food is Chicken McNuggets and Life cereal and Frosted Flakes."

"Don't go to Blimpie's. They have the worst service."

APPENDIX

"I'm not into Teenage Mutant Ninja Turtles anymore. I grew out of that. I like Donatello, but I'm not a fan. I don't buy the figures anymore."

"The best television shows are on Friday night on ABC. It's called TGIF, and it's *Family Matters*, *Step by Step*, *Dinosaurs*, and *Perfect Strangers*, where the guy has a funny accent."

"The best candy is Skittles and Symphony bars and Crybabies and Warheads. Crybabies are great because if you eat a lot of them at once you feel so sour."

"Hyundais are Korean cars. It's the only Korean car. They're not that good because Koreans don't have a lot of experience building cars."

"The best movie is *City Slickers*, and the best part was when he saved his little cow in the river."

"The Giants really need to get rid of Ray Handley. They have to get somebody who has real coaching experience. He's just no good."

"My dog, Sally, cost seventy-two dollars. That sounds like a lot of money but it's a really good price because you get a flea bath with your dog."

"The best magazines are *Nintendo Power*, because they tell you how to do the secret moves in the video games, and also *Mad* magazine and *Money Guide*—I really like that one."

"The best artist in the world is Jim Davis, who draws Garfield."

"The most beautiful woman in the world is not Madonna! Only Wayne and Garth think that! She looks like maybe a . . . a . . . slut or something. Cindy Crawford looks like she would look good, but if you see her on an awards program on TV she doesn't look that good. I think the most beautiful woman in the world probably is my mom."

COLIN THINKS A LOT about money. This started when he was about nine and a half, which is when a lot of other things started—a new way of walking that has a little macho hitch and swagger, a decision about the Teenage Mutant Ninja Turtles (con) and Eurythmics (pro), and a

APPENDIX

persistent curiosity about a certain girl whose name he will not reveal. He knows the price of everything he encounters. He knows how much college costs and what someone might earn performing different jobs. Once, he asked me what my husband did; when I answered that he was a lawyer, he snapped, "You must be a rich family. Lawyers make $400,000 a year." His preoccupation with money baffles his family. They are not struggling, so this is not the anxiety of deprivation; they are not rich, so he is not responding to an elegant, advantaged world. His allowance is five dollars a week. It seems sufficient for his needs, which consist chiefly of quarters for Nintendo and candy money. He puts whatever is leftover into his Wyoming fund. His fascination is not just specific to needing money or having plans for money: It is as if money itself, and the way it makes the world work, and the realization that almost everything in the world can be assigned a price, has possessed him. "I just pay attention to things like that," Colin says. "It's really very interesting."

He is looking for a windfall. He tells me his mother has been notified that she is in the fourth and final round of the Publisher's Clearinghouse Sweepstakes. This is not an ironic observation. He plays the New Jersey lottery every Thursday night. He knows the weekly jackpot; he knows the number to call to find out if he has won. I do not think this presages a future for Colin as a high-stakes gambler; I think it says more about the powerful grasp that money has on imagination and what a large percentage of a ten-year-old's mind is made up of imaginings. One Friday, we were at his school, and one of his friends was asking him about the lottery, and he said, "This week it was $4 million. That would be I forget how much every year for the rest of your life. It's a lot, I think. You should play. All it takes is a dollar and a dream."

UNTIL THE LOTTERY comes through and he starts putting together the Wyoming land deal, Colin can be found most of the time in the backyard. Often, he will have friends come over. Regularly, children from the neighborhood will gravitate to the backyard, too. As a technical matter of real-property law, title to the house and yard belongs to Jim and Elaine Duffy, but Colin adversely possesses the backyard, at least from four o'clock each afternoon until it gets dark. As yet, the fixtures of teenage life—malls, video arcades, friends' basements, automobiles—either hold little interest for him or are not his to have.

He is, at the moment, very content with his backyard. For most intents and purposes, it is as big as Wyoming. One day, certainly, he will grow and it will shrink, and it will become simply a suburban backyard, and it won't be big enough for him anymore. This will happen so fast that one night he will be in the backyard, believing it a perfect place, and by the next night he will have changed and the yard as he imagined it will be gone, and this era of his life will be behind him forever.

Most days, he spends his hours in the backyard building an Evil Spider-Web Trap. This entails running a spool of Jim's fishing line from every surface in the yard until it forms a huge web. Once a garbageman picking up the Duffys' trash got caught in the trap. Otherwise, the Evil Spider-Web Trap mostly has a deterrent effect, because the kids in the neighborhood who might roam over know that Colin builds it back there. "I do it all the time," he says. "First I plan who I'd like to catch in it, and then we get started. Trespassers have to beware."

One afternoon when I was visiting, Colin began building a trap. He selected a victim for inspiration—a boy in his class who had been pestering him—and began wrapping. He was entirely absorbed. He moved from tree to tree, wrapping; he laced fishing line through the railing of the deck and then back to the shed; he circled an old jungle gym, something he'd outgrown and abandoned a few years earlier, and then crossed over to a bush at the back of the yard. Briefly, he contemplated making his dog, Sally, part of the web. Dusk fell. He kept wrapping, paying out fishing line an inch at a time. We could hear mothers up and down the block hooting for their kids; two tiny children from next door stood transfixed at the edge of the yard, uncertain whether they would end up inside or outside the web. After a while, the spool spun around in Colin's hands one more time and then stopped; he was out of line.

It was almost too dark to see much of anything, although now and again the light from the deck would glance off a length of line, and it would glint and sparkle. "That's the point," he said. "You could do it with thread, but the fishing line is invisible. Now I have this perfect thing and the only one who knows about it is me." With that, he dropped the spool, skipped up the stairs of the deck, threw open the screen door, and then bounded into the house, leaving me and Sally the dog trapped in his web.

BE A JOKE UNTO YOURSELF

Village Voice
August 3, 1982

ANTELOPE, OREGON – The fact is, if you really love Bhagwan, you don't wear deodorant.

Everybody here, of course, really loves Bhagwan. To see him, they've come from Japan, England, Holland, Germany, and from all over the U.S.A.; paid $350; driven through the unsympathetic Oregon towns of Biggs, Wasco, Moro, Grass Valley, and Kent; crept past the creepy ghost town of Shaniko; coasted into the even more unsympathetic town of Antelope; then headed down twenty twisted miles of washboard country road through hills best suited to rattlesnakes and coyotes; and finally passed through three public safety checkpoints to get to the First Annual World Celebration in Bhagwan's new city of Rajneeshpuram. Thus committed, no one would dare risk getting booted out of the *satsang* or *darshon* ceremonies by one of the official sniffers up by the stage. Let them catch a whiff of perfume or Ban Roll-On on you, and you're out: Bhagwan may be enlightened, but he's also terrifically allergic. The sannyasins—his followers—are asked please to cut the asthmatic Great Master some slack and leave the scented stuff at home.

APPENDIX

There is much slack cut here at the festival, held July 2 through 8; much asked of the sannyasins and granted without a grumble. No protest is registered when the faithful are asked to not photograph or record prayer ceremonies, and in fact they line up later to buy tapes of the proceedings for $100 per video minute. There is no exasperation at the sky-high prices in the festival boutiques full of Bhagwan memorabilia. Some festivalgoers have spent several thousand dollars to get here, and still, you never, ever hear anyone carping about Bhagwan's stable of Rolls-Royces. Ask any of these perpetually red-clad troops whether it's all worth it and they're taken aback. Are you kidding? Is it *worth* it? To see Bhagwan is worth anything imaginable.

"It's so easy to love Bhagwan," smiles a UCLA student who has just been initiated. "He asks so little of us." In fact, there are only three tenets in Bhagwan's faith—wear your *mala* (a wooden bead necklace with his photograph in an amulet), dress only in the colors of the sun, and be aware. Being aware, his faithful will tell you straight-faced, can be very, very hard sometimes. Bhagwan woos most of his followers with some thirty-three million words' worth of wisdom, published in hundreds of books, which feature a hip mishmash of transactional analysis, Henny Youngman, Baba Ram Dass, Alex Comfort, and horse sense. Many of his disciples have supermarketed their way through a whole bevy of other masters before finding Bhagwan. They revel in his good humor ("For a Great Master, he's really funny!") and his flair for the vernacular. They love the fact that he doesn't ask them to give up anything—not sex, not money, not even cigarettes. It's a neat coincidence, because the fifty-year-old Bhagwan has gathered around himself a remarkably rich, handsome, lusty, swinging crowd. But this is spirituality without sweat, enlightenment without angst. No wonder the hottest Rajneesh bumper sticker is a quote of Bhagwan's: Be a Joke Unto Yourself.

Following Bhagwan seems like lightweight stuff, but there is at least some suggestion of a darker side. Encounter groups in his commune in India were rumored to be occasionally violent. Many of his teachings are anti-Semitic. His philosophies preach selfishness. His foundation, which collects donations from his followers, is fabulously rich, and at least a good chunk of the money is spent on Bhagwan's posh automobiles. But for most people following his path, those are only minor annoyances in the general spirit of Club Med camaraderie.

If the people of Antelope, Oregon, had had their way, the Bhagwan would have never settled here at all. He was not warmly received in these parts, in these little desert hill towns peopled with retirees and ranch hands. Bhagwan arrived a year ago, after a sudden and still mysterious departure from his commune in Pune, India. Some say he was scooting out on a tax rap, some that his health was deteriorating, some that the publicity about the encounter groups and his celebrated liberal attitude toward sex had gotten out of hand. At any rate, after departing India, he resurfaced on the Big Muddy Ranch in Central Oregon's Mutton Mountains—a one-hundred-square-mile spread so wrinkled with hills that if you could iron it out, it'd probably be twice that big. The land has been grazed to the bone by generations of cattle. The ranch, huge even by Wild West standards, didn't look like the kind of place that would do a whole lot of good for anyone or anything, but Bhagwan wanted it. His faithful heeded his call to the tune of $2.5 million in cash toward the $6 million purchase price. Three hundred and fifty believers soon followed him to his new arid home and set up a sophisticated kibbutz-like farm with cows, chickens, a vineyard, wheatfield, an airstrip, a school, a gas station, and homes. This would be official turf, and self-sufficient community for his creed, the Rajneesh Neo-Sannyas International Commune, mailing address Antelope, U.S.A.

You can make a lot of easy jokes about Antelope, a spit of a town with forty souls, a post office, and a general store. But you can't say the folks of Antelope aren't industrious. Within weeks of the ranch's sale last summer, they'd filed a ream of lawsuits to stop it, and they actually started their

APPENDIX

own appropriate cottage industries, manufacturing "Better Dead Than Red" bumper stickers, and tractor hats stamped with "Antelope Border Patrol" and a picture of the crosshairs of a rifle trained on a Rolls-Royce just like Bhagwan's own. Some even took to wearing necklaces like the sannyasins' *malas*, except instead of wooden beads they used bullets, and instead of Bhagwan's photograph they featured a grizzled cowboy named Boswan. Such is the skepticism that met the 7,000 celebrants at the week-long festival (the first of what will be an annual event) marking a year of work at the old Big Muddy, now the incorporated new city of Rajneeshpuram.

None of that matters to the thousands here. After all, it's Master's Day, the fifth and most important day of the festival. The deep valley floor is filled with thousands of rosy-hued worshippers strolling to evening services through sagebrush and thistle and rimrock and dew. Forget the three safety checkpoints, forget the three Jesus freaks who earlier in the day chased Bhagwan and tried to forcibly save his soul, forget the fact that the governor of Oregon has put the National Guard on alert. This afternoon, Bhagwan drove slowly down Nirvana Road in his milk-white Rolls-Royce while an Air Rajneesh plane flying overhead scattered 50,000 rose petals. A blonde Laguna Beach matron assures me it was gorgeous. Just gorgeous. She turns and fixes an adoring stare on the podium where Bhagwan will soon appear for the *darshon* ceremony. She tells me she found Bhagwan after a decade of dead-end therapy. His books and his simplicity got to her. Now she sends him $50 each month and spends long afternoons shopping for red clothes. Practice makes perfect: she's dressed to the nines in magenta silks and orange cottons, and opal glitter is sprinkled along the ridge of her cheeks. As Buddha Hall begins to fill (all two and a half acres of it, which will be converted into America's largest greenhouse after the ceremony), everyone is looking just as sharp as she is, in shimmering satin and orange gauze and sparkling silks run through with gold thread,

APPENDIX

in tunics and pegged pants and knickers and jumpsuits, harem pants and halter tops and miniskirts and vests.

For such a big crowd, it's remarkably quiet. There are only whispers at our end of the hall, and all of them are German. The Germans have embraced Bhagwan with gusto, and thousands of them have trooped all the way to Oregon to see him. They love him because, a striking young German man tells me, the Germans suffered so much in the last wars. "Maybe we've finally learned something," he says wistfully. His wistfulness right now has less to do with the tragedy of history than a circumstance of the moment: he came to the festival hoping to change his sannyasin name from Swami Deva Wolfgang to a more Sanskrit name, only to discover hordes of other people wanting to change their names too. Unless he squeezes in for an audience with someone in charge, it looks like he's stuck with Wolfgang.

The band is warming up in the back of the hall. It's an all-Bhagwan band, decked out in maroon T-shirts and faded red slacks, their *malas* slung sideways, like guitar straps, to stay out of the way. Like Bhagwan's philosophy, the music is a two-fisted hodgepodge—the equipment on the stage includes acoustic guitars, stand-up bass, a sitar, a glossy red rock-and-roll drum kit, congas, a fiddle, and a set of cowbells.

Suddenly, Bhagwan's bodyguards appear. They wear flak jackets, walkie-talkies, thick-handled revolvers, and dead-pan stares, a disconcerting sight amid this high-color, low-friction crowd. During the festival Bhagwan is guarded by a five-man force from a Portland security agency of Vietnam vets called the Golden Centurions. There's an excited buzz in the hall as the final Centurion appears and takes his place in a suspended scaffolding. He's wearing a red Lacoste shirt! Red, one of Bhagwan's prescribed colors! Of course, it's only a coincidence, but the crowd of true believers sees it as a cause for celebration, and the buzz becomes a giggle and finally an explosion of applause. Then Bhagwan appears.

He sneaks up on the podium because he's driven behind it silently in one of his Rolls-Royces and has the door opened for him without a creak by a long, tall *sannyasin* wearing a red Stetson. Bhagwan looks much older than his years. He has a long, gray beard and hair, round prominent eyes, and uncannily smooth skin. He glides on stage and settles into an Ozzie Nelson-style overstuffed armchair. The crowd begins to sing. "This life/our celebration/Of the joy we've come to know/My love for you Bhagwan/Is overflowing!!" The tune is chantlike and soothing, and it goes on for a good eight minutes, just one verse repeated over and over and over. The bare floor of Buddha Hall gets mighty hard; most people brought a cushion or scrap of rug to sit on.

Bhagwan hasn't spoken publicly since early last spring, when he entered the final and silent phase of his work. He does speak to his inner circle, namely Ma Anand Sheela, his wise-cracking, tough-minded business director. Most significantly, he told her to expect worldwide poverty in 1984 and world destruction in 1993. But otherwise, he no longer addresses his followers like he did in Pune, and Sheela is charged with passing his word along to the group. She drives a Mercedes.

The singing continues: songs about surrender, silent love, dancing, the wind, taking it easy, and getting on a soul train with Bhagwan. It is punctuated by a violent thunderstorm that boils up out of the mountains and hills. Every smack of thunder spurs the group on, and by the time we get to the last song (title: "Yes Bhagwan Yes") the tempo and volume have made noticeable gains. Through all of this, Bhagwan sits peacefully and without visible emotion. He is loving the festival, Sheela says. It's like we're all his lovers and all his lovers have come home.

After the songs and fifteen minutes of meditation, the ceremony is over. The band breaks into a galloping boogie tune, and everyone leaps up and begins spiraling and jiggling their way to the edge of Buddha Hall, to jostle for a good view. At the end of each prayer service, Ma Anand Sheela drives Bhagwan around the hall's perimeter while he passes a cool eye over his disciples. Half of the marvel is seeing an enormous, perfectly clean Rolls-Royce crawling around a mucky mountain field. And the cars are always clean—after each of his rides, Bhagwan's personal staff scrub them down to remove any dust or pollen that might aggravate his allergies. The Rolls-Royces have been the source of much negative press. "It used to bother me," admits a swami who came to Bhagwan by way of liberal Jewish parents, Columbia University, a teaching stint in Harlem, and experiments with drugs. "But then I look around and see all the happiness Bhagwan has given to all these people, and I think, why shouldn't he have Rolls-Royces? It's like a joke, or maybe a test. It's a test to see how loving we can be. So it doesn't really bother me anymore. Really, it doesn't." Sheela is even firmer. When asked why Bhagwan needs seventeen Rolls, she snaps, "Why shouldn't he have seventeen Rolls-Royces? And I wish you people would get it right. He's got twenty-two Rolls-Royces, and we'll give him 350 if that's what he wants. We won't be happy until every Rajneeshi has two Rolls in their garage and the world will see just how well we are living."

The festival's 7,000 attendees are housed and fed in one of three "sleeping fields" called Socrates, Zarathustra, and Buddha. But tonight is special, so we all gather for a huge communal dinner in Buddha Field. Like the entire seven-day gathering, the dinner is a wonder of organization. There are thirty tidy lines for food, scores of coffee urns and wastebaskets, trays of cheese, cherries, melon, and ice cream sandwiches. Till dawn, there is chanting and singing, and from the tents you can hear laughing and hooting till the sun comes up.

Breakfast had been scheduled for seven a.m., right before the morning ceremony, but so many people were skipping breakfast to line up for a good seat that the cooks relented and started serving around six. It is a splendid morning, the last day of the festival. It's hard to get used to the sight of all these brilliantly clothed people in the middle of this bleached-out canyon, or all these golden tents, 1,800 of them, set up on platforms in neat rows across the meadows. The Rajneesh Foundation bought all of them, as well as the fleecy sleeping bags and cushions and tent lamps and leased the orange school buses that ferry the festivalgoers around the enormous ranch. All in all, it cost more than $3 million for the celebration.

The ceremony begins with a series of announcements: someone has lost their *mala*, Dutch people flying out today should pick up their tickets, someone's wife has called with an urgent message. Then there is a long meditation and a reading from Bhagwan's work. Today's tale is about the Buddha in all of us, and about a tiger cub raised by goats who becomes a vegetarian. Giggles ripple through the hall; even the reader can barely finish the story. Bhagwan is on the stage flanked by his bodyguards, and he too is cracking a shy smile. His long, gray beard makes him look ancient, but the smile is as sweet as a baby's.

After the ceremony, new members join the group. Today three hundred are pledging allegiance to Bhagwan, which brings the festival's new membership total close to a thousand. The initiates kneel in the center of Buddha Hall. Around them, rows and rows of sannyasins beam and applaud. To join Bhagwan's ranks, one merely fills out an application and then goes through this ceremony. A few people who might not seem certain are interviewed to make sure they're serious. A few others are urged to go through therapy before they join.

Two of Bhagwan's lieutenants perform the ceremonies. One is in a flowing pink tunic and pants; the other, mustachioed and suave, is wearing a pink Ralph Lauren polo shirt, a pink cotton Lacoste sweater, and magenta tapered slacks. They sit in armchairs at the head of the circle. The initiates scramble up on their knees, get their third eye massaged, receive their *malas* and a certificate saying they're in like Flynn. The certificate also lists their new sannyasin name and its English translation. The initiation takes about 45 seconds per person. Fifty-eight of them giggle as they walk away; four weep openly; one man quakes violently, one woman shrieks; three shake their heads and say either "Oh, wow" or "Oh, boy"; several grow misty-eyed; countless look shy and a little embarrassed.

After the initiation, there's dynamic meditation, a popular activity that combines dancing, hyperventilation, and complete release (which often

APPENDIX

results in participants wetting their pants, screaming, or writhing fiendishly). Then we're off to lunch, an ordinary affair of vegetables and rice, finished off with the extraordinary surprise of Bhagwan fortune cookies. The messages: "Elephants always dream about flying." "Sex has been called the original sin—it is neither original nor sin." "Just try to be a human being." These are all signed Bhagwan Shree Rajneesh. There's an odd one, too: "You can't tell how deep a puddle is until you step into it," signed "Murphy's Law No. 2."

One woman who tells me she has been living at one of Bhagwan's meditation centers in France chuckles at her cookie's fortune: a gentle reminder from Bhagwan that sucking your thumb is better than smoking. She's chuckling because she's just lit up her third postprandial cigarette. She's not alone; it seems like half the people here are smoking. "The wonderful thing about Bhagwan," sighs an Irish squire, who says he's selling his castle and donating the money to the group, "is that he doesn't ask you to renounce anything. He's not interested in denial. He says, why be a beggar when you can be an emperor. I like that. Renouncing is negative."

What about charity? It's a question that stumps the lunch group, until a New Yorker who has also been living in the French center breaks in. "It's not like that. Bhagwan gives so much. I did all that stuff, fresh-air camps for inner-city kids, that sort of thing. Bhagwan gives us unconditional love. It's hard to explain." Hard only if you don't read Bhagwan's praise of super-capitalism and self-promotion. "We love money," Sheela reminds the reporters that quiz her about well-heeled disciples. "It's a part of life. Religion can only be for rich persons. When you're hungry, you can't think of the divine. When your stomach is full and you don't know what else to do, you think of art and God. Bhagwan has the answer for the poor. He says get off your fat ass and start working. *Move* your ass! You're in the country of capitalism. Why not? You can do it too. Life offers everyone what is available—it's up to you to take advantage."

Take advantage they do, of the festival's more earthly distractions—rafting, horseback riding, swimming, hiking, not to mention shopping

APPENDIX

at Noah's Ark Boutiques, one in each of the Socrates, Zarathustra, and Buddha sleeping fields. Sales in the boutiques are averaging $75,000 to $100,000 each day. Separate annexes sell nothing but Bhagwan videos and cassettes. In the main boutiques, there are racks and racks of pink, red, and orange designer clothes, one with expensive, full-length dresses under a sign saying, "Nice for *Darshon* and *Satsang*!" There are pillowcases silkscreened with a photo of Bhagwan sleeping. There are Frisbees, lighters, lecture cushions, purses, wallets, and baseball caps commemorating the festival. There are $70 wristwatches with Bhagwan's face for the face. There are coffee cups featuring Bhagwan drinking coffee; coasters made of photos of Bhagwan sipping what looks like whiskey. There are book bags with his picture above the statement "I Am Happening to You." Across the way, in sundries, there are bottles of Kwell and fine-toothed combs for nabbing lice; three-packs and twelve-packs of condoms. "You only want the three-pack?" marvels the cashier to a bearded young man. "Come on, Swami! Think positive!" He leaves with the twelve-pack and a two-dollar toothbrush, which has been printed along the handle with the legend, "BUDDHA BRUSH—RAJNEESHPURAM."

The lines at the cash registers are long. They are also snail-slow, because every few minutes the line stops cold while a couple of sannyasins embrace in a long, soulful, full-body hug. Sometimes even three or four will join in and the whole line will clot. Spontaneous hugging is a regular ranch activity—on the way to *satsang*, in line for the bathroom, at lunch, on the bus.

The most popular afternoon recreation is the ranch tour, a bus ride around the huge spread to show off the work that's been done. As we start down Hasid Road, a yelp comes from the back of the bus. It's the Master! He's coming down the road! The bus driver pulls over and lets everyone out to watch Bhagwan drive by. "This is the Rolls-Royce *darshon*," whispers a young German man, Swami Prem Shivam. Every afternoon, Bhagwan drives to the nearby town of Madras for exercise. The

APPENDIX

locals complain that he drives like a maniac and has ended up in ditches several times, but his closest disciples insist it's wonderful for him to get out, considering he spent his last twenty years in India in little more than one room. Throughout the festival, the sannyasins line the road at 2:15 to watch as Bhagwan, wearing a little ski cap and flowing robes, drives away to Madras.

The work on the ranch is astonishing. Where there had been nothing but empty grazing land, there are now thousands of chickens, newly planted fruit trees, dairy cows, horses, a bakery, new bridges, homes for the sannyasins who live here permanently. "We have worms being raised right now that we'll put in the greenhouse," says the tour guide. "They'll get in there and do Kundilini Yoga and there will be so much great energy that the plants will just, well, *explode!*" Before the festival began, the tour used to drive right up to Bhagwan's simple prefab ranch home. Now, the guides only describe it, proudly mentioning its solar-heated indoor swimming pool, and the flock of pure white peacocks that live on the grounds, each wearing bells around its ankles so that they might make music when Bhagwan walks outside. "He's so simple," says Ma Anand Sheela. "He likes the best of everything, you know."

This part of the country has long been prized by survivalists, who believe it could outlast an apocalyptic war. Bhagwan has urged his followers to learn self-sufficiency, and that is clearly the aim of the ranch. Land-use watchdogs in Oregon fiercely opposed the ranch's incorporation as a city, and even more fiercely oppose permitting thousands of people to move here permanently. Many of Bhagwan's disciples, though, believe that his unconditional ever-flowing love will spirit them to the ranch for good, where they might wait out the war he says is coming.

But in the meantime, what are they here for? What, besides dancing and socializing and getting showered with rose petals? For enlightenment, of course—eternal peace, ultimate truth, satisfaction. Right? "No way," laughs Ma Anand Sheela. "I just love the circus—every morning driving Bhagwan around and watching his face grinning and dressing him so gorgeously! Just imagine, if I were enlightened, I'd be beyond that, and I'd miss all of it. No, I could have a million lifetimes, and it wouldn't matter as long as I got to see Bhagwan the way I see him every day."

DEVOTION ROAD

The New Yorker
April 17, 1995

The biggest, nicest thing a travelling gospel group might pray for is a bus. Usually, gospel groups consider themselves blessed if they book a show, and truly blessed if they can also find a way to get there; sometimes they get the call but they don't have a ride. Flying is rarely an option, because it costs too much, and because gospel concerts are often in places that are underserved by airlines, like Demopolis, Alabama, and Madison, Georgia. The Jackson Southernaires, who have been singing in gospel programs around the country virtually every weekend for the last fifty years, used to travel from show to show crowded into whatever car they could get their hands on, and they thanked God if the car got them to the program and back before it broke down. In 1965, they sang in a gospel competition in Detroit, and a fan of theirs bet a fan of the Mighty Clouds of Joy a substantial sum that the Southernaires would win. The Mighty Clouds were heavy favorites but the Southernaires prevailed, and their fan was so grateful that he bought them a bus with some of his winnings. The Southernaires are now on their third bus. In a previous life, their bus worked for Trailways; now it is painted silver and white, has a license plate that says "BUCKLE UP WITH JESUS," and has "The Jackson Southernaires" stencilled in large, loopy script on the back and both sides.

The bus attracts attention. Once, at a diner in Florida, a truck driver who was hauling a carnival ride from Tampa to Birmingham came over to the Southernaires' table, introduced himself, and said, "I heard you-all sing thirty years ago, in a union hall in Suffolk, Virginia, and I been dreaming of meeting you ever since." Then he clapped his hands to his chest and exclaimed, "Thank Jesus for causing me to see your bus!" Another time, in Jackson, Mississippi, which is the group's base of operations, Mack Brandon, the Southernaires' driver, was outside checking the engine and the tires, and a woman pulled over to take a picture of the bus for her gospel scrapbook. She asked Mack to pose beside the front tire. He was in work clothes and didn't feel photogenic, but she persisted. Not long ago, I asked him if he had ever seen the photograph, and he said, "And *how*! That lady and me got engaged."

Sometimes the bus becomes a source of problems. Once, the Southernaires broke down somewhere between Nashville and Louisville and needed three days to raise the money for repairs. Another time, in Richmond, Virginia, the transmission blew up, but, fortunately, Willis Pittman—the lead singer in Willis Pittman and the Burden Lifters—lives in Richmond and is a mechanic, and he fixed the transmission for free. One night, in the middle of Ohio, a tire blew out and they ran out of gas at the same moment. A farmer heard the commotion and came out of his house, then went into his barn, found a tire that fitted the wheel, filled a can of gas, jacked up the bus, replaced the tire, filled the gas tank, pulled them back onto the road with his tractor, and then showed them his Ku Klux Klan membership card and asked them to be on their way.

The gospel audience is probably the poorest of any mass audience in the country, and there are a thousand ways, like working at a Kmart or doing construction, that most gospel singers could make more money than they do singing gospel; and most gospel singers don't make enough from their music to live on. It is a matter of devotion. Gospel music has complicated origins, but it primarily came out of the Southern black Church of God in Christ and the Holiness movement of the Methodist Church; musically, it is a union of English revival hymns and African song styles—call-and-response, moaning, shouting. In the thirties, gospel singers started travelling a circuit of auditoriums, churches, grange halls, and tent meetings, and through more than half a century the gospel highway has hardly changed. There are gospel records, but for most of the audience gospel is more a form of public worship and performance than something you listen to at home.

Over the past year, the Jackson Southernaires, as they have for most of the last five decades, left home nearly every Thursday and spent the weekend on the road. They sang in almost every state and in Ontario, in places as tiny as Blytheville, Arkansas, and as big as Brooklyn; they sang in half-empty church halls and in packed theatres; and last year, for the first time, they sang in France and were treated like stars. Not long ago, I travelled with the Southernaires on the gospel circuit. The first night on the road, I couldn't sleep, so I sat on the steps at the front of the bus and talked to Mack. We were on our way to Demopolis, Alabama, a rundown town in the center of the state. Mack said, "We're going way out in the country. You wait and see—people'll be coming to the show on mules." Mack has been a gospel-bus driver for twenty-five years. He started with Reverend Julius Cheeks and the Sensational Nightingales, and then he drove for Willie Neal Johnson and the Gospel Keynotes, and then, four years ago, he joined the Southernaires. Until 1965, he drove for Trailways. His home is in Roxboro, North Carolina, but he often stays at the Stonewall Jackson Motel, in Jackson, Mississippi. He said that his professional zenith was in 1981, after Willie Neal was nominated for a gospel Grammy, when the Gospel Keynotes rode to the ceremony in a limousine. "It wasn't just the limousine," he said. "When they came to pick me up, I opened the door, and there was Dionne Warwick. It was a completely beautiful experience. I opened the door, I saw Dionne, and I wanted to *die*."

APPENDIX

When Mack gets tired, James Burks drives. That's his No. 2 job with the Southernaires; his No. 1 job is to play bass guitar and sing backup. Everyone in the group doubles up. Granard McClendon, the guitar player, who is slim and glib and is a sharp dresser, negotiates for the motel rooms when they pull into a town, and he also chooses which of their six sets of matching uniforms they will wear each night. During my trip with the group, Melvin Wilson sang tenor ("high") and falsetto ("top") and was also the sound engineer. He has satiny dark skin and a plump, pumpkin-shaped face. When Melvin was a teen-ager, in Robersonville, North Carolina, his father managed a gospel group called the Dynamic Powell Brothers. No one knew that Melvin could sing—not even Melvin. One day, he was riding home with the Dynamic Powell Brothers from a show and he just opened his mouth and let go. His voice was as cool and clear as water; the Dynamic Powell Brothers hired him on the spot. When I travelled with the Jackson Southernaires, the keyboard player was Gary Miles. (Melvin and Gary recently left to join another group, and have been replaced by Tony Nichols and Daryl Johnson.) Gary also hauled equipment out of the bus for shows and hauled it back afterward. In his off-road life, he is an actor. He has been an extra on "Murder, She Wrote" and "Magnum, P.I." Both times, he was cast as an officious waiter. He has skinny arms, a wide trunk, a nutty laugh, and an air of astonishment.

Maurice Surrell drums and sings and is the Southernaires' enforcer; that is, he writes up members of the group when they infract Southernaire rules. The rules take up fifteen typewritten pages. They were established years ago by Luther Jennings, one of the original Southernaires, who is now retired from gospel and teaches math at a high school in Jackson. Luther wanted the Southernaires to be known as the gentlemen of the gospel circuit, so his rules are strict and the fines are steep: twenty-five dollars for a wrinkled uniform, twenty-five dollars for unshined shoes, a hundred dollars for cursing, a hundred dollars for bringing a young lady to the restaurant where the group is eating, twenty-five dollars for hitting the wrong note in a song. Luther did not believe in leniency; if he transgressed, he fined himself. Luther was also the Southernaires' debt collector. Sometimes concert promoters were so moved by the Southernaires' performances that they misplaced the money they owed the Southernaires. This had a way of irritating Luther, so he usually carried one or more of the guns he owned—a single-action revolver, a bolt-action rifle, a .22, a .32, a Winchester, two .25-calibre revolvers, some twelve-gauge shotguns, two .357s, two .45s, and a couple of dainty handguns—which he could lay down, as if he were setting the table, when he went to collect from the promoter at the end of a show.

The Southernaires have two lead singers—Roger Bryant and Huey Williams. Roger is an ordained minister and an emphatic public speaker, so he is responsible for going onstage before each concert and urging the members of the audience to buy a Southernaires record or video before they leave. He has full cheeks, gap teeth, a sidelong glance, and parchment-colored skin. His hair is puffy and moldable; it looks different every day. His voice is choked and explosive. Onstage, Roger is a pacer, an arm-swinger, a hip-slapper, a fist-shaker, and a screamer. He is now thirty-nine years old. When he was small, he was in a group called the Sunbeam Jrs. His father, a foundry worker and preacher in Saginaw, Michigan, would stand him up on the kitchen table and beat him to make him sing.

Huey Williams is fifty-five. He has been with the group for twenty-nine years, and now when people think of the Southernaires they mostly think of Huey. He grew up in the country south of Jackson. Before he became a full-time gospel singer, he did construction work in Detroit and in New Orleans, but his enthusiasms are strictly rural. He once told me that people refer to him as the coon-hunting gospel singer. Currently, he has six Walker hounds; they live in big dog pens behind his house, in McComb, Mississippi. On his days off, Huey usually takes the dogs hunting or attends to hunting-related errands. One time when I visited him in McComb, we spent the day driving across the state to the taxidermist, to pick up a bobcat Huey had shot. Huey is a tall man with a broad chest and the steep cheekbones of a Cherokee. He has big dimples, blue eyes, and a thin mustache. He wears two chunky gold rings and a thick gold cuff; his hands are long and elegant, and his nails are smooth and shiny. The first time I met him, he took my chin in his hands, tilted it toward him, and said, "Take a good look at my face. Have you ever in your life seen blue eyes on a black man?" His speaking voice is sometimes brisk and commanding and sometimes whispery and intimate, and always tonic. I have heard him sing in a bass voice, which is so deep that it sounds like burping, and in a shrieking, afflicted tenor, and in a buttery, pliant baritone. When he was around thirty, his voice was so supple he could do anything with it; he believes that at the time he was simply the best singer in the whole world. Before a performance, when he is encircled by his fans, he walks around like Goliath. In the morning, when he wakes up hoarse from the show and creaky from sleeping on the bus, he looks like someone who thinks a lot about retiring. His wife, Mamie, who is a machine operator at a General Motors plant in Mississippi, says, "I'm so used to him travelling I don't know what I'd do if he were here. He's got his dogs, I suppose. But, with him always being away, we don't have time to get into each other's hair."

On the road, at truck stops and diners, we ate Reese's peanut-butter cups; Reese's Pieces; Sour Cream 'n Onion Pringles potato crisps; 3 Musketeers; chicken, baked, simmered, stewed, smothered, potted in pies, or creamed à la king; chicken-fried steak; chicken-fried chicken; chicken even for breakfast sometimes, if we'd travelled all night after a show and never got dinner. Arriving in Columbus, Georgia, after driving since midnight, we had baked chicken at ten in the morning, which was the earliest I had ever eaten chicken in my life. Most often, the Southernaires take their meals at truck stops, which have telephones at the tables and showers for rent and sometimes Southernaires tapes for sale in racks near the cashiers. "Truck stops have beautiful food," Mack once explained to me. "Besides, we can get the bus serviced at the same time we eat."

APPENDIX

Now and then when I was with the Southernaires, I felt we spent more time arranging to eat, stopping to eat, ordering food to go, waiting to eat, and eating than we did at gospel shows. The night I began my travels with them, we left Jackson, drove about twelve miles, then pulled off at a truck stop and had dinner. It was a quarter to one in the morning. None of the Southernaires understood why I found this odd. The truck stop was fairly empty, and the nine of us spread out at five or six tables, so when Huey said grace our "Amen"s ping-ponged around the dining room. When the Southernaires' agent books a date for them, she tries to get the promoter to pay for their hotel and dinner, to supplement the small amount they are paid for the show. Sometimes the promoter offers to cook them dinner instead of underwriting it. In Madison, Georgia, an old man who was a friend of the promoter set up a booth outside the auditorium with paper, plates, napkins, an ancient deep fryer, and a CrockPot, and started cooking yellow perch and hot dogs for the group to have before the show. When I asked him if the fish was good, he gave me a funny look. Then he slapped a piece of perch across the palm of his hand and said, "Like I said, it don't got no bones."

At the concerts, I saw men wearing spats and women wearing hats such as I'd never seen before: a black porkpie with a turquoise veil and bow; a midshipman's white cap with little pearls sewn along the rim; a tricorne of orange faille; a green beanie; a purple derby, worn at a slant; a red saucer that had netting looped around the edge and a piece of stiff fabric shaped like a Dorito sticking straight up from the crown; a fuchsia-colored ten-gallon with an ostrich feather drooping from the hatband. The hats were on elderly ladies, who moved through the crowds like cruise ships. Teen-age girls came to the concerts, too, in flowered dresses or in jeans and tank tops, wearing their babies slung on their hips, the way hikers wear fanny packs, or jouncing them absent-mindedly, like loose change.

I heard people at gospel concerts call eyeglasses "helpers" and a gravel road "a dirty road," and I heard an infant called "a lap baby," and a gun called "a persuader," and dying called "making it over," and an embarrassed person described as "wanting to swallow his teeth," and a dead person described as someone who was "having his mail delivered to him by groundhogs." Everybody talked about Jesus all the time. He was called a doctor, a lawyer, a lily of the valley, a lamb, a shepherd, joy in the morning, a rock, a road, peace in the evening, a builder, a captain, a rose of Sharon, a friend, a father, and someone who is always on time. I met a man named Porkchop and a man named Midget and a little boy named Royriquez Clarencezellus Wooten. I heard other gospel groups perform: the Christian Harmonizers and the Sensational Harmonizers and the Harmonettes and the Religiousettes and the Gloryettes and the Gospel True Lights and the True Gospel Singers and the Brotherhood Gospel Singers and the Five Singing Sons and the Mighty Sons of Glory and the Fantastic Disciples and the Fantastic Soulernaires and the Fantastic Violinaires and the Sunset Jubilaires and the Pilgrim Jubilees and the Brown Boys and the Five Blind Boys and Wonder Boy and the Spiritual Voices. The concerts were like big public conversations. The exhortations that people called out to the singers most often were "Take your time!" and "Let Him *use* you!" The exhortations that Huey and Roger called out most often were "Do you believe in Jesus?" and "Can I get just one witness?" and "Are you with me, church?" and "You know, God is *able.*"

In Madison, Georgia, the Southernaires performed as part of a program given in a school auditorium. As soon as the concert began, a tiny woman in a peach-colored pantsuit got up from her seat and made her way over to the aisle, and then she spiralled around for about an hour, gasping "Thank you, Jesus! Thank you, Jesus!" with her eyes squeezed shut and her hands flapping in the air. People stepped around her carefully when they went to and from their seats. On the stage, a local group was performing, and one of the singers had raised her arms and turned her palms toward her face as she sang; she had six fingers on each hand, and each nail was painted coral pink. After the song, she leaned over the edge of the stage and said sharply, "Isn't Satan busy? Satan's a stubborn old mule. I remember when I would lay out all night on what they call the disco floor. Then something hit me in the head. The voice I heard, it was just like threading a needle." I saw only one white person besides myself at one concert—she was the desk clerk at the motel where we were staying, and Huey told her if she gave us good rooms he'd give her a free ticket. Huey introduced me to the audience one night, and afterward someone passed me a note that said, "We Welcome You, To Madison, Georgia. From: Hattie." I read it and looked up, and the woman who had written it fluttered her handkerchief at me, and during the next song she crossed the room and kissed me.

Marianna, Florida: We arrive at four-thirty in the morning, after driving all night. Granard will try to negotiate a half-day rate at a motel, since we will sleep for only a few hours and then will leave to set up the show, and after the show we'll get back on the bus and start driving to McCormick, South Carolina, for the next show. Even for a gospel group as well established as the Southernaires, every dollar makes a difference. One night, I found a scrap of paper on the bus on which someone had been doing calculations. It said, "Show, $1500. Records $232." When all was said and done, that appeared to be all they would make that evening, and they had to pay for their food and gas and lodging and split the remainder eight ways. The motels we drive by and consider around Marianna are squat, cinderblock buildings on weedy lots. At the first one we try, the night manager comes out and looks at the bus and then he tells Granard the motel is totally booked, even though the parking lot is empty. We stop at another motel, and Granard negotiates for ten minutes, until the clerk gives him a hospitable price. Mack pulls the bus behind the motel, where the parking lot turns into dirt and saw grass. My motel room is stale and dreary. There is a shopping program and a white gospel show on television, and a lizard, paralyzed but pulsating, on one corner of my door.

The next afternoon, the air is completely still. The street leading to Marianna High School is lined with palm trees, and not a frond is moving. The school is a pretty building with Mediterranean inclinations. Its walls are apricot brick. The lawns around it have been roasted. Some little blond girls are playing kickball in front of a bungalow next to the school. A few yards away, a group of old black men wearing short-sleeved white dress shirts and creased fedoras, their pants hiked up to their diaphragms, are standing and talking. When they see the bus, they hitch their pants up even higher and start trotting toward it, waving us around to the side of the school. Mack pulls up to a loading dock and yanks the gears until the bus wheezes and settles down.

Huey stands and stretches, half bent: he is too tall to unfold himself fully in the bus. He nudges Roger, who is listening to his Walkman, and then wipes his forehead, peers out, and says hoarsely, "I always do love Florida."

Through the loading-dock door comes Sister Lula Cheese Vann. She is a husky woman with the haughty bearing of a big shot. She is dressed in a salmon-colored luncheon suit, a dozen rings and pins and bracelets, and a structurally complex salmon-colored hat the size of a breadbox. In her right hand is a flyer for the evening's program. In her left is a quiver of paper fans, which are printed with an essay entitled "How to Get Along with People," and are sponsored by her full-time business, the Vann Funeral Home. By vocation, Sister Vann is a mortician; as an avocation she promotes gospel. She comes to the open door of the bus and says smartly, "Southernaires. Hello. Do you know who I am?"

Huey steps out and says "Sister *Vann*," in his most sultry voice, and shakes her hand. Sister Vann melts a little. The old men form a buzzy circle around them, giving orders and gesturing. Gary and Melvin step out, wearing work gloves, jeans, and T-shirts, and start shoving the equipment out of the belly of the bus. Mack is dragging the record crates up the ramp of the loading dock.

The hall of the school is cool and clattery. The front door is propped half open; a wedge of yellow late-afternoon light, of parched lawn, of palms, of shuttered bungalows, of tar-drizzled sidewalk, of little blond girls wandering by is showing through. The hall begins to fill. Mack, setting up the cassette table, is clowning with two young girls in fancy dresses. A brassy-voiced woman walks past them, hauling her teen-age daughter by the elbow. "I would like Sister Vann to give her a listen," the woman says to Mack. "Put her on the program. Yes, I would." Brother Alonzo Keys, a handsome chatterbox from Panama City, Florida, who is singing tonight, comes over to pay his respects to Huey and the Southernaires. Sister Gladys Madrick, who will open the gospel program, flounces by, trailed by three skittery young women in lavender dresses. The auditorium is medium-sized and tidy, with smooth gold seats and purple fittings. Three women are already seated, halfway back, and are flapping at one another with Sister Vann's fans.

By seven, Melvin has finished the sound check, so the Southernaires go back to the bus and change into the clothes they will wear for the hour or so before they change into the evening's uniforms—whichever of their six sets Granard has chosen. Melvin has put on a mustard-colored blazer, a mustard shirt, and a black tie. Huey is wearing a turquoise tunic. The last sunlight has deepened and now fades. The neighborhood is dead quiet and dim, except right here, in this little pocket, which is full of noise and commotion, with the school lights flaring, and someone in the auditorium already yelling, and Sister Gladys Madrick's organist starting to play.

The uniform that Granard chooses is the black double-breasted suit that they wear with a crisp white shirt, a tie with a purplish gardenia print, and smooth black shoes. Onstage in this uniform, they look polished, natty, and a little grave. Sister Vann introduces them: "I feel blessed. I never, never thought I'd get the Jackson Southernaires here in Marianna, and here they are. The Lord's been good to me." She pauses. "Now, before I start with the Southernaires I want to say to you-all that we got to stop this screaming and *crying* about the price of these tickets. This program costs seven dollars a ticket, and I can tell you, with God as my witness, that this is the cheapest the Jackson Southernaires have ever been anywhere they've gone. So give God a hand, would you, and quit this miserable complaining!" A smattering of applause. Sister Vann smiles wanly. Her funeral-home motto is "Concern for the Living, Reverence for the Dead." "I am so glad to be following in God's footsteps," she says. "And I'm glad God put love in my heart and I don't mind sharing it. Now, Marianna, the Jackson *Southernaires*!!"

Maurice taps the drum, and they begin. Each program opens with Roger singing "I've Been Changed." It's a song with a clunky, unlovely beat, but it always rouses the crowd. Singing it, Roger is coiled and ferocious. The auditorium is mostly full now, and the audience is clapping in time. When Roger finishes the song, he steps to one side, and Huey comes forward. "Say 'Amen,' Marianna," he says.

"Amen!"

"Say 'Amen' *again*." Huey flicks the microphone upward, looks forward, and then snaps the microphone to the right and his head the other way. It is a tiny gesture, but vivid—as if he has stolen a look at something and then torn himself away.

"Amen."

"Sing it, Huey. Sing it! Sing it!"

The woman next to me leans over and whispers, "Oh Lord, we got a loud one here."

"Let me ask you something," Huey says, stepping forward. "How many of you here know there is a heaven?"

"A-*men*."

Huey gives his testimony, about the night his house burned to the ground. It is a terrible true story: he lost everything he had, and his son could have died if Huey had not stumbled on him as the family was getting away. Around me, people are nodding and weeping. I have now heard Huey tell this many times—to me in private, and also at several shows—but each time the clenched and anguished look on his face seems fresh. After the story, he always sings "He Will Make a Way," which begins as a sweet, slow, melancholic exchange between singer and chorus, and then rises into a storm. In the last verse, Huey is shouting that God will make a way, that he always makes a way, and then he can't speak anymore, and he starts laughing, and sweat is running down his cheeks, and he turns his eyes upward, and he stares up past the auditorium ceiling, and tears stream down his face.

Huey steps back, exhausted, and Maurice starts the rattling drumbeat for "No Coward Soldier." Roger will take over until the end of the show. He bounds to the edge of the stage and starts singing. The woman next to me, who had taken my hand and held it through most of the show, now releases it gently, as if she were putting a hooked fish back in the water, and turns to me and says, "I'm sorry, baby, but I got to get *loose*." Then she jumps out into the aisle and bends forward from her waist and snaps in a staccato rhythm back and forth as Roger sings.

At that point, I get up and work my way along the row and across the far aisle and stand in the doorway by the side of the stage. It is almost midnight. Someone is frying catfish out front, and the peppery smell thickens the air. Someone with a wheezy cough is standing behind me. A big bug smacks into me, sizzles, and falls. I can see everything from where I am standing: a man in the front row pitched back in his seat and crying without making any noise; twin teen-agers in dotted sundresses fanning themselves a few rows behind him; Mack, at the back of the auditorium, sitting on the gray plastic crates that hold the group's records and tapes; a diapered baby in a sailor suit, draped over the shoulder of a slim woman in a yellow sheath; a woman, too wide to sit in an auditorium seat, teetering on a folding chair someone put out for her near the exit door; Roger, on the lip of the stage, taking little explosive bounces on the balls of his feet; Huey, behind him, leaning against the electric piano and running his hand over his hair, his expression a mingling of rapture, fatigue, and distraction, a sort of stillness absorbing him, as if he were in a different, quieter place; a banner over the stage showing the Marianna High School Fighting Bulldog mascot dressed in a snug purple crewneck; a toddler; a wheelchair; a tossed-away flyer; a flash of white in the crowd each time a woman flaps her handkerchief or a man raises his to dab his face—a flash as incandescent as a lit bulb or the luminous envelope of a flame.

Roger jumps off the stage and hollers, "What day did you get the Holy Ghost? Did you get it on a Monday? On a Tuesday? On a Wednesday? Did someone here get it on a Thursday?" One by one, people rise up like bubbles and float toward the stage, grab his hand, shake it hard, and then spin and dance away. He calls for anyone who got the Holy Ghost on Sunday; he sings that God don't need no coward soldiers. He shouts that he wishes he had a witness. He says he knows some people here tonight are going through something. He claps his left hand to his head and then whips it down and pounds his chest. The night is ending. The Southernaires' time is nearly over. They will be back on the bus and on the road to Jackson within the hour. The music is roaring. A little breeze is picking up outside, lifting bits of grass and gravel and blowing them away. Roger stamps his foot and screams, "*We will surely meet again someday!*"

ADS ON THE CUTTING EDGE

Boston Phoenix
January 29, 1985

It is no accident that Ginsu Products has sold in excess of three and a half million sets of Ginsu ("*As Seen On TV!*") knives. Since 1978, the knives ("*Complete Thirteen-Piece Set!*") have been promoted exclusively through a series of insistent, staccato television ads designed by Dial Media, an advertising agency based in Cranston, Rhode Island. At one time or another, Dial's ads have run in every television market in the United States, giving Ginsu ("*What A Clever Cleaver!*") an eighty-five percent name recognition—second only to stalwarts like Jell-O. So effective is Dial's mélange of speed-editing, testimonials, demonstration, and stop-and-chop visuals that these ads alone have landed a Ginsu ("*Amazing!*") set in one out of every one hundred homes in America.

That includes at least one NYNEX employee. I call directory assistance for Rhode Island in search of Ginsu.

"Directory assistance. What city?"

"Cranston. I'd like the number for Ginzu, G-i-n-z-u."

The operator clears her throat. "No, it's G-i-n-**s**-u."

"Are you sure?"

"Very sure. I have one myself."

Dial Media, situated in a squat brick building beside Route 95, is home to more than the Ginsu ("*The More You Use It, The Better It Cuts!*") dynasty: It is also marketing headquarters for a batch of other not-sold-in-any-store home appliances, including Miracle Painter, Miracle Duster, Miracle Slicer, Armourcote Cookware, ZipSnip cordless scissors, and the Suburbanite Squeeze Mop. And the Democratic National Committee, which came hat in hand to Cranston last year hoping Dial could produce some Miracle Voter.

A $7.95 value...

"Contrary to popular belief, Ginsu is not made in Japan," says Dial executive vice-president Edward Miccolis. He is sitting in the Dial screening room. Cassettes of the agency's direct-marketing miracles are stacked in front of him. "The name 'Ginsu' was made up," Miccolis continues. "It doesn't mean anything in Japanese. And the knives are made in Ohio."

"Where in Ohio?" I ask.

"I'd rather not say," says Miccolis. "I don't want to get into that heavy confidential stuff."

...for only $7.95!

The secret of Ginsu ("*This Is The Sharpest Knife Offer I've Ever Seen!*") is power: the blade is solid surgical steel, the handle indestructible plastic. The knives will cut through anything. And Dial's ads are all power: the demonstrations are dramatic, the pitch irresistible.

The Dial style was born in 1975 with Miracle Painter—a foam-rubber paint-pad-on-a-stick invented by a guy in Warwick. He sold only a couple before Dial got hold of the product and cooked up what would prove to be the first of its ad classics—the Man in the Tuxedo. The spot opens with a shot of a formally attired fellow running his paint pad over his ceiling. "This man is painting his ceiling," the narrator booms, "IN HIS TUXEDO!" The point is that Miracle Painter is dripless, affording one the opportunity, should one desire, to paint anything while wearing one's best.

Although the production values of the Miracle Painter spot are low rent, the characteristic Dial touch of class is evident. The camera catches odd, ill-lit angles of hands struggling with paint brushes on a rough wall—but the voiceover is always elegant. "Try painting stucco," the off-camera narrator urges. "First, the brush"—the hand slaps the thing against the wall. "ALMOST FUTILE!" The hand glides a Miracle Painter over the same wall. "Try *that* with a brush or roller," the narrator chides. But he's immediately conciliatory. "Money back," he oozes, "if not *delighted*!"

All this for only $19.99

Armourcote Cookware gave Dial another chance to polish its approach. In the Armourcote spot, the mythic man-in-the-tux structure is maintained, but substituting for the formal fellow is a woman's hand with long, slim fingers and a big diamond solitaire on a gold band. The hand stretches lazily, the ring glinting into the camera. "A diamond is the world's *hardest* surface," the narrator intones. He pauses. Suddenly, a just-plucked Perdue roaster, dropped from above, lands on top of this polished hand, pinning it to the counter. The narrator bellows: "But two years later, *you still can't cook on it!*" Next come lickety-split scenes of Armourcote triumph. To quote from the Armourcote Information Sheet:

- Burnt baked beans plop out of Saucepan
- Spatula pops burnt pudding mess from Cook&Serve Pan
- Burnt char removed from Dutch Oven with paper towel
- Muffins fly out of Muffin Pan
- Two forks lift meat loaf from Loaf Pan

Matched with the quick-cut scenes is the narrator's increasingly insistent voice. "Now how much would you pay for this?" he commands. "Don't answer until you see—" and the muffins go flying. By the finale, his fever pitch has acquired a mild sneer. "Well, *don't* just take *our* word for it," he sniffs. "Order *now*."

"We're bent on perfection," says James Cooney, Dial's assistant vice-president and creative director. "The ads need to grab your attention, and we'll do it any way we can. There's no psychological reason behind the way we do them."

Now only $29.99

But it is the spots for the Ginsu ("*The Incredible Knife That Changed The Way America Cuts!*") that made Dial.

Opening shot: a man in a karate outfit, framed to show only his torso, emits a kamikaze howl while blasting through a two-by-four with the flat of his hand. Cut. Same man, emitting a somewhat less enthusiastic howl, hauls off and karate-chops a red beefsteak tomato. *Splat*.

"One of our things is a good opening," says Cooney. "That opening represents one hundred hours of work."

The rest of the spot races through demonstrations shots—a Ginsu ("*You Get Them All!*") slicing through a tin can, chopping a log, cutting a nail, and halving a mushroom. For one low price, explains the narrator, you get the Chef's Knife, the Oriental Cleaver, and the Slicing Knife.

"*BUT WAIT! THERE'S MORE!*"

You also get the Fruit&Vegetable knife and two parers.

"*BUT WAIT! THERE'S MORE!*"

You also get a utility knife.

"*BUT WAIT! THERE'S MORE!*"

You also get six world-famous Ginsu steak knives.

APPENDIX

"When we first showed this spot," says Miccolis, "the phone lines in New York were so overloaded that the system shut down."

"Now everybody's using 'But wait, there's more,'" says Cooney, "but we're in the process of trademarking it."

"We've *revolutionized* those four words," says Miccolis. "We've revolutionized 'But wait, there's more.'"

Still only $39.99!

The first Ginsu ("*Cuts Pineapple!*") ad was almost too successful for its own good. It brought in almost 40,000 orders a day, but according to some customer mail, it was also inspiring youngsters to karate-chop Mom's tomato plants. "Please," pleaded one such customer, "could you use a watermelon instead?"

Done. The Ginsu ("*Cuts Cheese!*") II ad begins with a karate footchop through a huge watermelon. Then the frenzy of demonstration—the slicing of a radiator hose, the scoring of sheetrock. "*Look What It Does for Pizza!*"

Cooney smiles. "We got a letter from a lady who had a cast on her leg, and her leg started swelling. They tried everything—sawing it, even—and the cast wouldn't come off. She yelled, 'Quick, son! The Ginsu!' and he ran to the kitchen and got a Ginsu steak knife, and they sawed it off! She didn't have money to buy a new set, so we sent her one."

The Ginsu ("*Precision Honed!*") Oki II ad perfected the form. Shot on location in a Japanese steak house, the spot introduced the Dial benchmark of comment interruptus. A Japanese chef examines the knives and looks up. "*Now* how much would you pay for this set?" says the narrator. The chef opens his mouth to answer. "DON'T ANSWER YET!" barks the narrator, then reels off more of Ginsu's ("*Perfect in the Kitchen!*") good graces. The narrator and the chef go at it twice more before the ad wraps up, closing with the "beauty shot"—a staggered shot of all 13 Ginsu

("*Perfect for the Handyman!*") pieces fanned in tidy formation across a table top.

What could possibly be next? "We've gone as far as we can go with Ginsu," says Miccolis. "You can only sell so many Ginsu knives." He reconsiders. "Of course, there's a whole new generation out there. And everybody needs knives."

HARVARD SQUARE

The Boston Globe
March 2, 1986

Are you a hippie? A folkie? A member of the smarty-pants set? A truant teenager? A reader of books? A Boston University student? Are you hungry? In need of maps? Pipes? Poetry? Mediocre pizza? Newspapers? Not looking for a bathroom? Do you want to relive the '60s? The '70s? The early '80s? The '90s—that is, the 1790s? Do you want a parking ticket? Do you want ambience? Antiques? Overpriced small portions of food? Do you believe in tenure? Do you only associate with people with tenure? Do you consider it appropriate to play chess outdoors? Do you love to jaywalk constantly—against traffic? Do you, in fact, consider jaywalking your birthright? Do you consider yourself smarter than average? Do you yak about Herbert Marcuse over martinis? Do you go for subtitles? Footnotes? Large, underbaked, overpriced chocolate chip cookies? Do you find buckled brick sidewalks that cannot be navigated safely really charming—especially in winter? Do you find the idea of New York City just too awful to contemplate? Do you go to readings? Book signings? Have you ever matriculated at, applied to, or pretended to attend Harvard University? Do you toss around the term "Cantabrigian" with delight? Do you consider Boston an afterthought? Do you consider it at all? Have you ever been across the river for anything other than an occasional Red Sox game? Did you feel alien, awkward, or displaced?

Come home to Harvard Square. There are thousands of your kind there, hunched over the remaindered-book tables; drinking something au lait; ruminating about interesting stuff; considering another graduate degree; rejoicing in the knowledge that they are part of the intellectual, social, retail, philosophical, and vaguely apolitical political hub of the galaxy, if not the universe. It's like this: You move to Boston and it's just another real-estate transaction; you move to Harvard Square, and it's considered a moral achievement. That's the kind of place Harvard Square—or just the Square, if you will—is. It's more than square footage: It's a force field of meaning and nothingness and boutiques and being part of it obviates the need for much else to explain who and what you are.

But within the Square set are a score of different subsets, and that's why the place is such a likeable jumble. It is, for instance, one of the few places in the East where you can still find hippies; if you're a hippie, it's one of the few places you can still be outfitted properly (astrology books, backpacks, beards, acoustic music, and so on). Teenagers on leave from cigarette machines elsewhere form another of the Square's most appreciative cliques. And mostly the Square is host to lots of people who read with a vengeance, and who can't believe their good fortune to live in possibly the only place in America where bookstores outnumber television stores twenty-eight to one.

What's unique about Harvard Square is that it's always remained a little apart from the rest of the world. It didn't exactly sidestep eras; it was folky in the '50s, scruffy in the '60s, punky in the '70s, and throughout it has cultivated the beer-barfing bonhomie that makes for a college town. The difference between anywhere else and Harvard Square is that it's never been totally subsumed by the here-and-now, always maintaining a bit of anachronistic, scholarly daffiness that's made it the kind of place

APPENDIX

where listing "Runic Scholar and Oboist" as your occupation wouldn't land you in the loony bin.

Or so it's been so far. Will this era, which introduced franchises, fast food, and fancy haircuts to the Square, prove too much for the old dame? Will the TV store/bookstore ratio finally tilt? Will there always be room in the world for Harvard Square?

PHOTO CREDITS

18, 20, 21, 170	Courtesy of the Author
26	Arthur Orlean
52	Cathy Cheney
91	Oberto Gili, *Vogue* © Condé Nast
124	David Blum (top), Peter Sistrom (bottom)
194	Spike Jonze via Sandy Curiosity, Inc.
202	John Gillespie (top), Bei/Shutterstock (bottom left), L. Cohen/WireImage (bottom right)
215	Raymond Elman
216	John Gillespie
217	Peter Kramer
228	Jennifer May

ABOUT THE AUTHOR

SUSAN ORLEAN has been a staff writer at *The New Yorker* since 1992. She is the *New York Times* bestselling author of eight books, including *The Library Book*, *The Orchid Thief*, and *Rin Tin Tin*. She lives with her family in Los Angeles and can be reached at susanorlean.com and on Substack at susanorlean.substack.com.

Avid Reader Press, an imprint of Simon & Schuster, is built on the idea that the most rewarding publishing has three common denominators: great books, published with intense focus, in true partnership. Thank you to the Avid Reader Press colleagues who collaborated on *Joyride*, as well as to the hundreds of professionals in the Simon & Schuster advertising, audio, communications, design, ebook, finance, human resources, legal, marketing, operations, production, sales, supply chain, subsidiary rights, and warehouse departments whose invaluable support and expertise benefit every one of our titles.

Editorial
Jofie Ferrari-Adler, *VP and Co-Publisher*
Carolyn Kelly, *Editor*
Alexandra Silvas, *Editorial Assistant*

Jacket Design
Alison Forner, *Senior Art Director*
Clay Smith, *Senior Designer*
Sydney Newman, *Art Associate*

Marketing
Meredith Vilarello, *VP and Associate Publisher*
Caroline McGregor, *Senior Marketing Manager*
Katya Wiegmann, *Marketing and Publishing Assistant*

Production
Allison Green, *Managing Editor*
Hana Handzija, *Managing Editorial Assistant*
Jessica Chin, *Senior Manager of Copyediting*
Annalea Manalili, *Senior Production Editor*
Alicia Brancato, *Production Manager*
Carly Loman, *Interior Text Designer*
Cait Lamborne, *Ebook Developer*

Publicity
Alexandra Primiani, *Publicity Director*
Ilana Gold, *Publicity Director*
Eva Kerins, *Publicity Assistant*

Subsidiary Rights
Paul O'Halloran, *VP and Director of Subsidiary Rights*
Fiona Sharp, *Subsidiary Rights Coordinator*